CONTEMPORARY
Home Plans

Design 6636, see page 190

220 Sleek Designs For Modern Lifestyles

HOME PLANNERS, LLC
Wholly owned by Hanley-Wood, LLC
Tucson, Arizona

Published by Home Planners, LLC
Wholly owned by Hanley-Wood, LLC
Editorial and Corporate Offices:
3275 West Ina Road, Suite 110
Tucson, Arizona 85741

Distribution Center:
29333 Lorie Lane
Wixom, Michigan 48393

Rickard D. Bailey, *CEO and Publisher*
Cindy Coatsworth Lewis, *Director of Publishing*
Jan Prideaux, *Executive Editor*
Marian E. Haggard, *Editor*
Paul Fitzgerald, *Senior Graphic Designer*

Photo Credits
Front Cover: Oscar Thompson Photography, courtesy of The Sater
Design Collection, Inc.
Back Cover: Strode Eckert

First Printing, February, 1998

10 9   8   7   6   5   4   3   2

Library of Congress Catalog Card Number: 97-077084

ISBN softcover: 1-881955-42-7

On the front cover: Design 6636, with it's classically sleek interior, exhibits the finest of
Contemporary styling. For more information about this design, please see page 190.

On the back cover: Design 7408 exhibits the fine detail and smooth lines of a
Contemporary home, presenting angles and openness for a futuristic feeling. For more
information on this design, please see page 132.

Design 2858, see page 24

TABLE OF CONTENTS

ABOUT THE DESIGNERS

The Blue Ribbon Designer Series™ is a collection of books featuring the home plans of a diverse group of outstanding home designers and architects known as the Blue Ribbon Network of Designers. This group of companies is dedicated to creating and marketing the finest possible plans for home construction on a regional and national basis. Each of the companies exhibits superior work and integrity in all phases of the stock-plan business including modern, trendsetting floor planning, a professionally executed blueprint package and a strong sense of service and commitment to the consumer.

Alan Mascord Design Associates, Inc.

Founded in 1983 as a local supplier to the building community, Mascord Design Associates of Portland, Oregon began to successfully publish plans nationally in 1985. With plans now drawn exclusively on computer, Mascord Design Associates quickly received a reputation for homes that are easy to build yet meet the rigorous demands of the buyers' market, winning local and national awards. The company's trademark is creating floor plans that work well and exhibit excellent traffic patterns. Their motto is: "Drawn to build, designed to sell."

Larry E. Belk Designs

Through the years, Larry E. Belk has worked with individuals and builders alike to provide a quality product. After listening to over 4,000 dreams and watching them become reality all across America, Larry's design philosophy today combines traditional exteriors with upscale interiors designed for contemporary lifestyles. Flowing, open spaces and interesting angles define his interiors. Great emphasis is placed on providing views that showcase the natural environment. Dynamic exteriors reflect Larry's extensive home construction experience, painstaking research and talent as a fine artist.

Home Planners

Headquartered in Tucson, Arizona, with additional offices in Detroit, Home Planners is one of the longest-running and most successful home design firms in the United States. With over 2,500 designs in its portfolio, the company provides a wide range of styles, sizes and types of homes for the residential builder. All of Home Planners' designs are created with the care and professional expertise that fifty years of experience in the home-planning business affords. Their homes are designed to be built, lived in and enjoyed for years to come.

Donald A. Gardner Architects, Inc.

The South Carolina firm of Donald A. Gardner was established in response to a growing demand for residential designs that reflect constantly changing lifestyles. The company's specialty is providing homes with refined, custom-style details and unique features such as passive-solar designs and open floor plans. Computer-aided design and drafting technology resulting in trouble-free construction documents places the firm at the leading edge of the home plan industry.

The Sater Design Collection

The Sater Design Collection has a long established tradition of providing South Florida's most diverse and extraordinary custom designed homes. Their goal is to fulfill each client's particular need for an exciting approach to design by merging creative vision with elements that satisfy a desire for a distinctive lifestyle. This philosophy is proven, as exemplified by over 50 national design awards, numerous magazine features and, most important, satisfied clients. The result is an elegant statement of lasting beauty and value.

Home Design Services, Inc.

For the past fifteen years, Home Design Services of Longwood, Florida, has been formulating plans for the sun-country lifestyle. At the forefront of design innovation and imagination, the company has developed award-winning designs that are consistently praised for their highly detailed, free-flowing floor plans, imaginative and exciting interior architecture and elevations which have gained international appeal.

CONTEMPORARY HOME PLANS

CONTEMPORARY DESIGN

Anthropologists say that you can tell a lot about people by the type of homes they choose to live in. Contemporary architecture certainly tells a lot about some people's lifestyles. A style that consciously strives for modernity and an artistic expression, Contemporary architecture borrows heavily from Modernist and International styles. The emphasis on the future rather than the past is one of this style's principal characteristics.

Concrete, smooth-faced stone, large glass openings, geometric shapes and vivid colors define the style and give it special flavor. Elements from Europe and even Early American sometimes combine with Cubism and Modernist/International styles to produce dramatic results. Mix these styles with traces of Tudor, Georgian, Salt Box and Cape Cod, and you get an elegantly eclectic design known as Today's Contemporary.

The popular slogan "form follows function" has been transformed to the more recent "form and function are one," and is expressed in the way the indoor/outdoor relationships are defined. Typical features include terraces, patios, large glass viewing areas and private balconies—all designed neatly in private rear and side yards. The fronts are reserved for window space that provides plenty of natural light to interior rooms.

Indoors, Contemporary design caters to the pace of today's more frenetic lifestyle. With open spaces, efficient kitchens, many large bathrooms and multi-purpose rooms to provide the space for a variety of activities, Contemporary style adds adaptability to its impressive description.

While found throughout the United States, Contemporary architecture is prevalently rooted in the Pacific Northwest, California, the Southwest, and the Midwest. Evolutions of Contemporary design vary from region to region.

In the Northwest particularly, designers, builders and especially consumers showed early preference for Contemporary design. Today, Northwest Contemporary architecture reflects its woodsy surroundings and adaptation to the climate and materials of the region. A futuristic effect is achieved through combining the use of extended wood beams, exposed rafter tails, heavy shake roofs, dark-stained exteriors and wide overhangs with a simplified and streamlined form. As with all successful architecture, Northwest Contemporaries fit their settings and are built with materials readily available in the area. A good example of this can be seen with Design 7627 (page 88).

Generally, the composite Contemporary homes of the Southwest are simple, open, comfortable and informal. They incorporate Spanish and Native American design with Contemporary styling. Adobe, concrete block or masonry—often washed with a stucco finish to protect the surface—are usually employed. Southwestern Contemporaries often incorporate porches, sheltered "ramada" terraces, shady overhangs and large blank walls that face west away from the burning sun. Floors are often tile, quarry or scored concrete to weather the heat. Terraces and patios frequently feature fountains, pools and plants. Design 3403 (page 206) exhibits these features well and combines them with the flavor of International style.

Design 2534 (page 39) incorporates all of the elements when it comes to the Midwest Contemporary ranch: long, low lines, a sense of mass- or self-enclosure with rambling buildings of various rooflines and pitches all leaning toward a central point. Emphasis is placed on aesthetic values over disciplined art forms in quest of space, freedom, peace and the outdoors. Introduced after World War II, the Midwest ranch house combines design elements from east and west with practical substitution of Midwest materials.

The influence of Early American architecture is highly evident in the Northeast Contemporaries. Once-simple Cape Cod cottages of few rooms and basic needs have been expanded to larger, more complex homes. The openness, gathering space to the rear and multiple accesses to the terrace all point toward Contemporary architectural design in Design 2927 (page 127), while still evidencing the flavor of yesterday so popular in the Northeast.

A compromise is demonstrated in Southern Contemporary style. Elements of traditional styling are smoothed into modern lines. Traditional-style columns, balconies and cupolas are combined with sleek lines and interesting angles on Design 8001 (page 68). Originally designed for a sloping site, the home incorporates multiple levels inside, furthering the futuristic ambience.

The homes presented here represent a look toward tomorrow. They're a fine collection of the many forms and variations of what Contemporary design has become and encompass the potential for what it is yet to be. Ranging from ground-hugging, one-story ranches to lavish multi-level homes, the designs in this book provide the lover of Contemporary style with a vast choice of sizes and looks. So, peruse, compare and enjoy!

SINGULAR SUCCESS: *One-story homes with flair*

DESIGN 8644

Square Footage: 1,831

□ A two-story entry, varying rooflines and multi-pane windows add to the spectacular street appeal of this three-bedroom home. To the right, off the foyer, is the dining room surrounded by elegant columns. Adjacent is the angular kitchen, which opens to the bayed breakfast nook. The family room includes plans for an optional fireplace and accesses the covered porch. The master bedroom is tucked in the back of the home and features a walk-in closet and full bath with a dual vanity, spa tub and oversized shower. Two additional bedrooms share a full bath.

Design by
**Home Design
Services, Inc.**

Width 59'
Depth 55'-4"

Floor Plan Labels

Bedroom 2
12⁰ · 11⁰

Bath

desk

summer kitchen

lin

Bedroom 3
12⁰ · 11⁰

Family Room
19⁴ · 17⁰

Covered Patio

up

Bath

Master Bedroom
15⁰ · 13⁸

Nook

fireplace

Living Room
16⁰ · 13⁸

w.i.c.

Kitchen

dw

d

ref

pantry

Utility

w

wh

lin

s

lin

Bath

Dining
12⁰ · 11⁰

Garage

Foyer

Den / Study
13⁸ · 11⁰

Entry

window seat

Width 57'-6"
Depth 66'

Design by
Home Design
Services, Inc.

DESIGN 8673

Square Footage: 2,398

❏ A three-car garage gives this home large-scale appeal in less than 2,400 square feet. The casual areas of the home remain open to each other for lots of family time. The kitchen features a pantry and island work surface and works well with the nearby nook. Secondary bedrooms are nearby and enjoy a built-in desk and a roomy bath. Formal living and dining areas flow into a den or study. The master bedroom delights with lots of windows, two closets and a custom bath. Off the covered patio, a summer kitchen facilitates added pool-time fun.

J.N. HANSEN P.T.L.

Covered Patio

Bedroom 3
12⁰ · 10⁰

Bath

Master Bedroom
15⁴ · 14⁰

w.i.c.

Breakfast

volume ceiling

desk

w.i.c.

Bath

Bedroom 2
12⁴ · 11⁰

Family Room
volume ceiling
16⁰ · 16⁰

fireplace

ent

ent

ent

dw

Kitchen

Utility

w

d

ac

Bath

lin

ref

pan

lin

Living Room
volume ceiling
12⁰ · 11⁰

Foyer

down

dn

Dining
volume ceiling
12⁰ · 11⁰

Double Garage

wh

ac

Bedroom 4
12⁴ · 11⁰

Entry

up

Design by
Home Design
Services, Inc.

Width 65'
Depth 50'

DESIGN 8708

Square Footage: 2,221

☐ The raised foyer and living room bring an interesting change of levels to this ingenious plan. The family room, with a twelve-foot wall of sliding glass doors, brings the outside in, and the entertainment/fireplace wall brings wows from visitors. The efficient kitchen features a pantry and easy access to the sunny breakfast nook. Three secondary bedrooms are conveniently split with the rear bedroom, which doubles as a guest or in-law suite and shares a pool bath. The master suite, located off the nook is open and airy, with access to the patio. The master bath holds a corner soaking tub, an oversized shower, a large double vanity with make-up area and double walk-in closets.

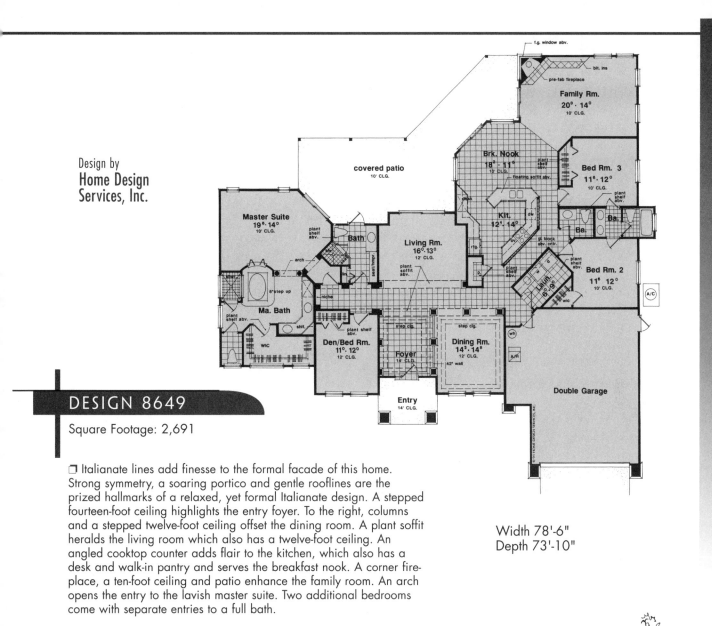

Design by
**Home Design
Services, Inc.**

Master Suite
19⁸·14⁰
10' CLG.

Bath

Living Rm.
16⁰·13⁰
12' CLG.

covered patio
10' CLG.

Family Rm.
20⁸·14⁰
10' CLG.

Brk. Nook
18³·11⁶
12' CLG.

Bed Rm. 3
11⁶·12⁰
10' CLG.

Kit.
12⁴·14⁰

Ma. Bath

Ba.

Bed Rm. 2
11⁶·12⁰
10' CLG.

Laun.
6·9

Den/Bed Rm.
11⁰·12⁰
12' CLG.

Foyer
14' CLG.

Dining Rm.
14³·14⁶
12' CLG.
42" wall

Double Garage

Entry
14' CLG.

A/C

DESIGN 8649

Square Footage: 2,691

❏ Italianate lines add finesse to the formal facade of this home. Strong symmetry, a soaring portico and gentle rooflines are the prized hallmarks of a relaxed, yet formal Italianate design. A stepped fourteen-foot ceiling highlights the entry foyer. To the right, columns and a stepped twelve-foot ceiling offset the dining room. A plant soffit heralds the living room which also has a twelve-foot ceiling. An angled cooktop counter adds flair to the kitchen, which also has a desk and walk-in pantry and serves the breakfast nook. A corner fireplace, a ten-foot ceiling and patio enhance the family room. An arch opens the entry to the lavish master suite. Two additional bedrooms come with separate entries to a full bath.

Width 78'-6"
Depth 73'-10"

© 91 HOME DESIGN SERVICES, INC.

J.N. HANSEN P.T.L.

DESIGN 8681

Square Footage: 2,322
Bonus Room: 370 square feet

❏ Grand Palladian windows create a classic look for this sensational stucco home. A magnificent view from the living room provides unlimited vistas of the rear grounds through a wall of glass, with the nearby dining room completing the formal area. The kitchen, breakfast nook and family room comprise the family wing, coming together to create the perfect place for casual gatherings. Two secondary bedrooms share a bath and provide complete privacy to the master suite, located on the opposite side of the plan. The master bedroom sets the mood for relaxation, and the lavish master bath pampers with a sumptuous soaking tub flanked by a step-down shower and a compartmented toilet. Bonus space may be completed at a later date to accommodate additional space requirements.

Design by
Home Design
Services, Inc.

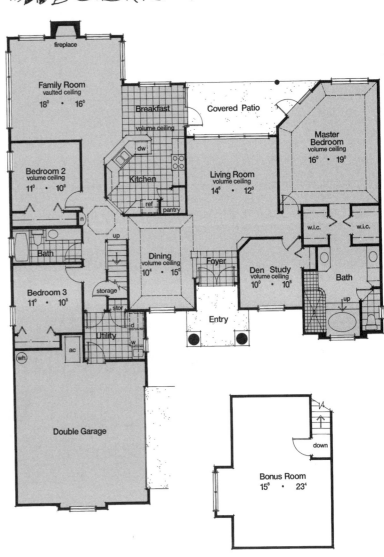

Width 60'
Depth 76'-8"

DESIGN 8709

Square Footage: 2,530

❑ This design is perfect for the growing family. The formal living and dining rooms separated by angular tile walkways are ideal for quiet evenings of dinner and conversation, while the huge island kitchen becomes the center of family gatherings. The secondary bedrooms share a "pullman" style bath just off the large family room, with a windowed media/fireplace wall. Note the large pantry just off the laundry room. The den/study can easily become a guest room, with use of the pool bath. The master wing comes complete with a windowed bed wall and an excellent master bath with an island tub, glass block shower, His and Hers vanities and walk-in closets. The courtyard-style garage layout makes for an easy fit on a small lot.

Bedroom 3
11⁰ · 10⁴

Family Room
15⁰ · 16⁰

Covered Porch

W.I.C.

Bath

Bedroom 2
12⁰ · 12⁰

Nook

Living Room
12¹⁰ · 14⁰

Bath

Master Bedroom
16⁰ · 15⁴

Kitchen

W.I.C. W.I.C.

Pan.

Bath

Utility

Dining
12⁸ · 15⁴

Foyer

Den/Study
12⁰ · 18⁰

Storage

Entry

2 Car Garage

Width 71'-10"
Depth 72'-8"

Design by
**Home Design
Services, Inc.**

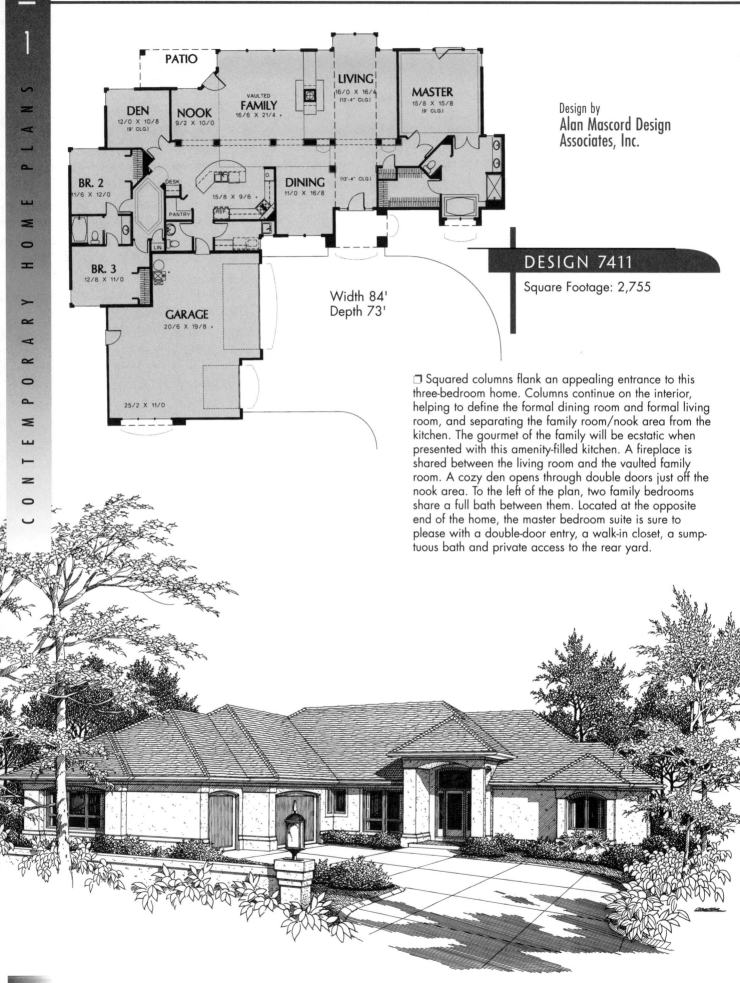

PATIO

DEN
12/0 X 10/8
(9' CLG.)

NOOK
9/2 X 10/0

VAULTED
FAMILY
16/6 X 21/4 *

LIVING
16/0 X 16/4
(13'-4" CLG.)

MASTER
15/8 X 15/8
(9' CLG.)

BR. 2
11/6 X 12/0

DESK

PANTRY

LIN

DINING
11/0 X 16/8

15/8 X 9/6 *

REF.

(13'-4" CLG.)

BR. 3
12/8 X 11/0

GARAGE
20/6 X 19/8 *

25/2 X 11/0

Width 84'
Depth 73'

Design by
**Alan Mascord Design
Associates, Inc.**

DESIGN 7411

Square Footage: 2,755

❏ Squared columns flank an appealing entrance to this three-bedroom home. Columns continue on the interior, helping to define the formal dining room and formal living room, and separating the family room/nook area from the kitchen. The gourmet of the family will be ecstatic when presented with this amenity-filled kitchen. A fireplace is shared between the living room and the vaulted family room. A cozy den opens through double doors just off the nook area. To the left of the plan, two family bedrooms share a full bath between them. Located at the opposite end of the home, the master bedroom suite is sure to please with a double-door entry, a walk-in closet, a sumptuous bath and private access to the rear yard.

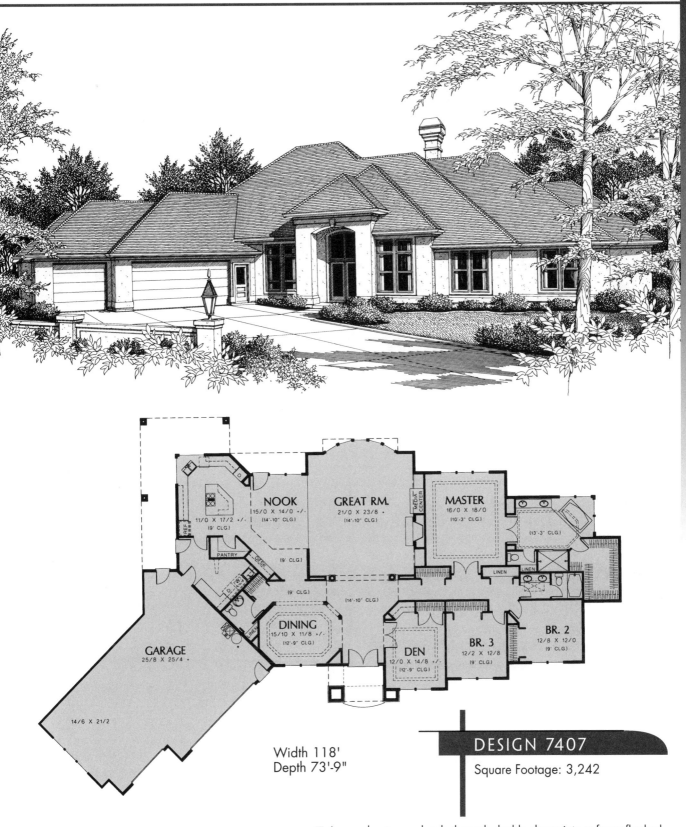

NOOK
15/0 X 14/0 +/-
(14'-10" CLG.)

11/0 X 17/2 +/-
(9' CLG.)

GREAT RM.
21/0 X 23/8
(14'-10" CLG.)

MASTER
16/0 X 18/0
(10'-3" CLG.)

(13'-3" CLG.)

MEDIA CENTER

PANTRY

DESK

(9' CLG.)

(9' CLG.)

LINEN

LINEN

(9' CLG.)

(14'-10" CLG.)

DINING
15/10 X 11/8 +/-
(12'-9" CLG.)

GARAGE
25/8 X 25/4 +/-

DEN
12/0 X 14/8 +/-
(12'-9" CLG.)

BR. 3
12/2 X 12/8
(9' CLG.)

BR. 2
12/8 X 12/0
(9' CLG.)

14/6 X 21/2

Width 118'
Depth 73'-9"

DESIGN 7407

Square Footage: 3,242

Design by
**Alan Mascord Design
Associates, Inc.**

❏ A grand entrance leads through double doors into a foyer flanked by a formal, octagonal dining room and a cozy den with a tray ceiling. The huge great room lies just ahead and features a fireplace, a built-in media center and a bowed window-wall. The island kitchen tempts the cook to stay all day, enjoying the corner sink with its window, the walk-in pantry and the nearby nook which offers access to the rear yard. Two family bedrooms share a full bath with a dual-bowl vanity and a large, hall linen closet. The master suite is sweet indeed, with a double door entry, a tray ceiling, a walk-in closet and a lavish master bath.

DESIGN 3560

Square Footage: 2,189

L

□ Simplicity is the key to the stylish good looks of this home's facade. A walled garden entry and large window areas appeal to outdoor enthusiasts. Inside, the kitchen forms the hub of the plan. It opens directly off the foyer and contains an island cooktop and a work counter with eating space on the living area side. A sloped ceiling, a fireplace and sliding glass doors to a rear terrace are highlights in the living area. The master bedroom also sports sliding glass doors to the terrace. Its dressing area is enhanced with double walk-in closets, a whirlpool tub and a seated shower. Two family bedrooms are found on the opposite side of the house. They share a full bath with twin vanities.

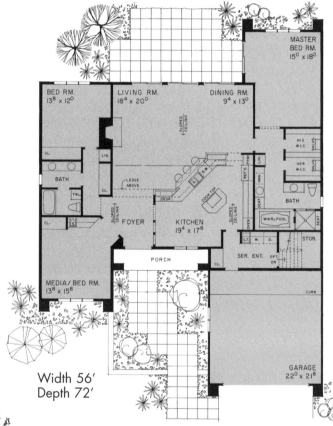

Width 56'
Depth 72'

Rear Elevation

QUOTE ONE®

Cost to build? See page 230
to order complete cost estimate
to build this house in your area!

Design by
Home Planners

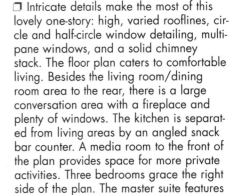

Square Footage: 2,916

L D

CONVERSATION
14⁰ x 20⁴ + BAY

DINING RM.
10⁶ x 14⁰

LIVING RM.
16⁰ x 19⁰

MASTER
BED RM.
13⁰ x 18⁰

SHWR

WHIRLPOOL

GLASS BLOCK

VAN.

SEAT

DRSG.

KITCHEN
17⁸ x 19⁸

COOK TOP

OVEN

POR. RM.

REF'G

PANTRY

CL.

HIS W.I.C.

HER W.I.C.

SHLVS

SHLVS

LIN.

CL.

FOYER

BATH

BED RM.
11² x 13⁰

D. W.

LAUND.

SER. ENT.

STOR.

MEDIA RM.
14⁰ x 12⁰

CL.

PORCH

BED RM.
11² x 13⁰

CL.

GARAGE
22⁸ x 21⁴ + STOR.

STOR.

Width 77'-10"
Depth 73'-10"

□ Intricate details make the most of this lovely one-story: high, varied rooflines, circle and half-circle window detailing, multi-pane windows, and a solid chimney stack. The floor plan caters to comfortable living. Besides the living room/dining room area to the rear, there is a large conversation area with a fireplace and plenty of windows. The kitchen is separated from living areas by an angled snack bar counter. A media room to the front of the plan provides space for more private activities. Three bedrooms grace the right side of the plan. The master suite features a tray vaulted ceiling and sliding glass doors to the rear terrace. The dressing area is graced by His and Hers walk-in closets, double-bowl lavatory, and compartmented commode. The shower area is highlighted with glass block and is sunken down one step. A garden whirlpool finishes off the area.

QUOTE ONE®

Cost to build? See page 230 to order complete cost estimate to build this house in your area!

Design by
Home Planners

Photo by Dave Rowland

This home, as shown in the photograph, may differ from the actual blueprints. For more detailed information, please check the floor plans carefully.

DESIGN 9453

Square Footage: 3,524

☐ Just about any "extra" you might ever wish for has been thoughtfully incorporated into this striking one-story home. Tray vaulted ceilings are found in the breakfast nook, sitting room, master bedroom, dining room and living room. The den and the foyer are raised also. Notice the entertainment center in the sunken family room and the area set aside for exercise with a built-in wet bar. The master suite has an unbelievably large walk-in closet and includes skylights and a spa in the bath. The rear terrace could be a fine precursor to a swimming pool.

Design by
Alan Mascord Design Associates, Inc.

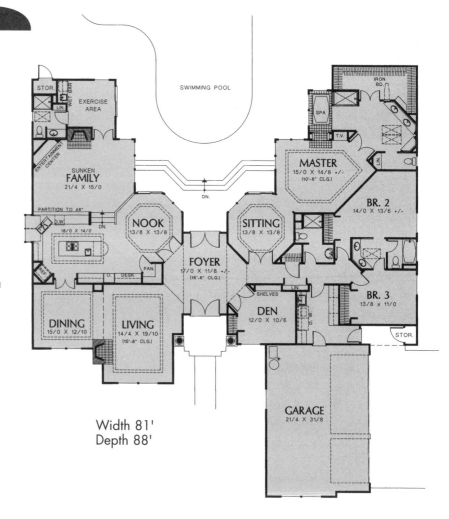

Width 81'
Depth 88'

DESIGN 9502

Square Footage: 1,865

MASTER
12/8 X 16/8

FAMILY
14/8 X 15/0

NOOK
8/0 X 9/8

SPA

LINEN

BR. 2
11/0 X 11/0

PANT.

KIT.
12/6 X 13/4

DINING
10/6 X 11/4
(9'-2" CLG.)

GARAGE
19/2 X 21/8

DEN/BR. 3
10/6 X 10/2

LIVING
12/6 X 14/8
(9'-2" CLG.)

D.W.

Width 50'
Depth 59'

❏ Don't let the small size of this home fool you. It adequately serves both formal and informal occasions. A living room and dining room are found to the right of the plan and are open to one another. Elegant ceilings may be found in both rooms. The well-planned kitchen is nearby and also serves a nook area and the casual family room. A cozy den—or use it as a third bedroom—has a double-doored entrance. The master suite is to the rear and opens through double doors. It is filled with unprecedented amenities for a smaller home, including a large walk-in closet and a dual-bowl vanity. One secondary bedroom has a full bath nearby.

Design by
Alan Mascord Design Associates, Inc.

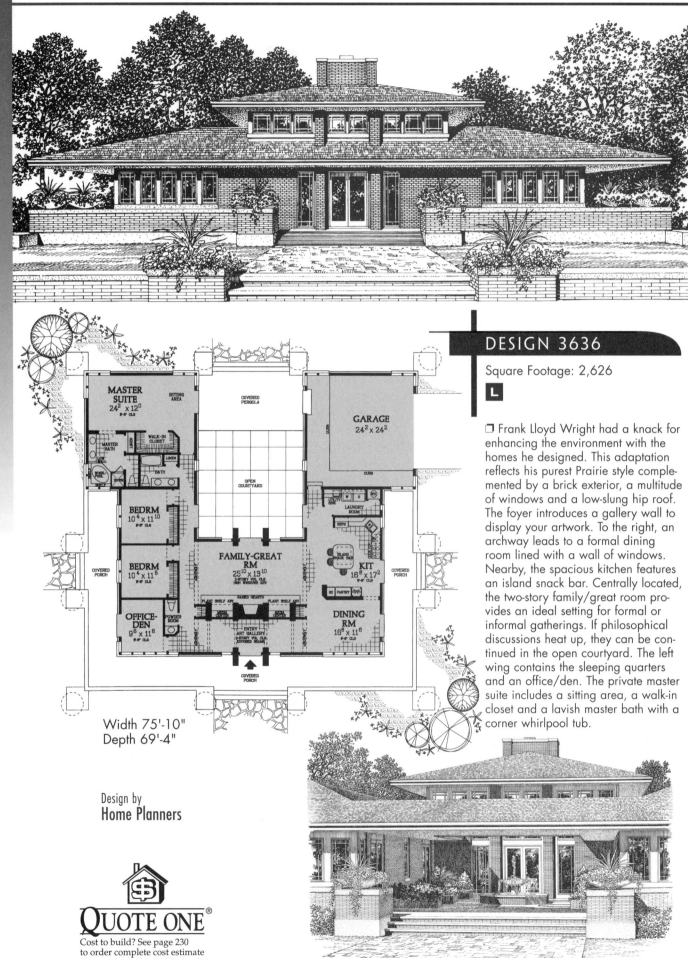

Square Footage: 2,626

L

❏ Frank Lloyd Wright had a knack for enhancing the environment with the homes he designed. This adaptation reflects his purest Prairie style complemented by a brick exterior, a multitude of windows and a low-slung hip roof. The foyer introduces a gallery wall to display your artwork. To the right, an archway leads to a formal dining room lined with a wall of windows. Nearby, the spacious kitchen features an island snack bar. Centrally located, the two-story family/great room provides an ideal setting for formal or informal gatherings. If philosophical discussions heat up, they can be continued in the open courtyard. The left wing contains the sleeping quarters and an office/den. The private master suite includes a sitting area, a walk-in closet and a lavish master bath with a corner whirlpool tub.

Width 75'-10"
Depth 69'-4"

Design by
Home Planners

Rear Elevation

This home, as shown in the photograph, may differ from the actual blueprints. For more detailed information, please check the floor plans carefully.

Photo by Andrew D. Lautman

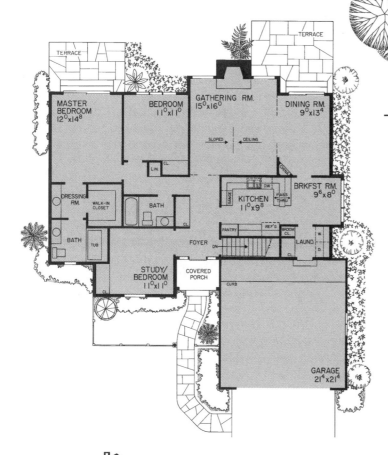

Width 51'-4"
Depth 55'-2"

Design by
Home Planners

DESIGN 2878

Square Footage: 1,530

L **D**

❏ This charming one-story traditional design offers plenty of livability in a compact size. Thoughtful zoning puts all sleeping areas to one side of the house, apart from household activity in the living and service areas. The home includes a spacious gathering room with a sloped ceiling, in addition to a formal dining room and a separate breakfast room. There's also a handy pass-through between the breakfast room and the large, efficient kitchen. The laundry is strategically located adjacent to the garage and the breakfast/kitchen areas for handy access. A master bedroom enjoys a private bath and a walk-in closet. A third bedroom can double as a sizable study just off the foyer.

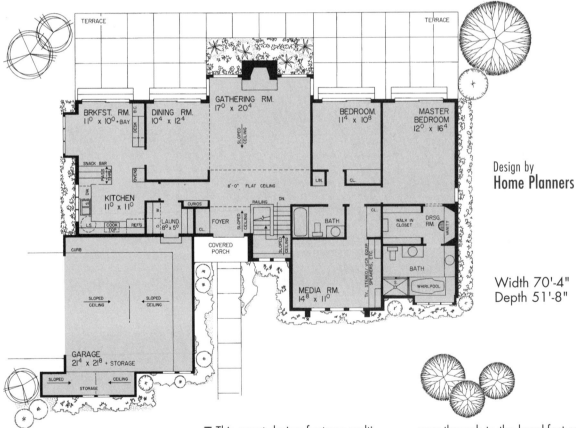

Design by
Home Planners

Width 70'-4"
Depth 51'-8"

DESIGN 2913

Square Footage: 1,835

❏ This smart design features multi-gabled ends, varied rooflines and vertical windows. It also offers efficient zoning by room functions and plenty of modern comforts for contemporary family living. A covered porch leads through a foyer to a large, central gathering room with a fireplace, a sloped ceiling and its own special view of the rear terrace. A modern kitchen with a snack bar features a pass-through to the breakfast room with a view of the terrace. There's also an adjacent dining room. A media room isolated along with the bedrooms from the rest of the house offers a quiet, private area for listening to stereos. The master bedroom suite includes its own whirlpool, sliding glass doors to the rear terrace and a walk-in closet. A large garage includes extra storage.

DESIGN 4293

Square Footage: 1,873

D

Design by
Home Planners

❏ Simple lines and a balanced sense of proportion dominate the look of this compact design. Approach over a welcoming bridge to an entry flanked by coat closets. The open great room, with clerestory windows, offers a fireplace and sliding glass doors to the rear deck. A country kitchen with island work area features plenty of space for a table and chairs. The deluxe master bedroom suite is complete with a walk-in closet, a dressing area, a pampering bath and sliding glass door to the rear deck. Two family bedrooms, to the front of the home, have access to a full bath.

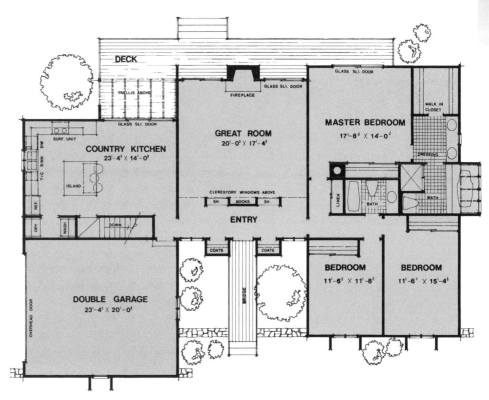

Width 68'
Depth 46'-8"

Alternate Elevation A

Alternate Elevation B

DESIGN 2505

Square Footage: 1,366

L D

❏ This design offers you a choice of three distinctively different exteriors. Blueprints show details for all three optional elevations. A study of the floor plan reveals a fine measure of livability. In less than 1,400 square feet, you'll find amenities often found in much larger homes. In addition to the two eating areas and the open planning of the gathering room, the indoor-outdoor relationships are of great interest. The basement may be developed at a later date for recreational activities.

QUOTE ONE®

Cost to build? See page 230 to order complete cost estimate to build this house in your area!

Design by
Home Planners

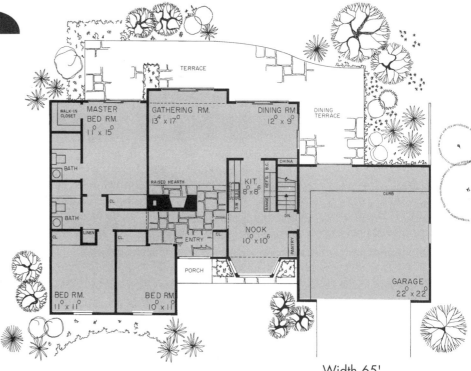

Width 65'
Depth 37'-4"

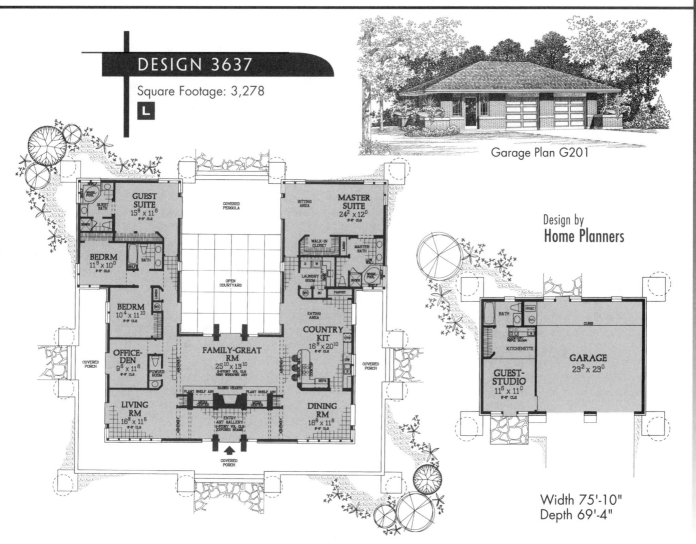

DESIGN 3637

Square Footage: 3,278

L

Garage Plan G201

Design by
Home Planners

Width 75'-10"
Depth 69'-4"

❏ The landscape harmonized so well with his designs that they often seemed as one. Yes, we're talking about the Wright stuff! This Prairie-style home—with its U-shaped design—maximizes indoor-outdoor livability. Note the access provided to the central, open courtyard from the family/great room, country kitchen, bedroom wing, master suite and guest suite. Inside, the master suite is split for privacy, enhanced with a sitting area, a walk-in closet and a luxurious master bath. Open planning combines the country kitchen with an eating area, a snack bar and a formal dining room nearby. The family-great room separates the sleeping quarters and formal living room. Guests will feel right at home with their own private suite and pampering guest bath. Plans for a detached garage with an optional guest suite are included with the blueprints.

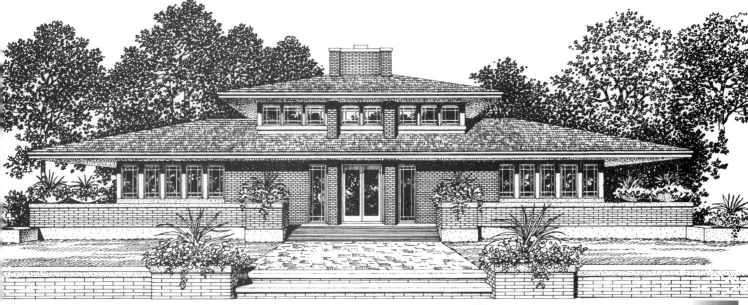

DESIGN 2858

Square Footage: 2,231

❐ This sun oriented design was created to face the south. The morning sun will brighten the living and dining rooms, along with the adjacent terrace. Sun enters the garden room by way of the glass roof and walls. In the winter, the solar heat gain from the garden room should provide relief from high energy bills. Solar shades allow you to adjust the amount of light that you want to enter in the warmer months. The kitchen has a snack bar and a serving counter to the dining room. The breakfast room with laundry area is also convenient to the kitchen. Three bedrooms are on the northern wall. The master bedroom has a large tub and a separate shower with a four-foot square skylight above. When this design is oriented toward the sun, it should prove to be energy-efficient and a joy to live in.

Design by
Home Planners

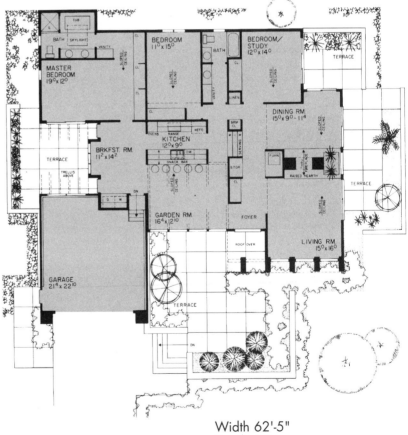

Width 62'-5"
Depth 62'

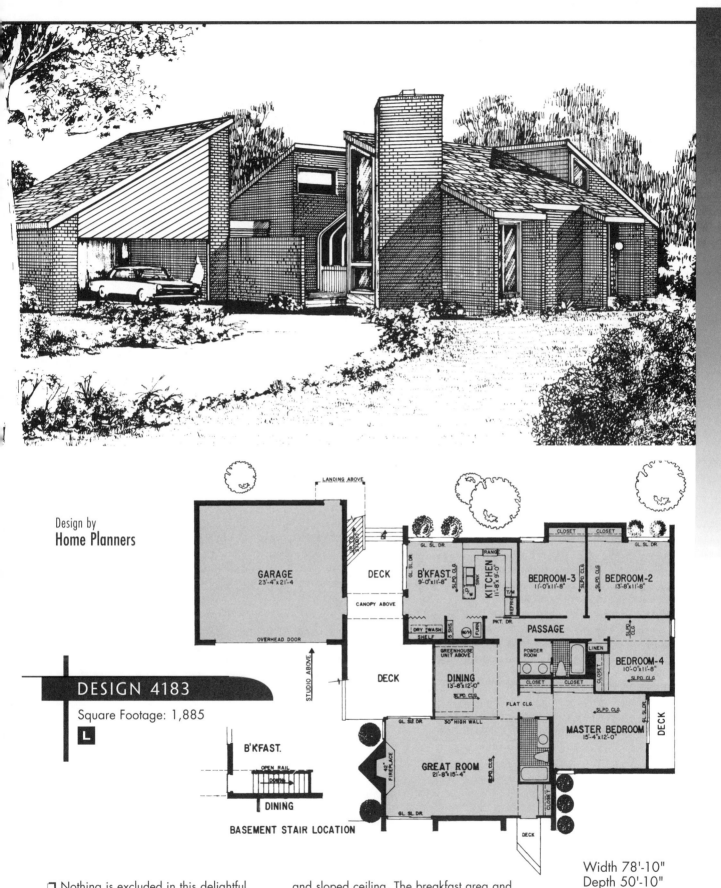

Design by
Home Planners

GARAGE
23'-4"x21'-4"

LANDING ABOVE

DECK

CANOPY ABOVE

OVERHEAD DOOR

DECK

STUDIO ABOVE

GL. SL. DR.

GL. SL. DR.

B'KFAST
9'-0"x11'-8"

KITCHEN
11'-8"x 9'-0"

RANGE

SINK

D/W

DRY WASH
SHELF

5 SHKS

W/H

FURN

GREENHOUSE
UNIT ABOVE

DINING
13'-8"x12'-0"

SLPD. CLG.

GL. SL. DR.

30" HIGH WALL

42"
FIREPLACE

GREAT ROOM
21'-8"x15'-4"

SLPD. CLG.

GL. SL. DR.

CLOSET   CLOSET

GL. SL. DR.

BEDROOM-3
11'-0"x11'-8"

BEDROOM-2
13'-8"x11'-8"

SLPD. CLG. SLPD. CLG.

PKT. DR.

PASSAGE

SLPD.
CLG.

BEDROOM-4
10'-0"x11'-8"

SLPD. CLG.

POWDER
ROOM

LINEN

CLOSET   CLOSET

CLOSET

FLAT CLG.

SLPD. CLG.

MASTER BEDROOM
15'-4"x12'-0"

DECK

CLOSET

DECK

DESIGN 4183

Square Footage: 1,885

L

B'KFAST.

OPEN RAIL

DOWN

DINING

BASEMENT STAIR LOCATION

Width 78'-10"
Depth 50'-10"

❏ Nothing is excluded in this delightful contemporary one-story. Enter the home from a deck entry to the oversized great room. A fireplace and sliding glass doors are nice accents here. The dining room is separated from this area by a divider wall. It is embellished with a greenhouse unit and sloped ceiling. The breakfast area and kitchen have access to the rear yard as well as to a side deck. Four bedrooms include three family bedrooms (two with sliding glass doors) and a master suite with private deck. This plan can be built with a basement included with blueprints.

DESIGN 2351

Square Footage: 1,862

❏ The extension of the wide overhanging roof of this distinctive home provides shelter for the walkway to the front door. A raised brick planter adds appeal to the outstanding exterior design. The living patterns offered by this plan are delightfully different, yet extremely practical. Notice the separation of the master bedroom from the other two bedrooms. While assuring an extra measure of quiet privacy for the parents, this master bedroom location may be ideal for a live-in relative. Locating the kitchen in the middle of the plan frees up valuable outside wall space and leads to interesting planning. The front living room is sunken for dramatic appeal and need not have any cross room traffic. The utility room houses the laundry and the heating and cooling equipment.

Width 56'-10"
Depth 48'-10"

Design by
Home Planners

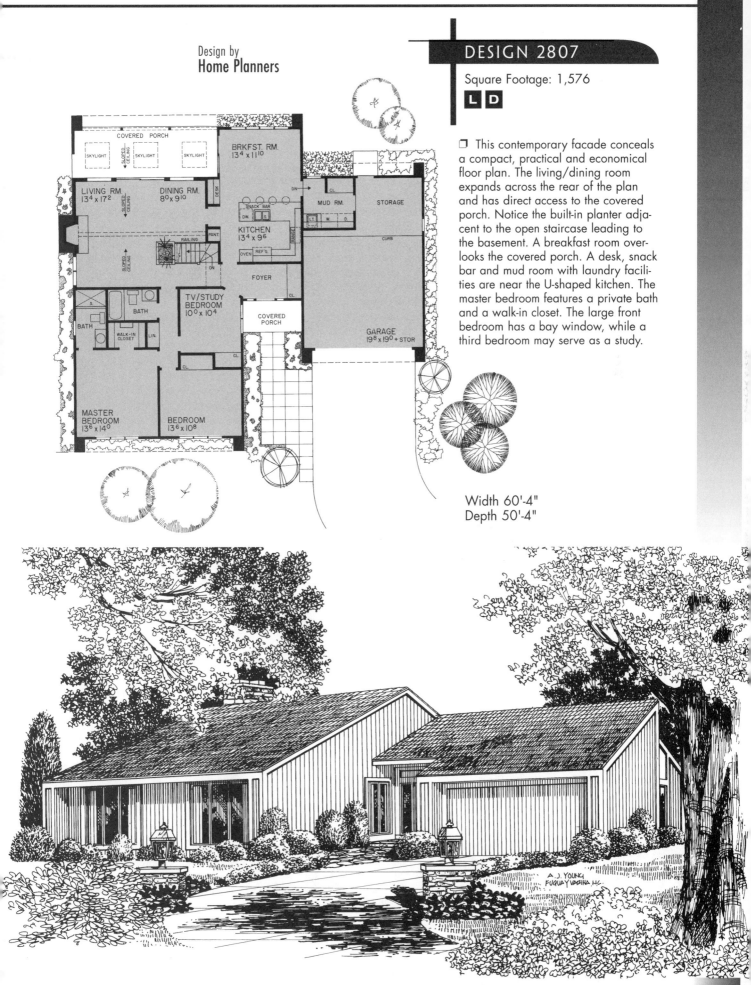

Design by
Home Planners

COVERED PORCH

SKYLIGHT | SLOPED CEILING | SKYLIGHT | SKYLIGHT

BRKFST. RM.
13⁴ x 11¹⁰

LIVING RM.
13⁴ x 17²

DINING RM.
8⁰ x 9¹⁰

DESK

CL.

MUD RM.

STORAGE

SNACK BAR

DW.

KITCHEN
13⁴ x 9⁶

LT. W. D.

RANGE

CURB

SLOPED CEILING

RAILING

PRNT.

OVEN | REF'G.

FOYER

CL.

DN

S.

BATH

TV/STUDY
BEDROOM
10⁰ x 10⁴

COVERED
PORCH

BATH

WALK-IN
CLOSET | LIN.

GARAGE
19⁸ x 19⁰ + STOR.

CL.

CL.

MASTER
BEDROOM
13⁶ x 14⁰

BEDROOM
13⁶ x 10⁸

❏ This contemporary facade conceals a compact, practical and economical floor plan. The living/dining room expands across the rear of the plan and has direct access to the covered porch. Notice the built-in planter adjacent to the open staircase leading to the basement. A breakfast room overlooks the covered porch. A desk, snack bar and mud room with laundry facilities are near the U-shaped kitchen. The master bedroom features a private bath and a walk-in closet. The large front bedroom has a bay window, while a third bedroom may serve as a study.

Width 60'-4"
Depth 50'-4"

A.J. YOUNG
FUQUAY VARINA, NC

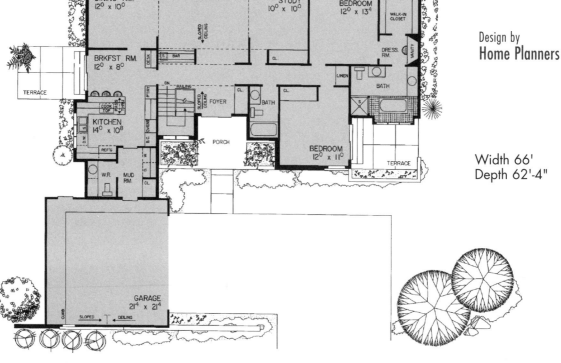

Design by
Home Planners

Width 66'
Depth 62'-4"

DESIGN 2918

Square Footage: 1,693

❏ Alternating use of stone and wood gives a textured look to this striking contemporary home with wide overhanging rooflines and a built-in planter box. The design is just as exciting on the inside, with two bedrooms, including a master suite, a study (or optional third bedroom), a rear gathering room with a fireplace and a sloped ceiling, a rear dining room and an efficient U-shaped kitchen with a pass-through to an adjoining breakfast room. A mud room and washroom are located between the kitchen and the spacious two-car garage. Plans for an optional basement are included.

Rear Elevation

Square Footage: 2,758
Greenhouse: 149 square feet

L D

❏ What a grand plan! This well-zoned beauty has nearly everything going for it. Start with the 340-square-foot country kitchen, which sports a fireplace, snack bar and greenhouse next door. Move to the media room, where there's a wall of built-ins, and then on to the combination living room/dining area (note the sloped ceiling, raised-hearth fireplace and doors leading to the terrace in back). Also check out the king-sized master suite with His and Hers walk-in closets and whirlpool tub made for two, and all the extra storage space.

QUOTE ONE®
Cost to build? See page 230 to order complete cost estimate to build this house in your area!

Width 81'-4"
Depth 78'-0"

Design by
Home Planners

DESIGN 2790

Square Footage: 2,075

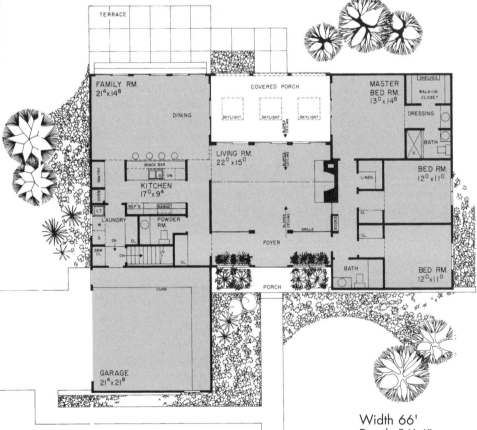

Width 66'
Depth 56'-4"

Design by
Home Planners

❒ Enter this contemporary hip-roofed home through the double front doors and immediately view the sloped-ceilinged living room with fireplace. This room will be a sheer delight when it comes to formal entertaining. It has easy access to the kitchen and also a powder room nearby. The work area will be convenient. The kitchen has an island work center with snack bar. The laundry is adjacent to the service entrance and stairs leading to the basement. This area is planned to be real a "step saver." The sleeping wing consists of two family bedrooms, bath and master bedroom suite. Maybe the most attractive feature of this design is the rear covered porch with skylights. It is accessible by way of sliding glass doors in the family/dining area, living room and master bedroom.

DESIGN 2789

Square Footage: 2,732

L D

TERRACE

COVERED PORCH

GATHERING RM.
21⁰x21⁶

DINING RM.
14²x11¹⁰

STUDY
11⁸x13⁴

MASTER
BED RM.
13⁰x18⁸

SHELVES

WALK-IN CLOSET

THRU FIREPLACE

DRESSING/BATH

VANITY

BREAKFAST
14⁰x11⁰

DESK   BAR

ROOMS CABINET

POWDER RM.

TUB

SEAT

BATH

WALK-IN CLOSET

LINEN

PATIO

PANTRY

FOYER

CL

BED RM.
11⁰x12⁰

BATH

BED RM.
11⁶x12⁰

KITCHEN
13⁰x10⁰

OVEN

REF G.

COVERED PORCH

STEP-UP

TUB

CEILING

CURB

GARAGE
31⁴x21⁸

Width 85'-10"
Depth 72'-4"

❐ An attached three car garage! What a fantastic feature of this three-bedroom contemporary design. And there's more. As one walks up the steps to the covered porch and through the double front doors the charm of this design will be overwhelming. Inside, a large foyer greets all visitors and leads them to each of the three areas, each down a few steps. The living area has a large gathering room with fireplace and a study adjacent on one side and the formal dining room on the other. The work center has an efficient kitchen with island range, breakfast room, laundry and built-in desk and bar. Then there is the sleeping area. Note the raised tub with sloped ceiling.

Design by
Home Planners

DESIGN 2871

Square Footage: 1,824
Greenhouse Area: 81 square feet
Total: 1,905 square feet

D

❐ A greenhouse area off the dining room and living room provides a cheerful focal point for this comfortable three-bedroom trend home. The spacious living room features a cozy fireplace and a sloped ceiling. In addition to the dining room, there's a less formal breakfast room just off the modern kitchen. Both kitchen and breakfast areas look out onto a front terrace. Stairs just off the foyer lead down to a recreation room. The master bedroom suite opens to a terrace. A mud room and a wash room off the garage allow rear entry to the house during inclement weather.

Design by
Home Planners

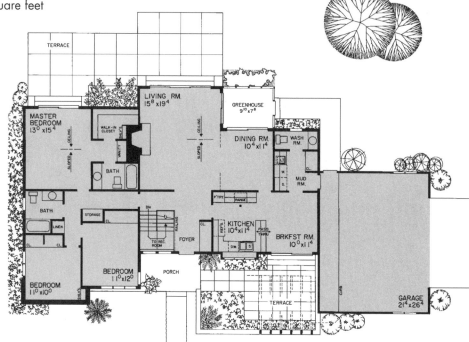

Width 80'-4"
Depth 43'

QUOTE ONE®

Cost to build? See page 230
to order complete cost estimate
to build this house in your area!

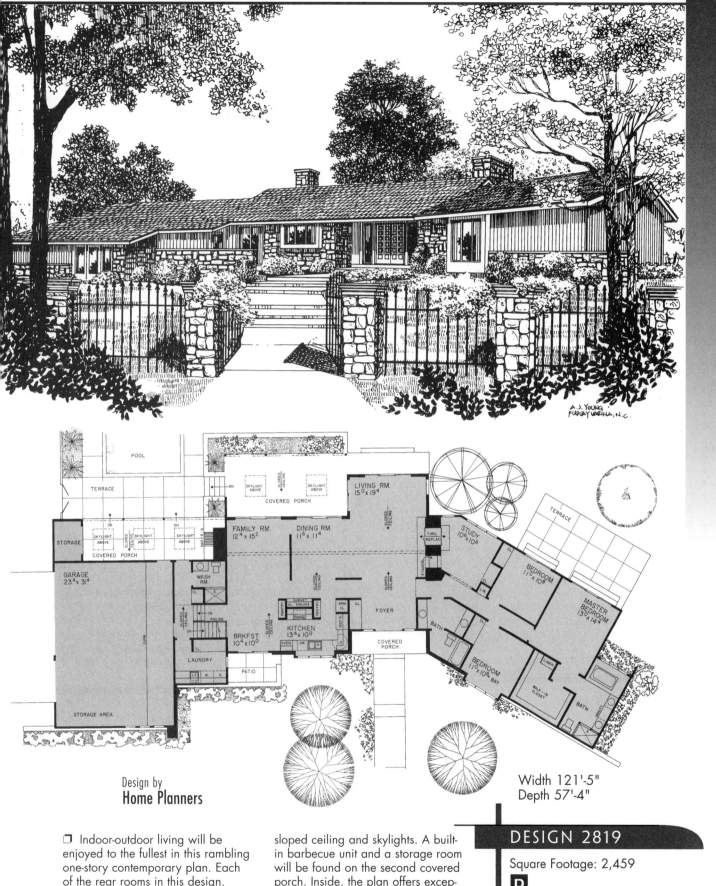

Design by
Home Planners

Width 121'-5"
Depth 57'-4"

DESIGN 2819

Square Footage: 2,459

☐ Indoor-outdoor living will be enjoyed to the fullest in this rambling one-story contemporary plan. Each of the rear rooms in this design, excluding the study, has access to a terrace or porch. Even the front breakfast room has access to a private dining patio. The covered porch off the living areas—family, dining and living rooms—has a sloped ceiling and skylights. A built-in barbecue unit and a storage room will be found on the second covered porch. Inside, the plan offers exceptional living patterns for various activities. Notice the through-fireplace that the living room shares with the study. A built-in etagere is nearby. The three-car garage has an extra storage area.

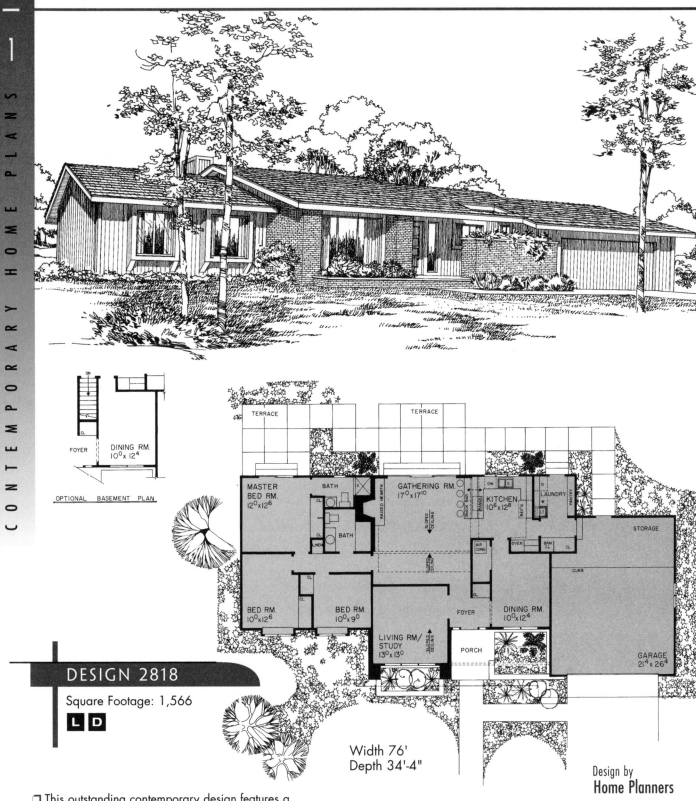

OPTIONAL BASEMENT PLAN

DINING RM. 10⁰ x 12⁴

FOYER

DN

TERRACE

TERRACE

MASTER BED RM. 12⁰ x 12⁶

BATH

GATHERING RM. 17⁰ x 17¹⁰

KITCHEN 10⁶ x 12⁸

LAUNDRY

PANTRY

RAISED HEARTH

SLOPED CEILING

SNACK BAR

RANGE

REF'G

DW

BATH

LINEN

CL

AIR COND.

SLOPED CEILING

OVEN

BRM CL

STORAGE

CURB

BED RM. 10⁰ x 12⁶

BED RM. 10⁰ x 9⁰

LIVING RM/ STUDY 13⁰ x 13⁰

FOYER

PORCH

DINING RM. 10⁰ x 12⁴

GARAGE 21⁴ x 26⁴

DESIGN 2818

Square Footage: 1,566

L D

Width 76'
Depth 34'-4"

Design by
Home Planners

❏ This outstanding contemporary design features a recessed front entry with covered front porch. Note the planter court with privacy wall. The rear gathering room has a sloped ceiling, raised-hearth fireplace, sliding glass doors to the terrace and a snack bar with pass-through to the kitchen. In addition to the gathering room, there is the living room/study. This room could be utilized in a variety of ways depending on your family's choice. The formal dining room is convenient to the kitchen. Three bedrooms and two closely located baths are in the sleeping wing. This plan includes details for the construction of an optional basement.

QUOTE ONE®

Cost to build? See page 230
to order complete cost estimate
to build this house in your area!

DESIGN 2864

Square Footage: 1,387

L D

☐ Projecting the garage to the front of a house is very economical in two ways. One, it reduces the required lot size, and two, it will protect the interior from street noise. Many other characteristics of this design deserve mention as well. A formal dining area opens to a spacious gathering room with a large, centered fireplace; both areas offer a sloped ceiling. The well-appointed kitchen has an adjacent breakfast room and a counter snack bar. The study contains a wet bar. Sliding glass doors in three rooms open to the terrace.

Quote One®

Cost to build? See page 230 to order complete cost estimate to build this house in your area!

Design by
Home Planners

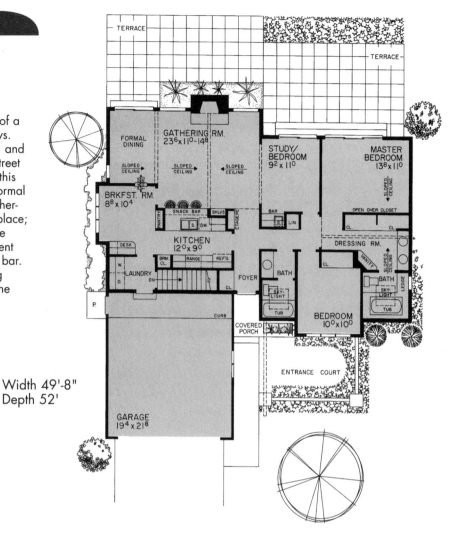

Width 49'-8"
Depth 52'

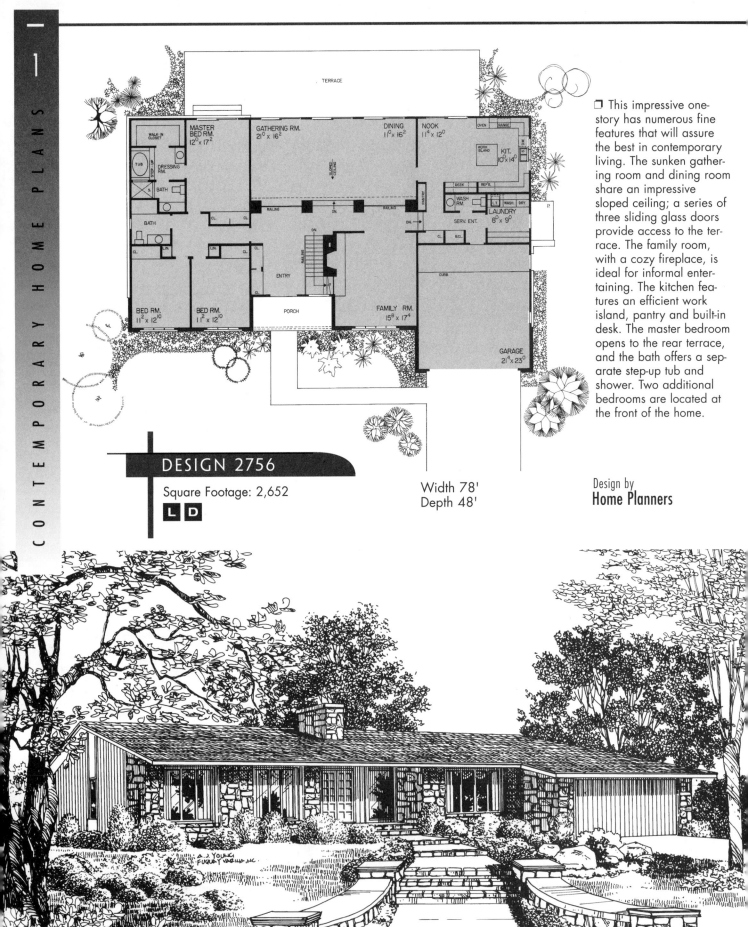

□ This impressive one-story has numerous fine features that will assure the best in contemporary living. The sunken gathering room and dining room share an impressive sloped ceiling; a series of three sliding glass doors provide access to the terrace. The family room, with a cozy fireplace, is ideal for informal entertaining. The kitchen features an efficient work island, pantry and built-in desk. The master bedroom opens to the rear terrace, and the bath offers a separate step-up tub and shower. Two additional bedrooms are located at the front of the home.

DESIGN 2756

Square Footage: 2,652

L D

Width 78'
Depth 48'

Design by
Home Planners

DESIGN 2671

Square Footage: 1,589

❑ The rustic exterior of this one-story home features vertical wood siding. The entry foyer is floored with flagstone and leads to the three areas of the plan: the sleeping, living and work center. The sleeping area features three bedrooms. The master bedroom utilizes sliding glass doors to the rear terrace. The living area, consisting of gathering and dining rooms, also enjoys access to the terrace. The work center is efficiently planned. It houses the kitchen with a snack bar, the breakfast room with a built-in china cabinet and stairs to the basement. Special amenities include a raised-hearth fireplace and a walk-in closet in the master bedroom.

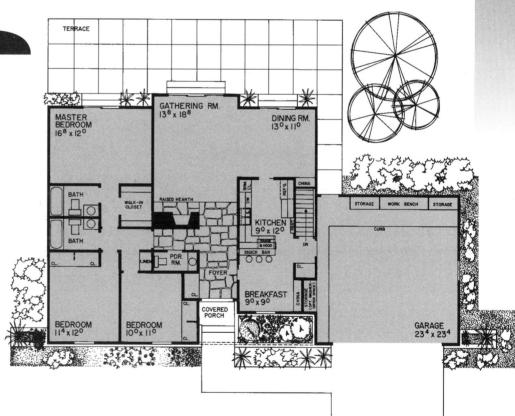

Width 68'
Depth 40'-5"

Design by
Home Planners

QUOTE ONE®
Cost to build? See page 230
to order complete cost estimate
to build this house in your area!

DESIGN 2343

Square Footage: 3,110

❏ If yours is a growing active family the chances are good that they will want their new home to relate to the outdoors. This distinctive design puts a premium on private outdoor living. And you don't have to install a swimming pool to get the most enjoyment from this home. Developing this area as a garden court will provide the indoor living areas with a breathtaking awareness of nature's beauty. Notice the fine zoning of the plan and how each area has its sliding glass doors to provide an unrestricted view. Three bedrooms plus a study are serviced by three baths. The family and gathering rooms provide two great living areas. The island kitchen with nearby nook is sure to please.

Design by
Home Planners

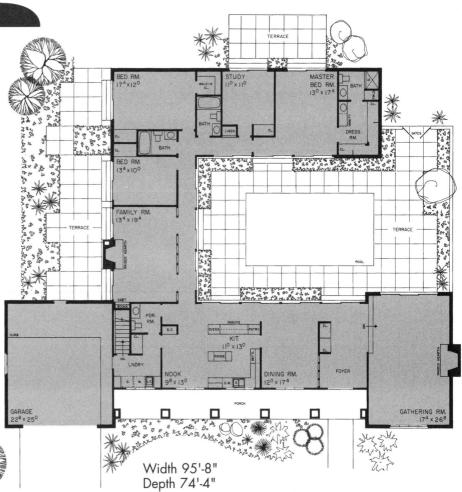

Width 95'-8"
Depth 74'-4"

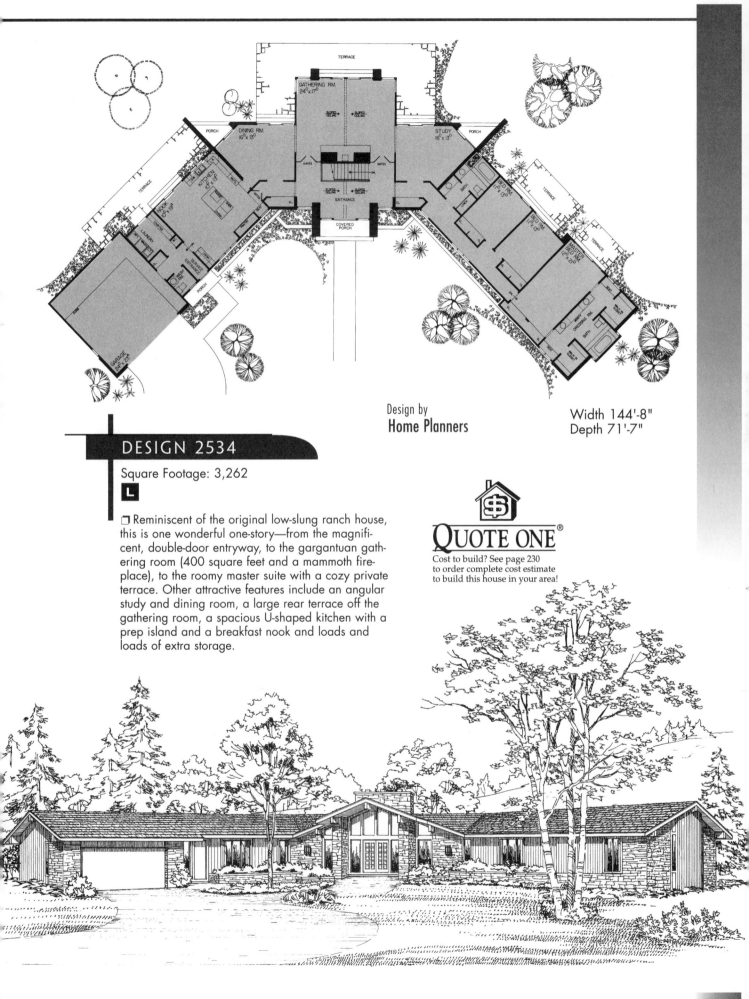

Design by
Home Planners

Width 144'-8"
Depth 71'-7"

DESIGN 2534

Square Footage: 3,262

L

❏ Reminiscent of the original low-slung ranch house, this is one wonderful one-story—from the magnificent, double-door entryway, to the gargantuan gathering room (400 square feet and a mammoth fireplace), to the roomy master suite with a cozy private terrace. Other attractive features include an angular study and dining room, a large rear terrace off the gathering room, a spacious U-shaped kitchen with a prep island and a breakfast nook and loads and loads of extra storage.

QUOTE ONE®

Cost to build? See page 230
to order complete cost estimate
to build this house in your area!

DESIGN 2226

Square Footage: 3,578

❑ Containing over 3,500 square feet, space for living is abundant. Each of the various rooms is large. Further, each major room has access to the outdoors. The efficient inside kitchen is strategically located in relation to the family and dining rooms. Observe how it functions with the enclosed atrium to provide a snack bar. Functional room dividers separate various areas. Study closely the living area. A two-way fireplace divides the spacious living room and the cozy library highlighted by built-in cabinets and bookshelves. A hobby room with laundry adjacent will be a favorite family activities spot.

Design by
Home Planners

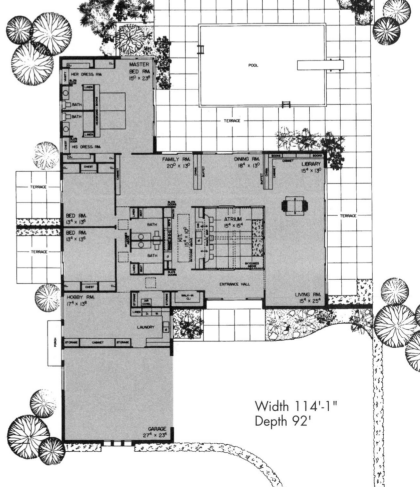

Width 114'-1"
Depth 92'

TWICE AS NICE: *Attractive two-story designs*

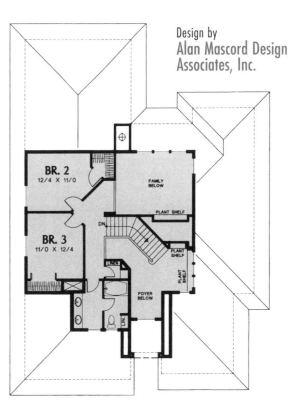

❏ Looking for a grand entrance? The entry to this contemporary home is so grand, you could ride in on a camel's back. Inside, a large foyer offers a gracious introduction to the formal living and dining rooms joined for effective entertaining. An adjacent gourmet kitchen with an island cooktop is strategically located to serve formal and informal areas with equal ease. Nearby, a two-story family room with a built-in media center and corner fireplace shares space with a sunny nook, perfect for informal get-togethers. The private master suite features a walk-in closet with a built-in ironing board and a luxurious master bath with a relaxing spa tub. A den, a powder room and a laundry room complete the first floor. The second floor contains two bedrooms and a full bath.

DESIGN 9581

First Floor: 1,896 square feet
Second Floor: 568 square feet
Total: 2,464 square feet

Design by
Alan Mascord Design Associates, Inc.

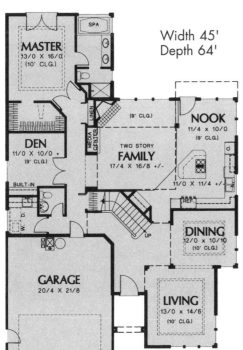

Width 45'
Depth 64'

MASTER
13/0 X 16/0
(10' CLG.)

SPA

DEN
11/0 X 10/0
(9' CLG.)

LINEN

MEDIA CENTER

NOOK
11/4 x 10/0
(9' CLG.)

(9' CLG.)

TWO STORY
FAMILY
17/4 X 16/8 +/-

11/0 X 11/4 +/-

BUILT-IN

W D

REF.

UP

DINING
12/0 x 10/10
(10' CLG.)

GARAGE
20/4 X 21/8

LIVING
13/0 x 14/6
(10' CLG.)

BR. 2
12/4 X 11/0

FAMILY BELOW

PLANT SHELF

BR. 3
11/0 X 12/4

DN

PLANT SHELF

LINEN

PLANT SHELF

FOYER BELOW

LIN

DESIGN 7421

First Floor: 1,255 square feet
Second Floor: 982 square feet
Total: 2,237 square feet

Design by
**Alan Mascord Design
Associates, Inc.**

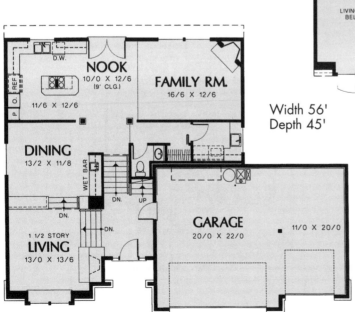

Width 56'
Depth 45'

☐ This Mediterranean-flavored contemporary is sure to please with its many amenities. From the raised foyer, a living room with the option for a fireplace and a 1½-story ceiling flows into the formal dining room. A spacious family room, with a corner fireplace and windows to the rear yard, works well with the island kitchen and eating nook. Upstairs, three family bedrooms share a full bath. A master bedroom suite features a walk-in closet and a private bath. A three-car garage shelters the family fleet.

DESIGN 9552

First Floor: 1,317 square feet
Second Floor: 1,146 square feet
Total: 2,463 square feet

☐ This home's master bedroom suite contains many fine design features, including a luxury bath with a vaulted ceiling, a spa tub, dual lavatories and a roomy walk-in closet. Other fine elements include a columned formal living and dining area. This area also includes a boxed ceiling and a fireplace. A gourmet kitchen accommodates the most elaborate—as well as the simplest—meals. A large family room is nearby. Family and guests will find three secondary bedrooms comfortable. Bedroom 2 enjoys an elegant window while Bedroom 3 contains a walk-in closet.

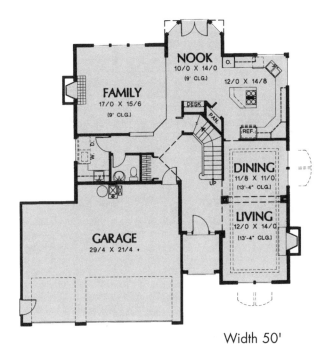

Width 50'
Depth 54'

Design by
Alan Mascord Design
Associates, Inc.

DESIGN 7424

First Floor: 1,127 square feet
Second Floor: 1,042 square feet
Total: 2,170 square feet

◻ An elegantly arched, brick entryway ushers you into this delightful four-bedroom home. The two-story living room opens directly off the foyer and features a fireplace and a corner full of windows. The island kitchen offers ease in serving with a nearby bayed nook and adjacent dining room. A cozy family room has a second fireplace and sliding glass doors to the rear yard. Upstairs, three spacious family bedrooms share a full bath, while the master suite comes complete with a walk-in closet and a lavish bath.

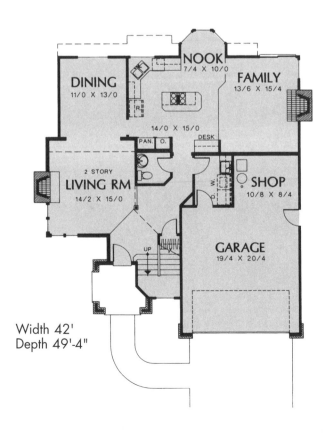

SPA

VAULTED
MASTER
12/8 X 16/8

BR. 2
13/4 X 10/0

LIVING RM.
BELOW

BR. 3
13/4 X 10/0

DN.

FOYER
BELOW

LIN

BR. 4
14/4 X 10/0

NOOK
7/4 X 10/0

DINING
11/0 X 13/0

FAMILY
13/6 X 15/4

14/0 X 15/0

PAN. O.

DESK

2 STORY
LIVING RM
14/2 X 15/0

W.

SHOP
10/8 X 8/4

UP

GARAGE
19/4 X 20/4

Design by
**Alan Mascord Design
Associates, Inc.**

Width 42'
Depth 49'-4"

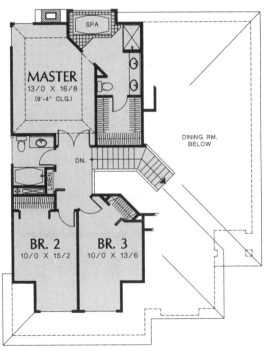

MASTER
13/0 X 16/8
(9'-4" CLG.)

SPA

BR. 2
10/0 X 15/2

BR. 3
10/0 X 13/6

DN.

LINEN

DINING RM.
BELOW

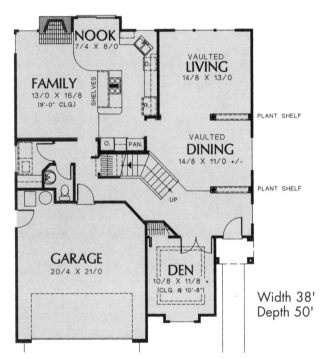

NOOK
7/4 X 8/0

VAULTED
LIVING
14/8 X 13/0

FAMILY
13/0 X 16/8
(9'-0" CLG.)

SHELVES

PLANT SHELF

VAULTED
DINING
14/8 X 11/0 +/-

O.   PAN.

PLANT SHELF

UP

GARAGE
20/4 X 21/0

DEN
10/8 X 11/8 +
(CLG. @ 10'-8")

Width 38'
Depth 50'

Design by
Alan Mascord Design Associates, Inc.

❏ This contemporary two-story home with stucco finish is packed with many amenities. The formal part of the home is characterized by a high vaulted ceiling with columns and plant shelves defining the dining area. A pair of French doors opens off the entry leading to the den (notice the high-stepped vaulted ceiling here). The functional kitchen with attached nook complements the casual family room—rounding out the first floor. Upstairs are the spectacular master suite as well as two additional bedrooms.

DESIGN 9426

First Floor: 1,257 square feet
Second Floor: 854 square feet
Total: 2,111 square feet

DESIGN 8674

First Floor: 1,816 square feet
Second Floor: 703 square feet
Total: 2,519 square feet

❒ No matter where you're building, this design offers two exteriors to heighten possibilities. The double-door entry opens to the combined formal living and dining areas. Nearby, the kitchen enjoys ample space for gourmet-meal preparations, as well as an attached breakfast nook. In the family room, a volume ceiling and a fireplace are sure to please. The master bedroom, located at the rear of the first floor, has access to the covered patio. It also sports a bath with a double-bowl lavatory, a garden tub and a large walk-in closet.

On the second floor, three bedrooms enjoy peace and quiet and share a hall bath. An option for a loft is included in the set blueprints.

Design by
Home Design Services, Inc.

Width 45'
Depth 67'-6"

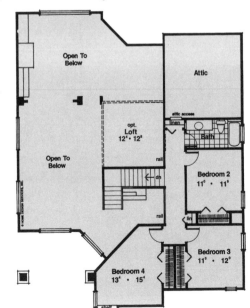

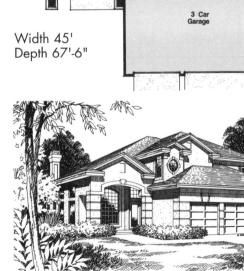

Alternate Elevation

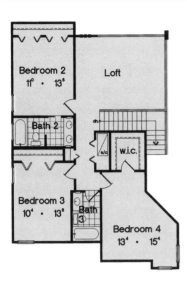

Floor plan labels (second floor / upper left):
Bedroom 2 11⁰ · 13⁸
Loft
Bath 2
w.i.c.
Bedroom 3 10⁴ · 13⁸
Bath 3
Bedroom 4 13⁴ · 15⁴

Floor plan labels (first floor / right):
Covered Patio
Pool Bath
service
Family Rm. 16⁸ · 15⁰
media
Master Suite 14⁸ · 15⁸
Nook
Kitchen
Dining Rm. 16⁴ · 10⁰
w.i.c.
Master Bath
ref
Living Rm. 16⁴ · 13⁸
storage
Laundry
Pwdr.
Foyer
w.h. a/c
Entry
2 Car Garage 28⁸ · 19⁸

© HOME DESIGN SERVICES, INC.

DESIGN 8704

First Floor: 1,844 square feet
Second Floor: 1,017 square feet
Total: 2,861 square feet

Width 45'
Depth 67'-8"

❑ The excitement begins upon entering the foyer of this home where an impressive staircase is its focal point. From there you view the formal spaces of the living and dining rooms with vaulted ceilings. Passing through an archway you enter the family room with its impressive media/fireplace wall. Just off the nook is a sliding glass door to the covered patio where a wet bar can be found as well as a pool bath. The kitchen is a gourmet's dream, with loads of pantry storage and planning desk. A built-in wall of shelves and arches just off the nook welcome you to the master wing. The suite is generously sized and has a wonderful bed wall of high transom glass, as well as sliding glass doors to the patio. The second floor is impressive with three large bedrooms, two of which share a bath, and one bedroom having a private bath. A spacious loft works well as a games, study or library room or it can be a fifth bedroom.

Design by
Home Design
Services, Inc.

J.N. HANSEN S.DG

DESIGN 8707

First Floor: 1,703 square feet
Second Floor: 889 square feet
Total: 2,592 square feet

❐ The gathering room is the heart of this design, and all other spaces move from its core. The large kitchen with a sunny, bayed nook is bathed in light through walls of glass, while the formal dining room has French doors that open onto a private patio. The hub of family activity is the gathering room, and it is sized for large gatherings indeed. It comes complete with a fireplace/media wall which soars two stories with niches and glass transoms. The master wing entry is tucked away under the ascending staircase for privacy. The suite features a bay window sitting area with a view to the deck area. The bath boasts loads of closet space, and His and Her vanities flank a soaking tub and shower. The second floor can become a three-bedroom affair, or you are able to make Bedroom 4 a game loft, or a second master suite with its own bath.

First Floor Plan:

Deck

Sitting

Master Suite
17⁰ · 14⁰

w.i.c.

media · media
Covered Patio

Gathering Rm.
15¹⁰ · 25⁰

Dining Rm.
11² · 13⁸

Master Bath

Kitchen

Laun. · Pwdr · niche
Foyer

Entry · Nook

2 Car Garage
21⁶ · 23⁴

Width 44'
Depth 64'-8"

Second Floor Plan:

Loft/Bedroom
14⁴ · 11¹⁰

Bath 2

Bedroom 2
11⁴ · 11⁸

Bath 3

w.i.c.

Bedroom 3
12⁰ · 11⁸

Design by
Home Design
Services, Inc.

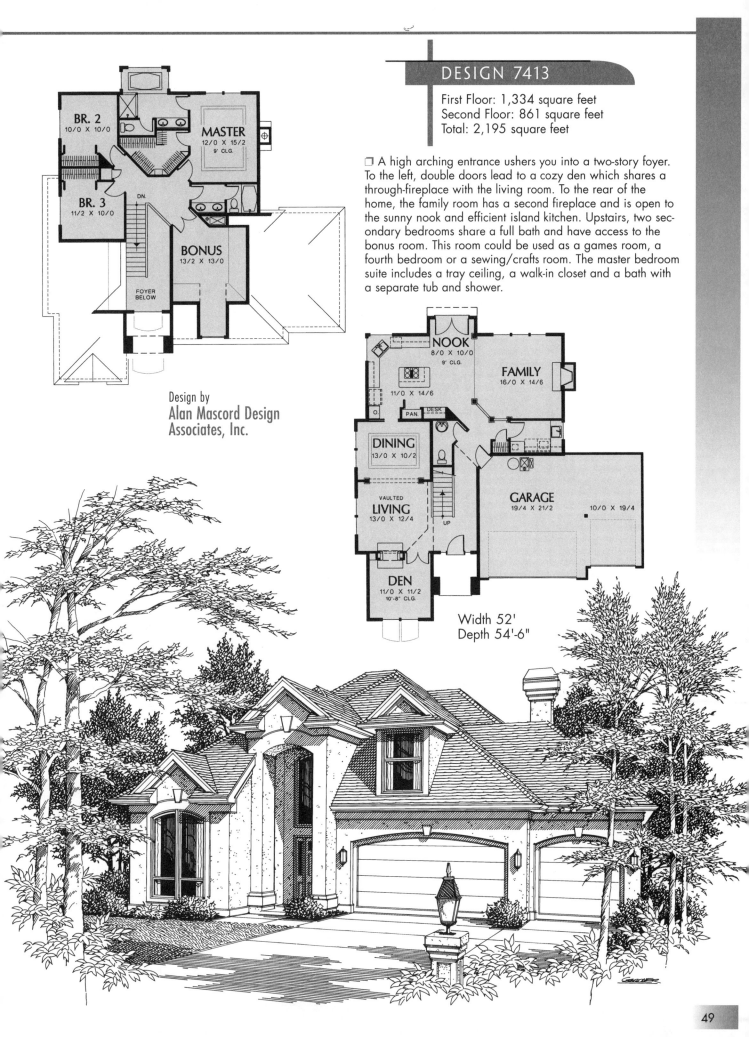

DESIGN 7413

First Floor: 1,334 square feet
Second Floor: 861 square feet
Total: 2,195 square feet

☐ A high arching entrance ushers you into a two-story foyer. To the left, double doors lead to a cozy den which shares a through-fireplace with the living room. To the rear of the home, the family room has a second fireplace and is open to the sunny nook and efficient island kitchen. Upstairs, two secondary bedrooms share a full bath and have access to the bonus room. This room could be used as a games room, a fourth bedroom or a sewing/crafts room. The master bedroom suite includes a tray ceiling, a walk-in closet and a bath with a separate tub and shower.

BR. 2
10/0 X 10/0

MASTER
12/0 X 15/2
9' CLG.

BR. 3
11/2 X 10/0

DN.

BONUS
13/2 X 13/0

FOYER
BELOW

Design by
Alan Mascord Design Associates, Inc.

NOOK
8/0 X 10/0
9' CLG.

FAMILY
16/0 X 14/6

11/0 X 14/6

PAN.   DESK

DINING
13/0 X 10/2

GARAGE
19/4 X 21/2   10/0 X 19/4

VAULTED
LIVING
13/0 X 12/4

UP

DEN
11/0 X 11/2
10'-8" CLG.

Width 52'
Depth 54'-6"

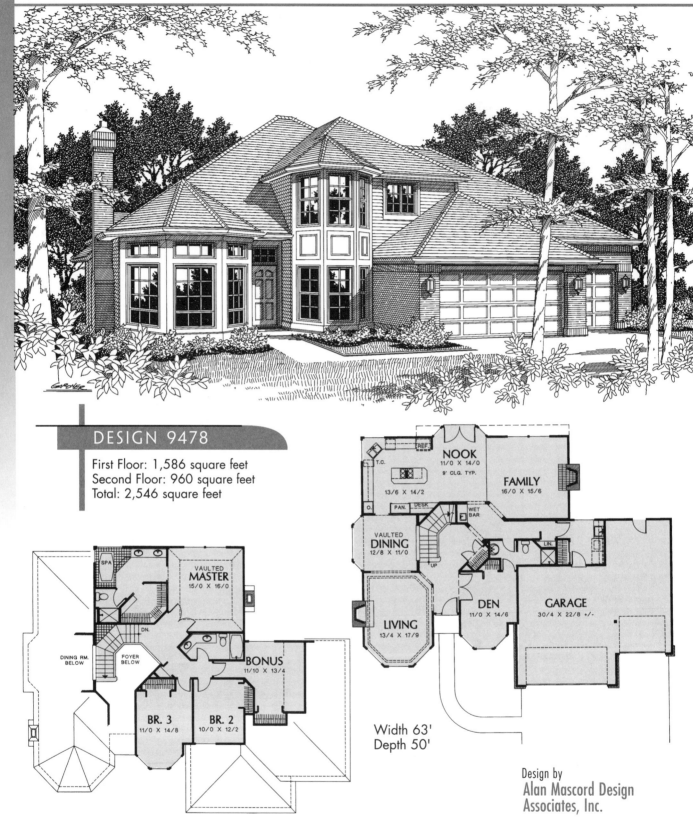

DESIGN 9478

First Floor: 1,586 square feet
Second Floor: 960 square feet
Total: 2,546 square feet

SPA

VAULTED
MASTER
15/0 X 16/0

DN.

DINING RM.
BELOW

FOYER
BELOW

BONUS
11/10 X 13/4

BR. 3
11/0 X 14/8

BR. 2
10/0 X 12/2

REF.

NOOK
11/0 X 14/0
9' CLG. TYP.

T.C.

13/6 X 14/2

FAMILY
16/0 X 15/6

O.

PAN.

DESK

WET
BAR

VAULTED
DINING
12/8 X 11/0

UP

LIN.

DEN
11/0 X 14/6

GARAGE
30/4 X 22/8 +/-

LIVING
13/4 X 17/9

Width 63'
Depth 50'

Design by
**Alan Mascord Design
Associates, Inc.**

This exquisite plan features two tower structures that enhance its dramatic facade. Inside, it contains a beautifully functioning room arrangement that caters to family lifestyles. The living areas radiate around the central hallway which also contains the stairway to the second floor. The living room is large and open, convenient for both casual and formal occasions and opens onto the formal dining room which is graced by a bay window. The nearby den is further enhanced by a second bay window and an attached full bath, making the room perfect for use as a guest suite. Three bedrooms upstairs include two family bedrooms and a grand master suite with a bath fit for a king. An oversized walk-in closet and vaulted ceiling are found here. Bonus space over the garage can be developed at a later time to suit changing needs.

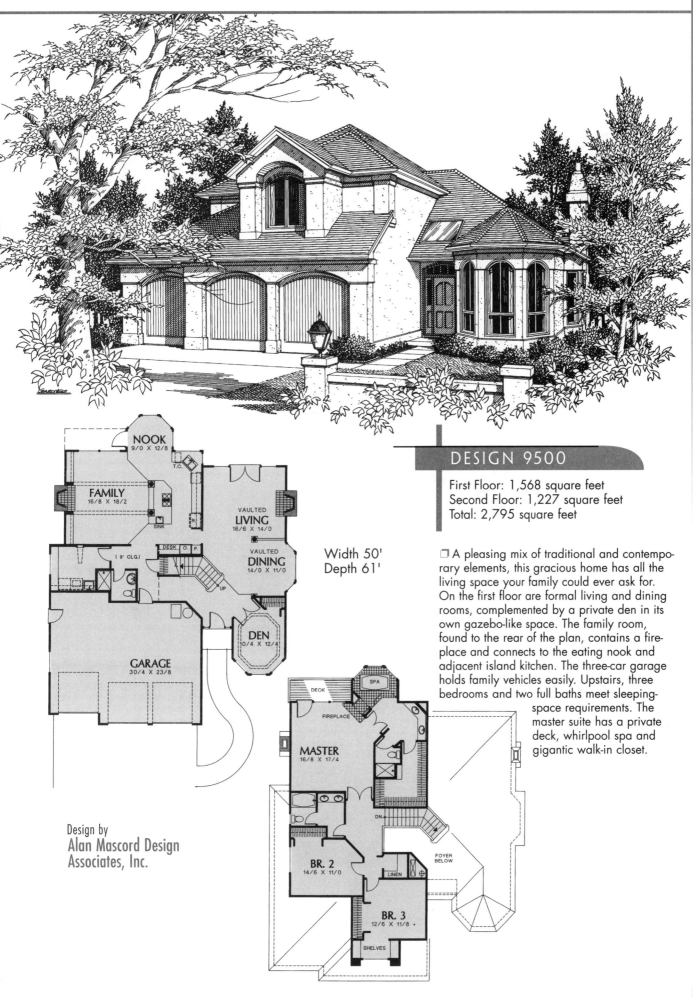

DESIGN 9500

First Floor: 1,568 square feet
Second Floor: 1,227 square feet
Total: 2,795 square feet

Width 50'
Depth 61'

❏ A pleasing mix of traditional and contemporary elements, this gracious home has all the living space your family could ever ask for. On the first floor are formal living and dining rooms, complemented by a private den in its own gazebo-like space. The family room, found to the rear of the plan, contains a fireplace and connects to the eating nook and adjacent island kitchen. The three-car garage holds family vehicles easily. Upstairs, three bedrooms and two full baths meet sleeping-space requirements. The master suite has a private deck, whirlpool spa and gigantic walk-in closet.

NOOK
9/0 X 12/8

FAMILY
16/8 X 18/2

VAULTED
LIVING
16/6 X 14/0

VAULTED
DINING
14/0 X 11/0

(9' CLG.)

DESK

DEN
10/4 X 12/4

GARAGE
30/4 X 23/8

Design by
Alan Mascord Design Associates, Inc.

DECK

SPA

FIREPLACE

MASTER
16/8 X 17/4

DN.

BR. 2
14/6 X 11/0

FOYER
BELOW

LINEN

BR. 3
12/6 X 11/8 +

SHELVES

DESIGN 9496

First Floor: 1,784 square feet
Second Floor: 742 square feet
Total: 2,526 square feet

BR. 3
11/0 X 11/8

GREAT RM.
BELOW

BR. 4
10/4 X 13/0

LINEN

DN.

DN.

LIN.

BR. 2
12/2 X 11/0

FOYER
BELOW

DINING RM.
BELOW

Design by
**Alan Mascord Design
Associates, Inc.**

MASTER
14/8 X 14/8
[9'-7" CLG.]

VAULTED
GREAT RM.
16/0 X 17/8

9/0 X 16/0

SPA

NOOK
10/0 X 14/4

DESK

PAN

UP

UP

W.D.

BUILT-IN

DEN
11/6 X 12/6 +/-

PLANT SHELF
OVER

UP

VAULTED
DINING
10/6 X 12/8

GARAGE
21/8 X 29/4 +/-

Width 64'
Depth 60'

❏ This stately contemporary home makes a grand statement inside and out. A volume entry leads to the two-story dining room with a plant shelf and skylights above. The great room with a fireplace flanked by windows is also vaulted. The kitchen provides a desk, a large pantry, an island cooktop and an adjacent breakfast nook with access to a covered porch. Double doors open from the foyer to a den with a built-in cabinet. The master bedroom with cove ceiling, walk-in closet and an amenity-filled bath is conveniently located on the first floor. A two-way staircase leads to the second floor which provides three family bedrooms and a full bath.

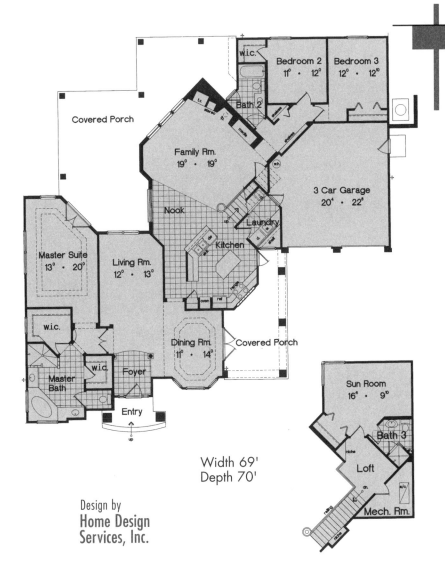

Covered Porch

Bedroom 2
11⁰ • 12⁰

Bedroom 3
12⁰ • 12⁰

w.i.c.

Bath 2

Family Rm.
19⁰ • 19⁰

3 Car Garage
20⁴ • 22⁸

Nook

Laundry

Master Suite
13⁰ • 20⁰

Living Rm.
12⁰ • 13⁰

Kitchen

w.i.c.

w.i.c.

Master Bath

Foyer

Dining Rm.
11⁰ • 14⁰

Covered Porch

oven ref

Entry
up

Width 69'
Depth 70'

Sun Room
16⁶ • 9⁰

Bath 3

Loft

Mech. Rm.

Design by
**Home Design
Services, Inc.**

DESIGN 8705

First Floor: 2,365 square feet
Second Floor: 364 square feet
Total: 2,729 square feet

❏ The columned foyer welcomes you into a series of spaces that reach out in all directions. The living room has a spectacular view of the huge covered patio area that's perfect for summer entertaining. The dining room has a tray ceiling and French doors which lead to a covered porch. A secluded master suite affords great views of the pool through French doors and also has a tray ceiling. The master bath is complete with His and Hers walk-in closets and a soaking tub. The family wing combines an island kitchen, nook and family gathering space with the built-in media/fireplace wall being the center of attention. While two secondary bedrooms share the versatile pool bath, a staircase which overlooks the family room takes you up to the sun room complete with bath, making this a very desirable kids' space.

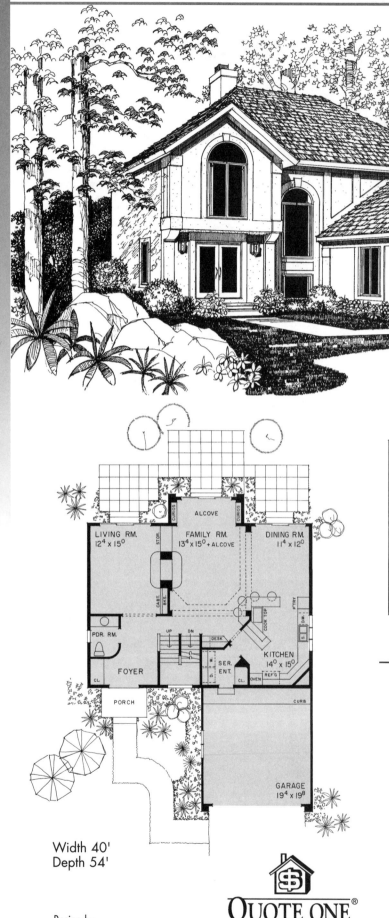

Width 40'
Depth 54'

Design by
Home Planners

Quote One®

Cost to build? See page 230
to order complete cost estimate
to build this house in your area!

DESIGN 3562

First Floor: 1,182 square feet
Second Floor: 927 square feet
Total: 2,109 square feet

L D

❏ Interesting detailing marks the exterior of this home as a beauty. Its interior makes it a livable option for any family. Entry occurs through double doors to the left side of the plan. A powder room with curved wall is handy to the entry. Living areas of the home are open and well-planned. The formal living room shares a through fireplace with the large family room. The dining room is adjoining and has a pass-through counter to the L-shaped kitchen. Special details on this floor include a wealth of sliding glass doors to the rear terrace and built-ins throughout. Upstairs are three bedrooms with two full baths.

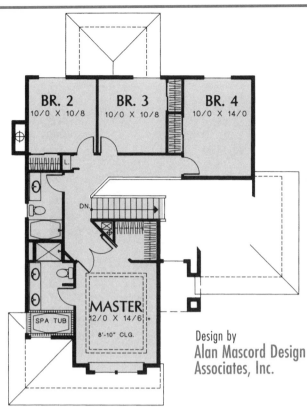

First Floor: 960 square feet
Second Floor: 968 square feet
Total: 1,928 square feet

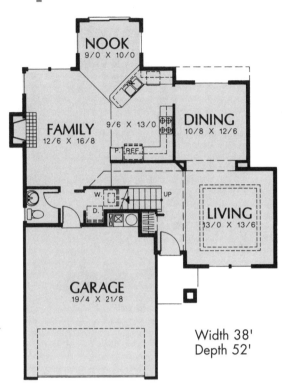

BR. 2
10/0 X 10/8

BR. 3
10/0 X 10/8

BR. 4
10/0 X 14/0

DN.

MASTER
12/0 X 14/6

8'-10" CLG.

SPA TUB

L.

Design by
Alan Mascord Design Associates, Inc.

NOOK
9/0 X 10/0

FAMILY
12/6 X 16/8

9/6 X 13/0

DINING
10/8 X 12/6

P. REF.

W.

D.

UP

LIVING
13/0 X 13/6

GARAGE
19/4 X 21/8

Width 38'
Depth 52'

❏ In accordance with modern home-building demands, this design incorporates a fully functional floor plan in less than 2,000 square feet. A grand living room opens up from the foyer and flows into the dining room. The kitchen offers easy access to both the family room and the bumped-out nook. A powder room sits across the hall from the utility room. Highlighted by the master bedroom with its double-door entry and bath with spa tub, the second floor provides four bedrooms to serve the growing family well.

DESIGN 9466

First Floor: 1,333 square feet
Second Floor: 843 square feet
Total: 2,176 square feet

❏ Brick columns flank the two-story entry and highlight the back of windows nearby, giving this design plenty of curb appeal. This efficient home incorporates all of the features demanded by today's discriminating home buyer. The spacious kitchen includes an island, large pantry, desk and nook area. Opening directly off the nook is a large family room with fireplace. Formal living takes place in the living and dining rooms located on the left side of the plan. Also found conveniently on the main floor is a den with a pair of French doors. The upper floor of this home includes three generous bedrooms.

NOOK
7/4 X 12/0

DINING
11/0 X 13/8

OVEN

FAMILY
18/0 X 13/4

12/2 X 13/4

(9' CEILING)

PANTRY   DESK

VAULTED
LIVING
13/4 X 15/8

DEN
12/0 X 10/8

UP

GARAGE
19/4 X 21/8

Width 46'
Depth 51'

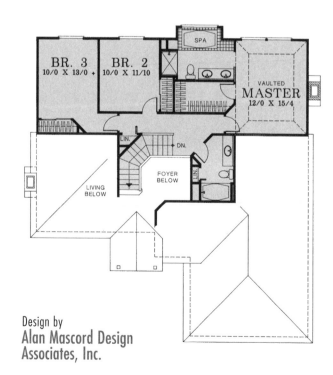

SPA

BR. 3
10/0 X 13/0 +

BR. 2
10/0 X 11/10

VAULTED
MASTER
12/0 X 15/4

LIN.

DN.

LIVING
BELOW

FOYER
BELOW

Design by
Alan Mascord Design Associates, Inc.

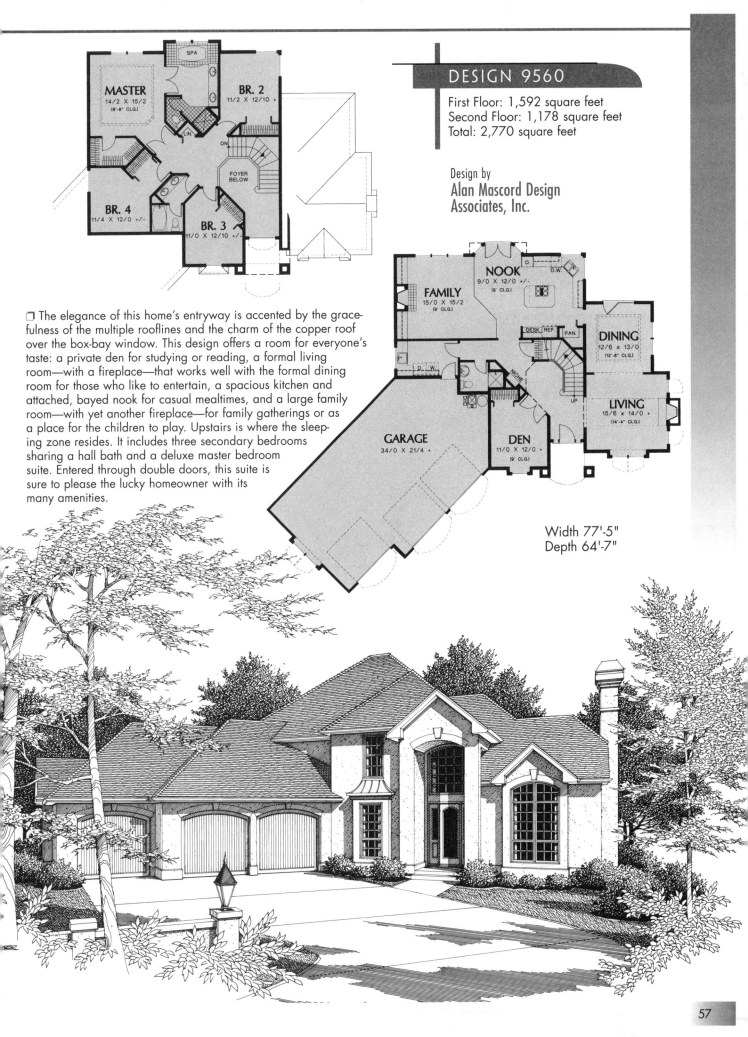

DESIGN 9560

First Floor: 1,592 square feet
Second Floor: 1,178 square feet
Total: 2,770 square feet

Design by
Alan Mascord Design Associates, Inc.

MASTER
14/2 X 15/2
(9'-8" CLG.)

BR. 2
11/2 X 12/10 +/-

SPA

LIN

DN

BR. 4
11/4 X 12/0 +/-

FOYER BELOW

BR. 3
11/0 X 12/10 +/-

❏ The elegance of this home's entryway is accented by the gracefulness of the multiple rooflines and the charm of the copper roof over the box-bay window. This design offers a room for everyone's taste: a private den for studying or reading, a formal living room—with a fireplace—that works well with the formal dining room for those who like to entertain, a spacious kitchen and attached, bayed nook for casual mealtimes, and a large family room—with yet another fireplace—for family gatherings or as a place for the children to play. Upstairs is where the sleeping zone resides. It includes three secondary bedrooms sharing a hall bath and a deluxe master bedroom suite. Entered through double doors, this suite is sure to please the lucky homeowner with its many amenities.

NOOK
9/0 X 12/0 +/-
(9' CLG.)

O.

D.W.

FAMILY
15/0 X 15/2
(9' CLG.)

DESK REF PAN.

DINING
12/6 x 13/0
(12'-8" CLG.)

D. W.

NICHE

UP

LIVING
15/6 x 14/0 +
(14'-4" CLG.)

GARAGE
34/0 X 21/4

DEN
11/0 X 12/0 +
(9' CLG.)

Width 77'-5"
Depth 64'-7"

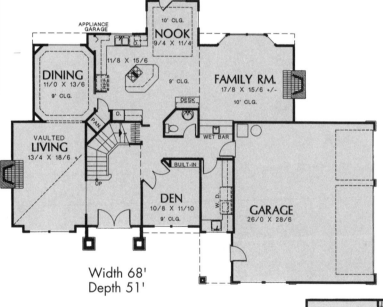

APPLIANCE GARAGE

10' CLG.

NOOK
9/4 X 11/4

11/8 X 15/6

DINING
11/0 X 13/6

9' CLG.

9' CLG.

DESK

10' CLG.

FAMILY RM.
17/8 X 15/6 +/-

VAULTED LIVING
13/4 X 18/6

WET BAR

BUILT-IN

UP

W.D.

DEN
10/8 X 11/10

9' CLG.

GARAGE
26/0 X 28/6

Width 68'
Depth 51'

DESIGN 9400

First Floor: 1,618 square feet
Second Floor: 1,212 square feet
Total: 2,830 square feet
Bonus Room: 376 square feet

Design by
**Alan Mascord Design
Associates, Inc.**

□ This attractive European-style plan is enhanced by a stucco finish and arched windows complementing the facade. The two-story foyer, with its angled stair, opens to the dramatically vaulted living room on one side and den with French doors on the other. An efficient L-shaped island kitchen works well with the formal dining room to its left and a sunny nook to the right. A bayed family room with a warming hearth completes this floor. Upstairs a sumptuous master suite includes spa tub, shower, twin vanities and large walk-in closet. Two family bedrooms share a full skylit bath with twin vanities. Over the garage is a vaulted bonus room, perfect as a game or hobby room.

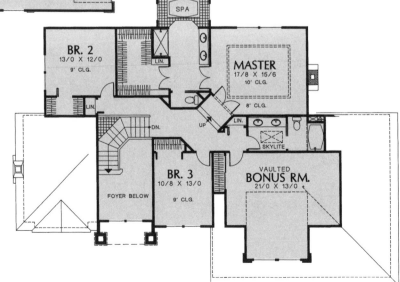

SPA

BR. 2
13/0 X 12/0

9' CLG.

LIN.

MASTER
17/8 X 15/6

10' CLG.

LIN.

8' CLG.

DN.

UP

LIN.

SKYLITE

BR. 3
10/8 X 13/0

9' CLG.

FOYER BELOW

VAULTED BONUS RM.
21/0 X 13/0

DESIGN 8635

First Floor: 982 square feet
Second Floor: 982 square feet
Total: 1,964 square feet

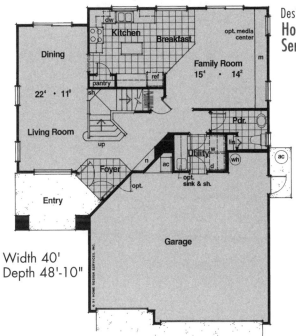

Design by
**Home Design
Services, Inc.**

Dining

22⁴ · 11⁰

Living Room

Foyer

Entry

Width 40'
Depth 48'-10"

Garage

Kitchen
Breakfast
opt. media center
dw
pantry
ref
sh
up
Family Room
15⁴ · 14²
m
Pdr.
lin.
Utility
w
ac
opt.
opt. sink & sh.
d
wh
ac

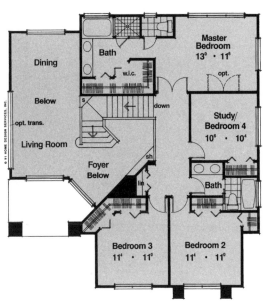

Dining
Below

opt. trans.

Living Room

Foyer
Below

Bath
w.i.c.
down
s
sh
lin

Master Bedroom
13⁰ · 11⁶
opt.

Study/
Bedroom 4
10⁶ · 10⁴

Bath

Bedroom 3
11⁴ · 11⁰

Bedroom 2
11⁴ · 11⁰

☐ This two-story has it all! Remarkable views as you enter this home are only the beginning. Every major living area on the first floor has a view of the rear yard. The formal living and dining area is the perfect place for entertaining and special candlelight dinners. The island kitchen has a commanding view of the breakfast and family areas, as well as the rear yard. The second floor boasts four bedrooms, with the master suite overlooking the rear yard. The California closet layout in the master bath makes efficient use of space and maximizes storage. The other three bedrooms are perfect for the kids, and one of the bedrooms can double as a master sitting room or den. Blueprints come with options for two different exteriors.

Alternate Elevation

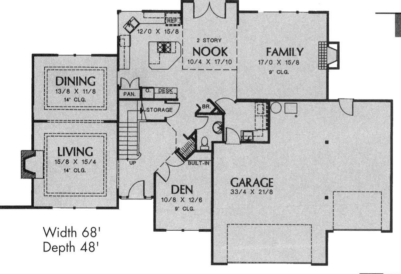

Width 68'
Depth 48'

First Floor: 1,600 square feet
Second Floor: 1,123 square feet
Total: 2,723 square feet

Design by
**Alan Mascord Design
Associates, Inc.**

❏ Beyond the Contemporary-style facade of this home lies a highly functional floor plan. First-floor living areas include formal living and dining rooms, a private den, and large family room that connects directly to the breakfast nook and island kitchen. A powder room off the entry hall accommodates guests. Direct entry to the laundry room and kitchen is gained from the three-car garage. The upper level contains three bedrooms, including a master suite with a nine-foot tray ceiling. These private quarters encompass a huge walk-in closet, a whirlpool spa and a double vanity in the bath.

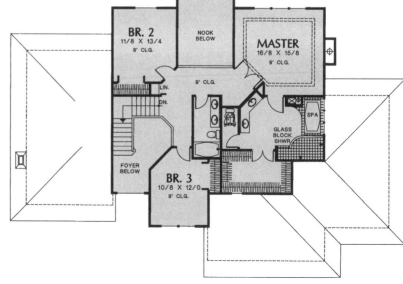

❏ Elegantly arched windows are echoed by an arch over the entryway. The two-story foyer opens directly to the formal two-story living room, which is graced by a fireplace and plant shelves. The adjacent formal dining room is also two-story and works well with the island kitchen. The family room, located to the rear of the home, offers a second fireplace and accessibility to the bayed nook. Upstairs, three family bedrooms—two with walk-in closets—share a full bath. The master suite features a tray ceiling, private balcony, large walk-in closet and a pampering bath.

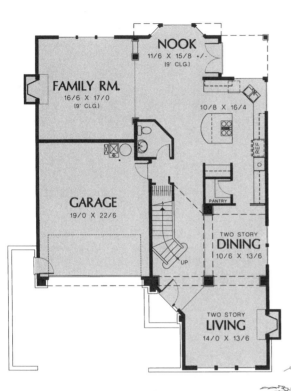

Width 40'
Depth 58'

DESIGN 7420

First Floor: 1,400 square feet
Second Floor: 1,320 square feet
Total: 2,720 square feet

Design by
Alan Mascord Design Associates, Inc.

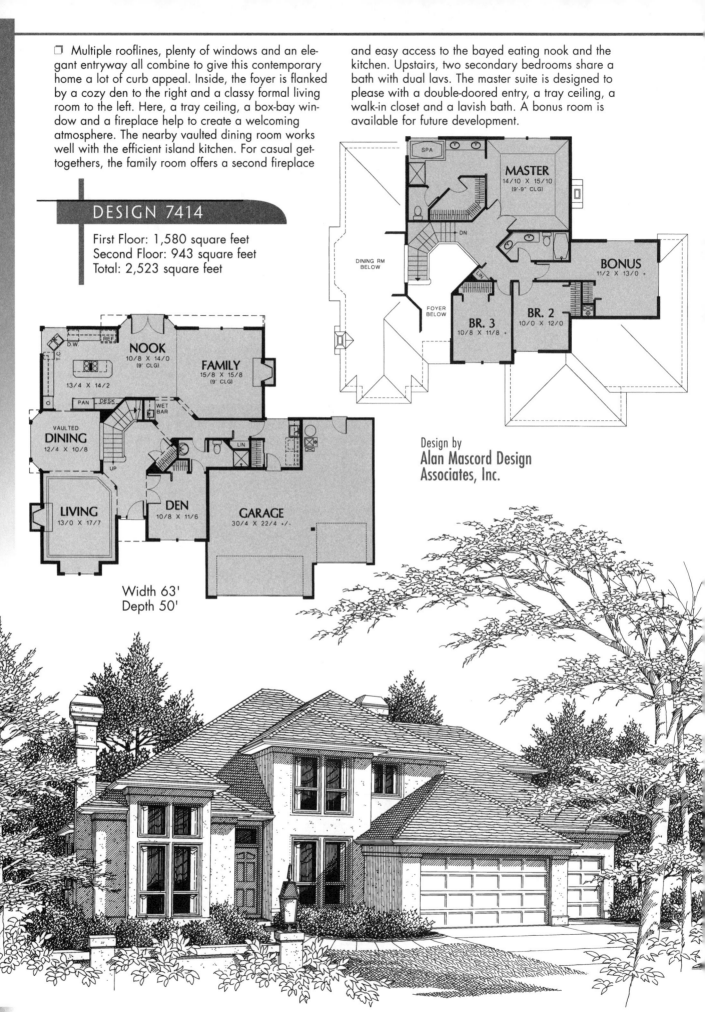

◻ Multiple rooflines, plenty of windows and an elegant entryway all combine to give this contemporary home a lot of curb appeal. Inside, the foyer is flanked by a cozy den to the right and a classy formal living room to the left. Here, a tray ceiling, a box-bay window and a fireplace help to create a welcoming atmosphere. The nearby vaulted dining room works well with the efficient island kitchen. For casual get-togethers, the family room offers a second fireplace

and easy access to the bayed eating nook and the kitchen. Upstairs, two secondary bedrooms share a bath with dual lavs. The master suite is designed to please with a double-doored entry, a tray ceiling, a walk-in closet and a lavish bath. A bonus room is available for future development.

DESIGN 7414

First Floor: 1,580 square feet
Second Floor: 943 square feet
Total: 2,523 square feet

Width 63'
Depth 50'

Design by
**Alan Mascord Design
Associates, Inc.**

DESIGN 9595

First Floor: 1,575 square feet
Second Floor: 1,338 square feet
Total: 2,913 square feet

❒ This Contemporary home is impressive from the first glance. A two-story bay window graces both the cozy den on the first floor and the deluxe master suite on the second floor. Inside, to the right of the foyer is the formal living room, enhanced by another bay window and by a warming fireplace. This room opens to the rear of the plan into a formal dining room which is just steps away from a large and efficient island kitchen. Casual living is comfortable in the attached nook, with the nearby family room sporting a second fireplace. Upstairs, three family bedrooms offer plenty of storage and share a hall bath. The master suite is impressive with its tray ceiling, large walk-in closet, twin vanities and corner spa. A three-car garage easily holds the family fleet.

Design by
Alan Mascord Design Associates, Inc.

Width 66'
Depth 48'

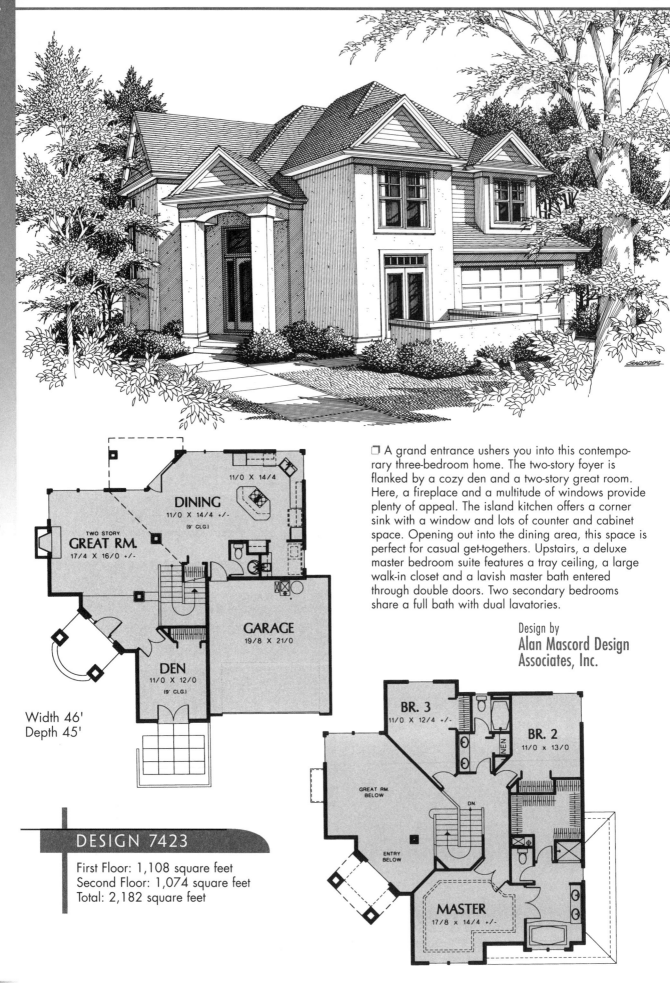

A grand entrance ushers you into this contemporary three-bedroom home. The two-story foyer is flanked by a cozy den and a two-story great room. Here, a fireplace and a multitude of windows provide plenty of appeal. The island kitchen offers a corner sink with a window and lots of counter and cabinet space. Opening out into the dining area, this space is perfect for casual get-togethers. Upstairs, a deluxe master bedroom suite features a tray ceiling, a large walk-in closet and a lavish master bath entered through double doors. Two secondary bedrooms share a full bath with dual lavatories.

Design by
Alan Mascord Design Associates, Inc.

DINING
11/0 X 14/4 +/-
(9' CLG.)

TWO STORY
GREAT RM.
17/4 X 16/0 +/-

11/0 X 14/4

GARAGE
19/8 X 21/0

DEN
11/0 X 12/0
(9' CLG.)

Width 46'
Depth 45'

BR. 3
11/0 X 12/4 +/-

BR. 2
11/0 x 13/0

GREAT RM.
BELOW

LINEN

DN

ENTRY
BELOW

MASTER
17/8 X 14/4 +/-

DESIGN 7423

First Floor: 1,108 square feet
Second Floor: 1,074 square feet
Total: 2,182 square feet

DESIGN 3456

First Floor: 1,130 square feet
Second Floor: 1,189 square feet
Total: 2,319 square feet

Design by
Home Planners

□ This volume-look home's angled entry opens to a wealth of living potential with a media room to the right and formal living and dining rooms to the left. Remaining exposed to the dining room, the living room pleases with its marbled hearth and sliding glass doors to the back terrace. A covered porch, accessed from both the dining and breakfast rooms, adds outdoor dining possibilities. The kitchen utilizes a built-in desk and a snack bar pass-through to the breakfast area. A large pantry and closet lead to the laundry near the garage. Upstairs, four bedrooms accommodate the large family well. In the master suite, amenities such as a sitting area and a balcony add definition. The master bath sports a whirlpool and a walk-in closet.

Width 40'-7"
Depth 57'-8"

QUOTE ONE®

Cost to build? See page 230
to order complete cost estimate
to build this house in your area!

DESIGN 6681

First Floor: 906 square feet
Second Floor: 714 square feet
Tower Loft: 86 square feet
Total: 1,706 square feet

❏ A unique tower with an observation deck will make this design a standout in any location. Inside, an impressive entry with a wrapping stair leads to three levels of livability. The main level includes a gallery leading to a formal dining room and a counter-filled kitchen on the left and a vaulted great room on the right. Five French doors on the main level access a covered porch spanning the width of the home. The upper level houses the master suite, with a sumptuous bath and a private deck, a guest bedroom and a large hall bath. On the lower level, the two-car garage is split and offers additional storage space.

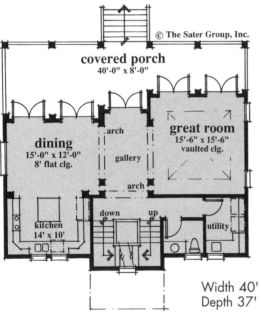

© The Sater Group, Inc.

covered porch
40'-0" x 8'-0"

dining
15'-0" x 12'-0"
8' flat clg.

arch

gallery

arch

great room
15'-6" x 15'-6"
vaulted clg.

kitchen
14' x 10'

down

up

utility

Width 40'
Depth 37'

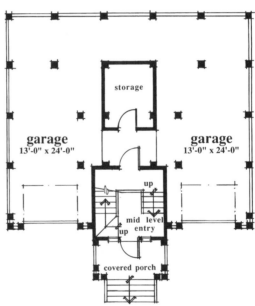

storage

garage
13'-0" x 24'-0"

garage
13'-0" x 24'-0"

mid level entry

up

up

covered porch

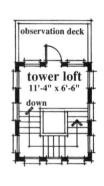

observation deck

tower loft
11'-4" x 6'-6"

down

Design by
The Sater Design Collection

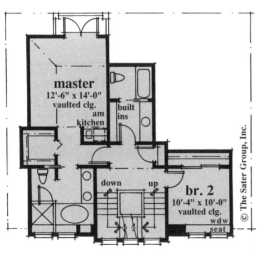

master
12'-6" x 14'-0"
vaulted clg.

am kitchen

built ins

down

up

br. 2
10'-4" x 10'-0"
vaulted clg.

w d w
seat

© The Sater Group, Inc.

Rear Elevation

Photo by Bob Greenspan

This home, as shown in the photograph, may differ from the actual blueprints. For more detailed information, please check the floor plans carefully.

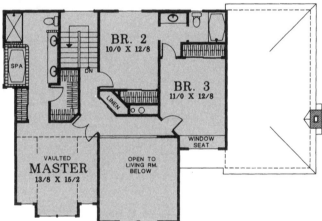

BR. 2
10/0 X 12/8

BR. 3
11/0 X 12/8

SPA

DN

LINEN

WINDOW SEAT

VAULTED
MASTER
13/8 X 15/2

OPEN TO LIVING RM. BELOW

DESIGN 9573

First Floor: 1,502 square feet
Second Floor: 954 square feet
Total: 2,456 square feet

Design by
Alan Mascord Design Associates, Inc.

❑ Come home to the spectacular views and livability offered by this lovely hillside home. It tucks a garage into the lower level with the two stories accommodating family living. A two-story living room shares a see-through fireplace with the formal dining room. Quiet time may be spent in the den, which has double doors opening onto the deck. The sunken family room also enjoys a fireplace that is visible to the country kitchen and breakfast nook. On the upper floor, a vaulted master suite is set apart from the two family bedrooms and has an ample dressing area and bath. The two family bedrooms share a private bath.

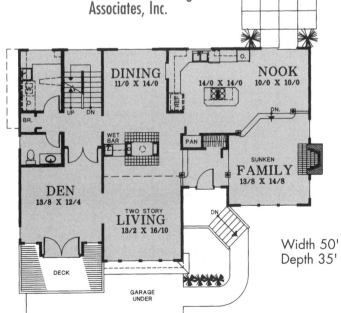

DINING
11/0 X 14/0

NOOK
10/0 X 10/0

UP   DN

BR.

WET BAR

PAN

SUNKEN
FAMILY
13/8 X 14/8

DEN
13/8 X 12/4

TWO STORY
LIVING
13/2 X 16/10

DN

DECK

GARAGE UNDER

Width 50'
Depth 35'

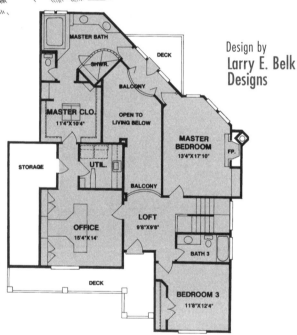

Design by
Larry E. Belk
Designs

DESIGN 8001

First Floor: 1,309 square feet
Second Floor: 1,343 square feet
Total: 2,652 square feet

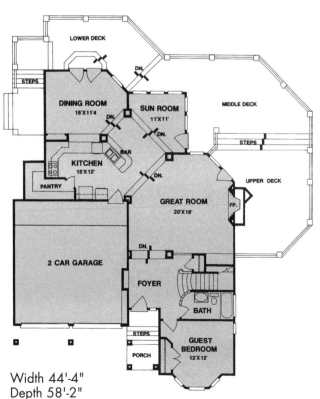

Width 44'-4"
Depth 58'-2"

❏ Clean, contemporary lines set this home apart and make it a stand out in any location. The metal roof and roof-top cupola rotated on a 45-degree angle add interest. Twin chimneys located on the right side of the house are constructed on a 45-degree angle to continue the theme. Stunning is the word when the front door opens on this home. Near the foyer, a 28-foot shaft opens from floor level to the top of the cupola. Remote control transoms in the cupola open automatically to increase ventilation. The great room, sun room, dining room and kitchen are all adjacent to provide areas for entertaining. Originally designed for a sloping site, the home incorporates multiple levels inside. Additionally, there is access to a series of multi-level outside decks from the dining room, sun room and great room. All these areas have at least one glass wall overlooking the rear. The master bedroom and bath upstairs are bridged by a pipe rail balcony that provides access to a rear outside deck. The master suite includes a huge master closet. Additional storage and closet area is located off the hallway to the office.

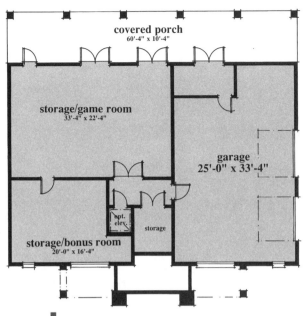

covered porch
60'-4" x 10'-4"

storage/game room
33'-4" x 22'-4"

garage
25'-0" x 33'-4"

opt. elev.

storage

storage/bonus room
20'-0" x 16'-4"

Rear Elevation

DESIGN 6684

Main Level: 2,385 square feet
Lower Level: 80 square feet
Total: 2,465 square feet

❒ Contemporary class is highly evident in this three-bedroom home. The varying angles and materials give the facade plenty of curb appeal. Inside, up a short flight of stairs from the foyer, a spacious great room is flooded with natural light from the wall of glass. Continuing the feeling of openness, the kitchen works well with the sunny dining area. Two secondary bedrooms have direct access to the laundry room and share a full hall bath. A study—or make it a fourth bedroom—is entered through double doors. The master bedroom suite is lavish with its amenities. Offering direct access to the rear covered porch, His and Hers walk-in closets and a sumptuous bath, this suite is sure to please.

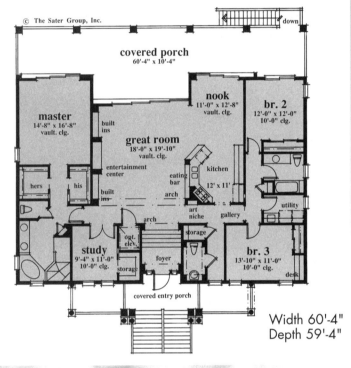

© The Sater Group, Inc.

down

covered porch
60'-4" x 10'-4"

master
14'-8" x 16'-8"
vault. clg.

built ins

nook
11'-0" x 12'-8"
vault. clg.

br. 2
12'-0" x 12'-0"
10'-0" clg.

great room
18'-0" x 19'-10"
vault. clg.

entertainment center

hers

his

built ins

kitchen
12' x 11'

eating bar

arch

art niche

gallery

utility

arch

opt. elev.

storage

storage

study
9'-4" x 11'-0"
10'-0" clg.

foyer

br. 3
13'-10" x 11'-0"
10'-0" clg.

desk

covered entry porch

Width 60'-4"
Depth 59'-4"

Design by
**The Sater
Design Collection**

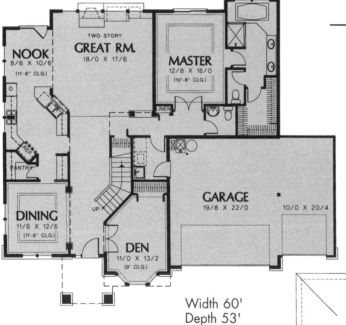

NOOK
8/6 X 10/6
(11'-6" CLG.)

TWO STORY
GREAT RM.
18/0 X 17/6

MASTER
12/8 X 16/0
(10'-8" CLG.)

LINEN

PANTRY

DINING
11/6 X 12/6
(11'-6" CLG.)

UP

GARAGE
19/8 X 22/0   10/0 X 20/4

DEN
11/0 X 13/2
(9' CLG.)

Width 60'
Depth 53'

GREAT RM.
BELOW

LINEN

DN.

FOYER
BELOW

BR. 3
11/0 X 14/0 +/-

BR. 2
11/0 X 15/0 +/-

DESIGN 7419

First Floor: 1,818 square feet
Second Floor: 698 square feet
Total: 2,516 square feet

Design by
**Alan Mascord Design
Associates, Inc.**

❏ Square columns flank the entry to this Contemporary three-bedroom home. The two-story great room is the focus of this design and provides a fireplace, a wall of windows and direct access to the efficient kitchen. A formal dining room, located at the front of the plan, offers a tray ceiling and works well with the kitchen. Across the hall through double doors, a bayed den is available for a quiet study. The master suite is located on the first floor for privacy and features a large walk-in closet, sliding glass doors to the rear yard and a sumptuous bath. Upstairs, two family bedrooms—each with a walk-in closet—share a full bath with dual lavatories.

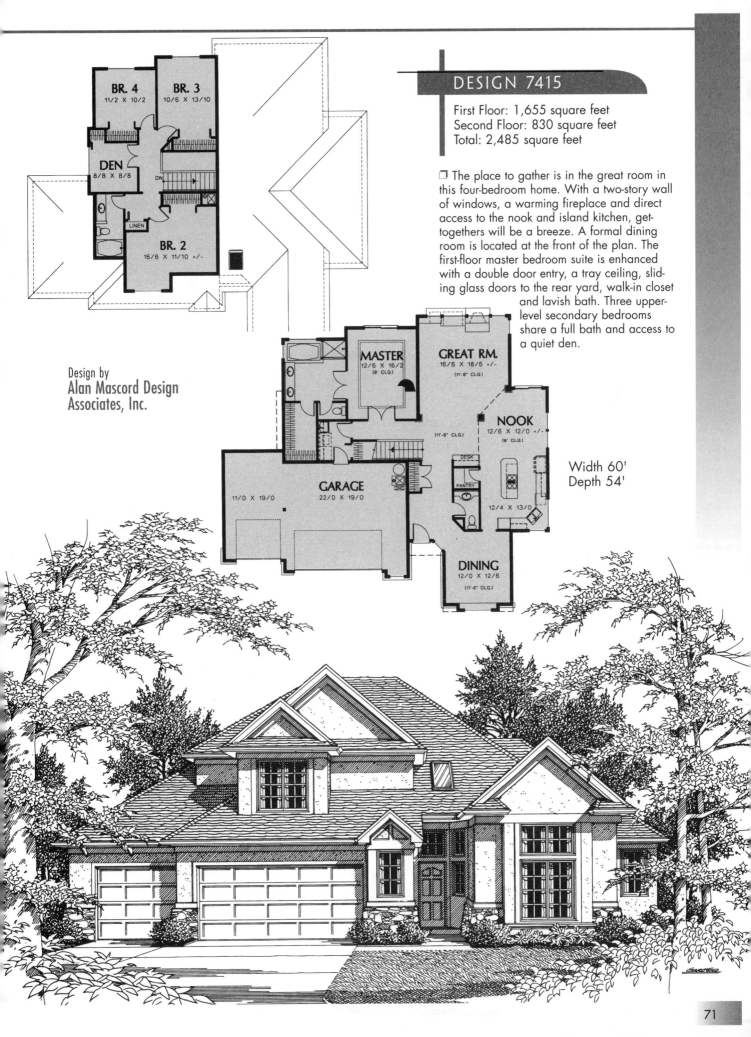

BR. 4
11/2 X 10/2

BR. 3
10/6 X 13/10

DEN
8/8 X 8/8

DN

LINEN

BR. 2
16/6 X 11/10 +/-

DESIGN 7415

First Floor: 1,655 square feet
Second Floor: 830 square feet
Total: 2,485 square feet

❏ The place to gather is in the great room in this four-bedroom home. With a two-story wall of windows, a warming fireplace and direct access to the nook and island kitchen, get-togethers will be a breeze. A formal dining room is located at the front of the plan. The first-floor master bedroom suite is enhanced with a double door entry, a tray ceiling, sliding glass doors to the rear yard, walk-in closet and lavish bath. Three upper-level secondary bedrooms share a full bath and access to a quiet den.

Design by
Alan Mascord Design Associates, Inc.

MASTER
12/6 X 15/2
(9' CLG.)

GREAT RM.
16/6 X 18/6 +/-
(11'-6" CLG.)

(11'-6" CLG.)

NOOK
12/6 X 12/0 +/-
(9' CLG.)

DESK

PANTRY

12/4 X 13/0

GARAGE
22/0 X 19/0

11/0 X 19/0

Width 60'
Depth 54'

DINING
12/0 X 12/6
(11'-6" CLG.)

71

NOOK
11/0 X 16/0 +/-
(9' CLG.)

VAULTED
FAMILY
17/0 X 14/2

13/6 X 17/0 +/-

O. REF

PAN.

GARAGE
19/8 X 21/8

10/8 X 19/4

W. D.

UP

DINING
13/0 X 11/0
(9' CLG.)

LIVING
13/0 X 15/4 +/-
(9' CLG.)

Width 50'
Depth 60'-6"

DECK

MASTER
13/0 X 16/0 +/-
(9'-4" CLG.)

SPA

FAMILY
BELOW
(8' CLG.)

BR. 2
11/2 X 12/2

NICHE

LIN

DN.

LIN

BR. 3
11/6 X 12/8 +/-

FOYER
BELOW

DEN
9/6 X 11/0

BR. 4
13/0 X 11/0

DESIGN 9553

First Floor: 1,466 square feet
Second Floor: 1,369 square feet
Total: 2,835 square feet

❏ Multi-pane windows and keystones enhance the beauty of this impressive two-story home. From the bay-windowed living room, to the casual family room, this plan caters to the active lifestyles of today's family. The large, U-shaped kitchen contains an island cooktop and a sunny nook nearby that supplies access to a covered porch. Upstairs, the master suite is designed for the ultimate in luxury. Three family bedrooms, a full bath and a den complete the second floor.

Design by
Alan Mascord Design Associates, Inc.

Width 62'
Depth 41'

Design by
Home Planners

Cost to build? See page 230
to order complete cost estimate
to build this house in your area!

DESIGN 3458

First Floor: 1,617 square feet
Second Floor: 725 square feet
Total: 2,342 square feet

L **D**

❏ With end gables, and five front gables, this design becomes an updated "house of seven gables." Meanwhile, brick veneer, the use of horizontal siding, radial head windows and interesting roof planes add an extra measure of charm. The attached, side-opening, two-car garage is a delightfully integral part of the appealing exterior. Designed for a growing family with a modest building budget, the floor plan incorporates four bedrooms and both formal and informal living areas. The central foyer, with its open staircase to the second floor, looks up to the balcony. The spacious family room has a high ceiling and a dramatic view of the balcony. In the U-shaped kitchen, a snack bar caters to quick, on-the-run meals. A pantry facilitates stocking-up on foodstuffs. A basement allows for bonus space should development of recreational, hobby or storage space come into play.

DESIGN 7418

First Floor: 1,786 square feet
Second Floor: 690 square feet
Total: 2,476 square feet

From the covered porch to the two-story window in the great room, this design is sure to please. The two-story foyer is flanked by a cozy den on the right and a formal dining room with a bay window on the left. A sunny nook is adjacent to the efficient kitchen which offers a snack bar and a corner sink. The first-floor master suite features a double-door entry, a tray ceiling, a walk-in closet and a bath with a corner tub and separate shower. Upstairs, two family bedrooms—each with a walk-in closet—share a full hall bath. A bonus room completes this level and is available for future development. A three-car garage easily shelters the family fleet.

NOOK
10/0 X 10/8
(11'-6" CLG.)

(2) STORY
GREAT RM.
16/0 X 20/8 +/-

MASTER
12/6 X 15/0
(14'-3" CLG.)

14/0 X 12/0 +/-

REF.
PAN.

DINING
11/0 X 12/0 +
(11'-6" CLG.)

UP

DEN
11/0 X 12/10
(11'-6" CLG.)

GARAGE
21/6 X 21/6

10/0 X 21/0

Width 60'
Depth 52'

GREAT RM.
BELOW

BONUS
12/0 X 13/0

DN.

BR. 3
11/10 X 12/6

FOYER
BELOW

LINEN

BR. 2
14/0 X 11/0

Design by
Alan Mascord Design Associates, Inc.

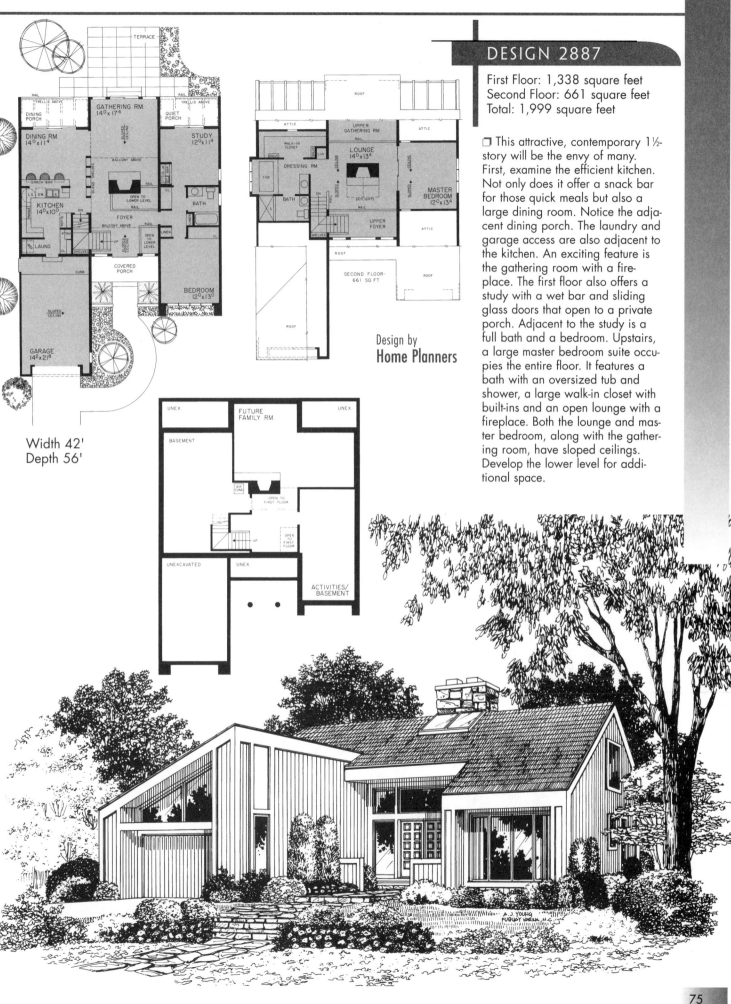

First Floor: 1,338 square feet
Second Floor: 661 square feet
Total: 1,999 square feet

❑ This attractive, contemporary 1½-story will be the envy of many. First, examine the efficient kitchen. Not only does it offer a snack bar for those quick meals but also a large dining room. Notice the adjacent dining porch. The laundry and garage access are also adjacent to the kitchen. An exciting feature is the gathering room with a fireplace. The first floor also offers a study with a wet bar and sliding glass doors that open to a private porch. Adjacent to the study is a full bath and a bedroom. Upstairs, a large master bedroom suite occupies the entire floor. It features a bath with an oversized tub and shower, a large walk-in closet with built-ins and an open lounge with a fireplace. Both the lounge and master bedroom, along with the gathering room, have sloped ceilings. Develop the lower level for additional space.

Design by
Home Planners

Width 42'
Depth 56'

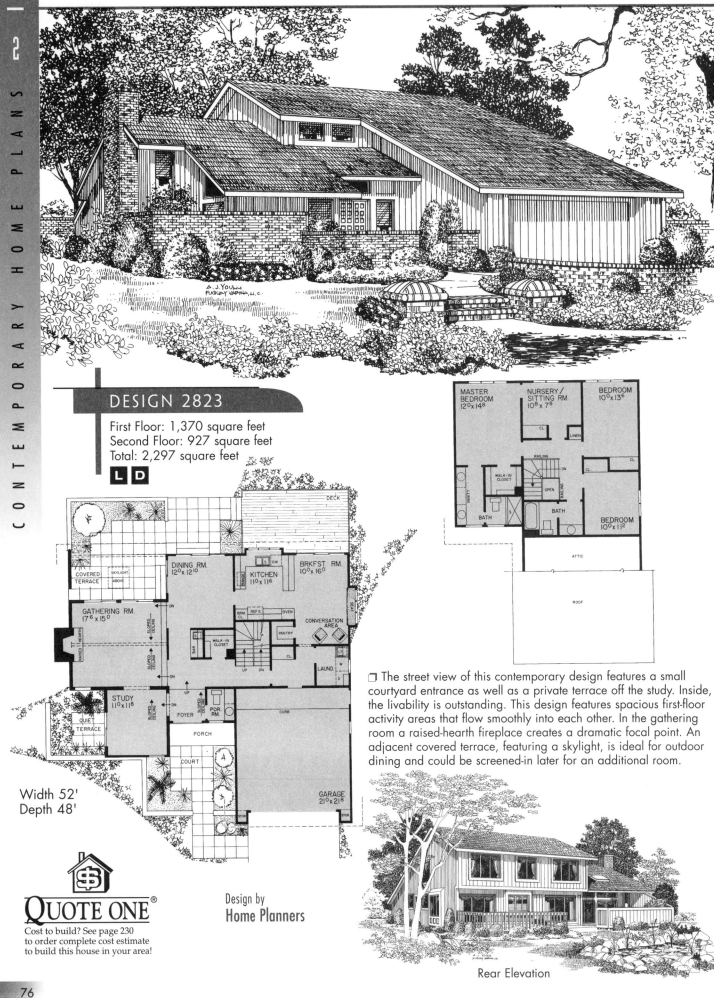

DESIGN 2823

First Floor: 1,370 square feet
Second Floor: 927 square feet
Total: 2,297 square feet

L **D**

Width 52'
Depth 48'

Floor Plan Labels

COVERED TERRACE
SKYLIGHT ABOVE
DINING RM. 12⁰ x 12¹⁰
KITCHEN 11⁰ x 11⁶
BRKFST. RM. 10⁰ x 16⁰
DECK
GATHERING RM. 17⁶ x 15⁰
RANGE
BRM. CL. REFG. OVEN
CONVERSATION AREA
BAR WALK-IN CLOSET PANTRY
UP DN LAUND.
STUDY 11⁰ x 11⁸
QUIET TERRACE
PDR. RM. FOYER
CURB
PORCH
COURT
GARAGE 21⁰ x 21⁸

MASTER BEDROOM 12⁰ x 14⁸
NURSERY / SITTING RM. 10⁸ x 7⁸
BEDROOM 10⁰ x 13⁶
RAILING
WALK-IN CLOSET OPEN
VANITY BATH BATH
BEDROOM 10⁰ x 11²
ATTIC
ROOF

☐ The street view of this contemporary design features a small courtyard entrance as well as a private terrace off the study. Inside, the livability is outstanding. This design features spacious first-floor activity areas that flow smoothly into each other. In the gathering room a raised-hearth fireplace creates a dramatic focal point. An adjacent covered terrace, featuring a skylight, is ideal for outdoor dining and could be screened-in later for an additional room.

QUOTE ONE®

Cost to build? See page 230 to order complete cost estimate to build this house in your area!

Design by
Home Planners

Rear Elevation

This home, as shown in the photograph, may differ from the actual blueprints.
For more detailed information, please check the floor plans carefully.

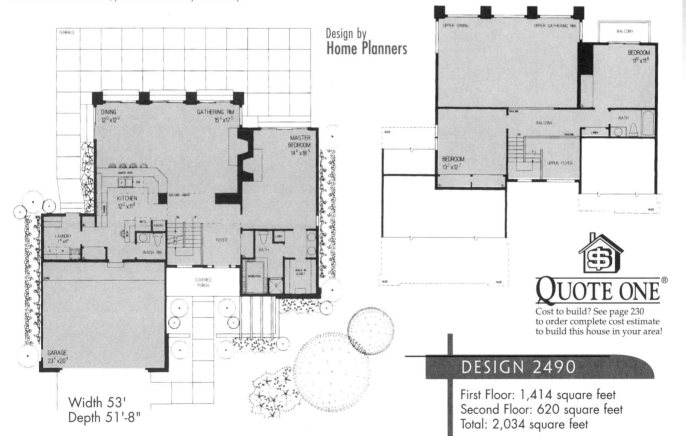

Design by
Home Planners

Width 53'
Depth 51'-8"

QUOTE ONE®
Cost to build? See page 230
to order complete cost estimate
to build this house in your area!

DESIGN 2490

First Floor: 1,414 square feet
Second Floor: 620 square feet
Total: 2,034 square feet

❏ Spacious living areas and luxury details give this contemporary home a sense of casual elegance. The oversized gathering and dining room is framed with windows to the rear terrace and accented with a fireplace. The spacious kitchen looks onto the gathering room and features a snack bar, planning desk and a nearby utility/laundry room. The beautiful master suite has its own fireplace, a walk-in closet and a whirlpool tub. Upstairs, a balcony overlooking the foyer and gathering room leads to the two secondary bedrooms and a full hall bath.

Photos by Andrew D. Lautman

This home, as shown in the photograph, may differ from the actual blueprints. For more detailed information, please check the floor plans carefully.

DESIGN 2822

First Floor: 1,363 square feet
Second Floor: 351 square feet
Total: 1,714 square feet

L

❒ Flexibility and livability are the hallmarks of this affordable plan, which is tailor-made for small families and empty-nesters. Basically a one-level design with second-floor possibilities, the room upstairs (see alternate layouts) can be nearly anything you want it to be: lounge, guest room, playroom for the kids or grandchildren, partitioned or open. Downstairs, a little space goes a long way. In less than 1,400 square feet is the great room with fireplace, separate dining room with adjacent porch, study-bedroom, and sizable master suite.

Design by
Home Planners

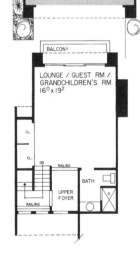

Width 54'-8"
Depth 54'

Rear Elevation

❏ Consider this compact contemporary with a flair for the dramatic. The entry, den and great room feature impressive vaulted ceilings. Note that the great room has a floor that is sunken two steps; the den is accessed through French doors from the entry. An elegant master suite features a spa tub, large shower and walk-in closet. Don't miss the additional shop or storage area built out along one side of the garage.

Design by
**Alan Mascord Design
Associates, Inc.**

DESIGN 9413

First Floor: 1,076 square feet
Second Floor: 819 square feet
Total: 1,895 square feet

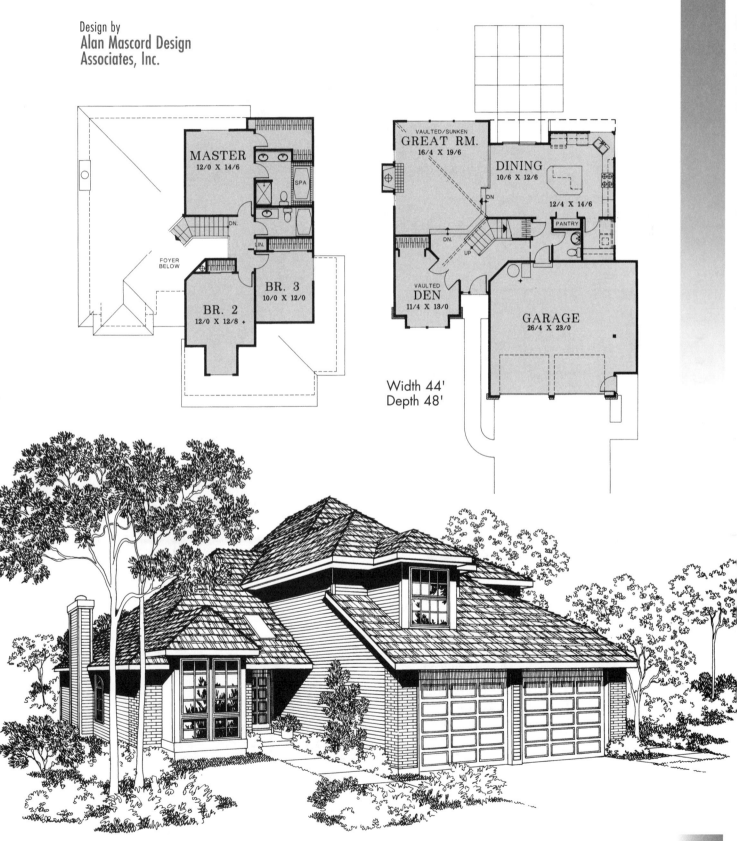

MASTER
12/0 X 14/6

SPA

DN.

FOYER
BELOW

BR. 3
10/0 X 12/0

BR. 2
12/0 X 12/8 +

VAULTED/SUNKEN
GREAT RM.
16/4 X 19/6

DINING
10/6 X 12/6

DN.

12/4 X 14/6

DN.

UP

PANTRY

VAULTED
DEN
11/4 X 13/0

GARAGE
26/4 X 23/0

Width 44'
Depth 48'

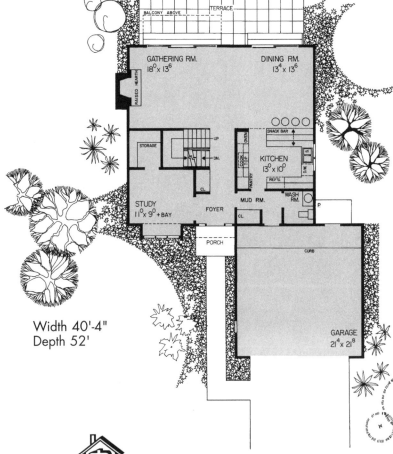

Width 40'-4"
Depth 52'

DESIGN 2711

First Floor: 975 square feet
Second Floor: 1,024 square feet
Total: 1,999 square feet

L **D**

❐ Sleek, affordable style. The large dining area, a U-shaped kitchen, the mudroom off the garage and a spacious master bedroom are key selling points for a young family. Two other bedrooms share a full hall bath on the second floor. Also note the private balcony off the master suite, a cozy study with a box-bay window and lots of storage space, a sunny terrace to the rear of the house and a sizable snack bar for the kids—and adults.

QUOTE ONE®

Cost to build? See page 230
to order complete cost estimate
to build this house in your area!

Design by
Home Planners

MASTER BED RM.
12-6 × 14-8

master bath

cl

walk-in closet

STUDY
11-4 × 5-6
clerestory above

(sloped ceiling to clerestory)

great room below

railing

foyer below

BALCONY
10-0 × 6-8

open to below

down

DECK
32-2 × 12-0

down

covered deck

DINING
12-6 × 13-0

GREAT RM.
13-4 × 19-10

fireplace

balcony above

BED RM.
11-0 × 11-0

cl

dry wsh

KITCHEN
12-6 × 10-4

ref.

cl

lin.

bath

storage

UTIL.
6-8 × 10-0

GARAGE
20-0 × 20-4

SUN RM.
12-6 × 11-0

balcony above

FOYER

down

up

BED RM.
12-4 × 10-6

cl

Width 60'-10"
Depth 48'-2"

DESIGN 7628

First Floor: 1,415 square feet
Second Floor: 585 square feet
Total: 2,000 square feet

☐ A two-story wall of windows floods the first-floor sun room and the second-story balcony off the master suite with natural light. The sloped-ceilinged great room is sure to please with a corner fireplace, a balcony overlook and two sets of sliding glass doors to the rear deck. The L-shaped, island kitchen works well with the large dining room which offers access to a small covered porch. Two family bedrooms share a full bath and complete this level. The second-floor master suite features a walk-in closet, an interior balcony overlooking the sun room, a private bath and an open study.

Design by
Donald A. Gardner Architects, Inc.

NATHAN INC.

Design by
Donald A. Gardner
Architects, Inc.

great room below
(sloped ceiling)

railing

BED RM.
14-0 × 11-0

cl   cl

LOFT

foyer
below

BED RM.
12-4 × 11-4

bath

walk-in
closet

down

ATTIC

down

DECK

SUN RM.
11-10 × 10-0

fireplace

DINING
14-0 × 12-0

GREAT RM.
14-0 × 20-0

MASTER
BED RM.
14-0 × 14-0

bath

balcony above

walk-in
closet

FOYER
6-0 × 8-0

cl

pd.
rm.

wash dry

storage

KITCHEN
14-0 × 13-8

sto.

down

up

UTILITY

© 1988 Donald A. Gardner Architects, Inc.

Width 52'-8"
Depth 60'-6"

GARAGE
20-0 × 19-8

DESIGN 9650

First Floor: 1,352 square feet
Second Floor: 576 square feet
Total: 1,928 square feet
Sun Room: 127 square feet

Rear Elevation

❏ This striking contemporary home retains some traditional flavor at the front exterior. Inside, the mood is modern and efficient. The formal dining room and the great room open to the sun room which has four skylights for passive solar heating. A spacious kitchen allows for a breakfast bar or separate table. The sun room, great room and master bedroom offer direct access to the deck which provides space for a hot tub. The luxurious master bath has a double-bowl vanity, shower and whirlpool tub. The second level has two spacious bedrooms sharing a full bath and a loft area overlooking the great room below. Ample attic storage space is provided over the garage.

DECK
33 - 6 × 10 - 0

spa

SUN RM.
14 - 0 × 8 - 10

LIVING RM.
13 - 4 × 18 - 10

FAMILY RM.
12 - 0 × 12 - 4

fireplace

fireplace

BED RM.
10 - 6 × 11 - 8

cl

BRKFST.
8 - 8 × 9 - 0

study above

storage

bath

KITCHEN
19 - 4 × 8 - 4

FOYER
9 - 10 × 10 - 4

cl

Width 62'
Depth 57'-4"

wash dry

storage

UTILITY
9 - 4 × 6 - 0

DINING
14 - 0 × 12 - 0

up

BED RM.
10 - 6 × 12 - 0

GARAGE
20 - 4 × 20 - 0

Design by
**Donald A. Gardner
Architects, Inc.**

DESIGN 7629

First Floor: 1,665 square feet
Second Floor: 848 square feet
Total: 2,513 square feet

open to sun room below

SUN RM.
BALCONY

(sloped ceiling to clerestory)

living room below

MASTER
BED RM.
14 - 0 × 14 - 6

fireplace

railing

bath

clerestory above

STUDY
9 - 10 × 7 - 8

BED RM.
10 - 6 × 10 - 6

walk-in closet

foyer below

down

master bath

lin.

☐ Multiple rooflines, a multitude of windows and sleek modern lines enhance the curb appeal of this four-bedroom home. The two-story foyer leads to either the formal dining room or the sloped-ceilinged living room which comes complete with a fireplace and two sets of sliding glass doors to the rear deck. The efficient kitchen is open to the bayed breakfast room and the family room. Here, a second fireplace brings cheer to casual gatherings, while the sliding glass doors lead to a two-story sun room. Two family bedrooms share a full bath on the first floor, and a third bedroom is upstairs and has its own bath. A deluxe master suite is also on the second floor and features a private bath, a fireplace, a walk-in closet and a balcony overlooking the sun room.

Rear Elevation

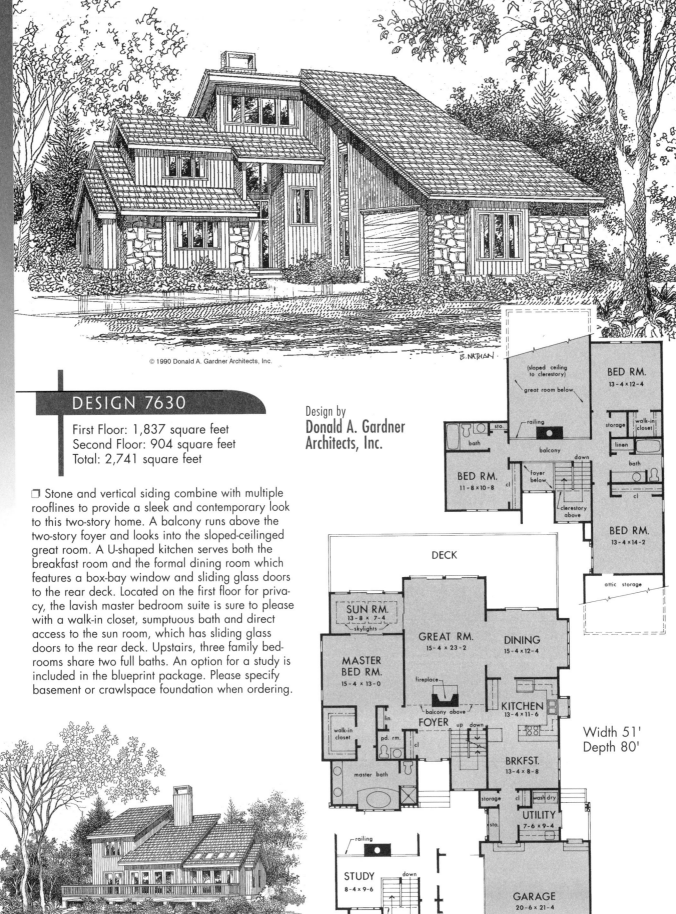

© 1990 Donald A. Gardner Architects, Inc.

B. NATHAN

DESIGN 7630

First Floor: 1,837 square feet
Second Floor: 904 square feet
Total: 2,741 square feet

Design by
Donald A. Gardner Architects, Inc.

❑ Stone and vertical siding combine with multiple rooflines to provide a sleek and contemporary look to this two-story home. A balcony runs above the two-story foyer and looks into the sloped-ceilinged great room. A U-shaped kitchen serves both the breakfast room and the formal dining room which features a box-bay window and sliding glass doors to the rear deck. Located on the first floor for privacy, the lavish master bedroom suite is sure to please with a walk-in closet, sumptuous bath and direct access to the sun room, which has sliding glass doors to the rear deck. Upstairs, three family bedrooms share two full baths. An option for a study is included in the blueprint package. Please specify basement or crawlspace foundation when ordering.

Width 51'
Depth 80'

Rear Elevation

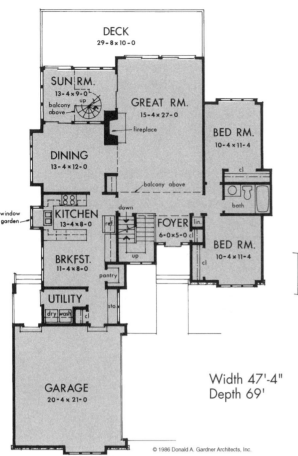

DECK
29-8 x 10-0

SUN RM.
13-4 x 9-0

balcony above

up

GREAT RM.
15-4 x 27-0

fireplace

BED RM.
10-4 x 11-4

DINING
13-4 x 12-0

balcony above

cl

window garden

KITCHEN
13-4 x 8-0

down

FOYER
6-0 x 5-0

lin.

cl

ref.

up

BED RM.
10-4 x 11-4

bath

BRKFST.
11-4 x 8-0

pantry

cl

UTILITY

sto.

dry | wash | cl

GARAGE
20-4 x 21-0

Width 47'-4"
Depth 69'

© 1986 Donald A. Gardner Architects, Inc.

Design by
**Donald A. Gardner
Architects, Inc.**

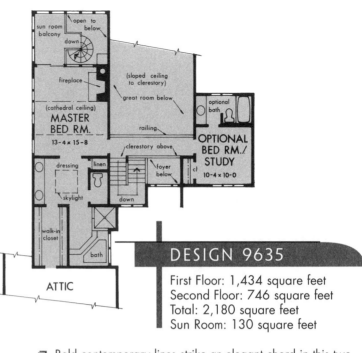

sun room balcony

open to below

down

fireplace

(sloped ceiling to clerestory)

great room below

optional bath

(cathedral ceiling)
**MASTER
BED RM.**
13-4 x 15-8

railing

**OPTIONAL
BED RM./
STUDY**
10-4 x 10-0

clerestory above

cl

dressing

linen

foyer below

skylight

down

walk-in closet

bath

ATTIC

DESIGN 9635

First Floor: 1,434 square feet
Second Floor: 746 square feet
Total: 2,180 square feet
Sun Room: 130 square feet

❏ Bold contemporary lines strike an elegant chord in this two-story plan. The entry foyer leads to a multi-purpose great room with a fireplace and sliding glass doors to a rear deck. The formal dining room is nearby and there is a connecting sun room. A U-shaped kitchen features an attached breakfast room and large walk-in pantry. Two bedrooms on this floor share a full bath. The master suite dominates the second floor. It features a large walk-in closet, double lavatories, a corner tub, and spiral stairs from its private balcony to the sun room below. The upstairs balcony connects it to a study or optional bedroom. Please specify basement or crawlspace foundation when ordering.

DESIGN 4153

First Floor: 893 square feet
Second Floor: 549 square feet
Total: 1,442 square feet

L D

❐ The rectangular shape of this design will make it an economical and easy-to-build choice for those wary of high construction costs. The first floor benefits from the informality of open planning: the living room and dining room combine to make one large living space. The partitioned kitchen is conveniently adjacent yet keeps the cooking process out of the living area. Also downstairs is the master bedroom and bath. The second floor houses two large bedrooms, a full bath and a balcony over the living room.

Design by
Home Planners

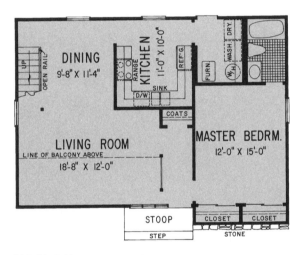

Width 36'
Depth 26'-4"

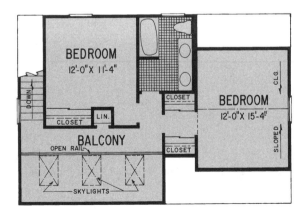

DESIGN 2782

First Floor: 2,060 square feet
Second Floor: 897 square feet
Total: 2,957 square feet

D

❑ What makes this such a distinctive four-bedroom design? This plan includes great formal and informal living for the family or when entertaining guests. The formal gathering room and informal family room share a dramatic raised-hearth fireplace. Other features of the sunken gathering room include: high, sloped ceilings, built-in planter and sliding glass doors to the front entrance court. The kitchen has a snack bar, built-ins, a pass-through to the dining room and easy access to the large laundry/washroom. The master bedroom suite is located on the main level for added privacy and convenience. There's even a study with a built-in bar. The upper level has three more bedrooms, a bath and a lounge that overlooks the gathering room.

Design by
Home Planners

Width 80'-8"
Depth 40'-4"

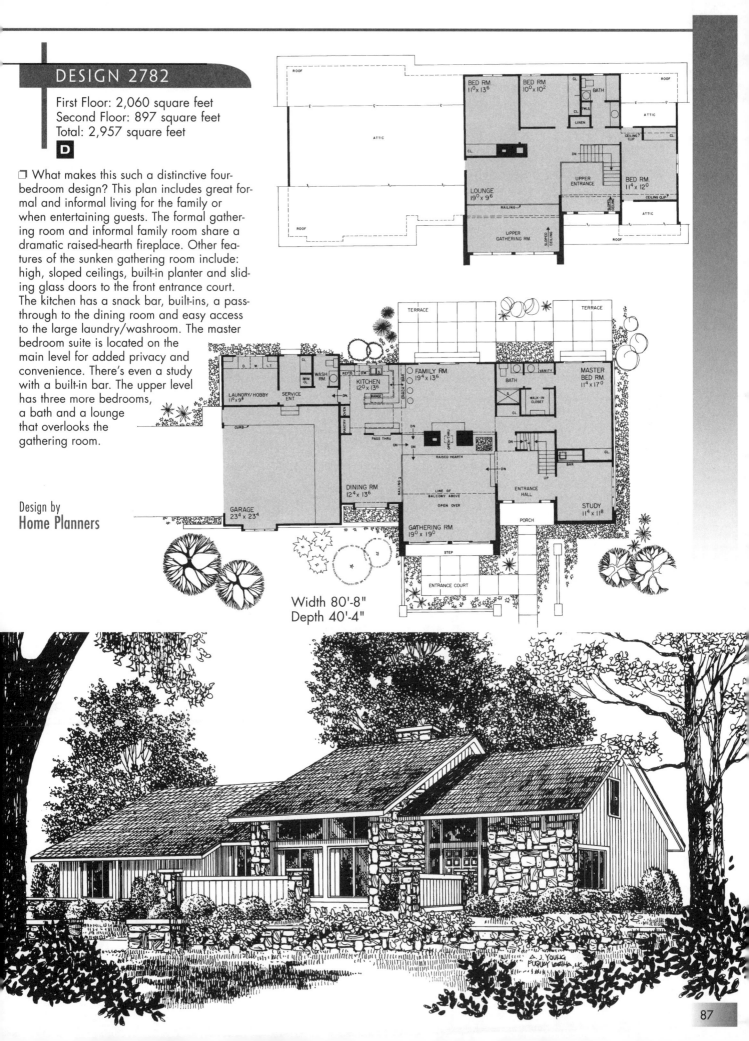

© 1988 Donald A. Gardner Architects, Inc.

NATHAN

Design by
**Donald A. Gardner
Architects, Inc.**

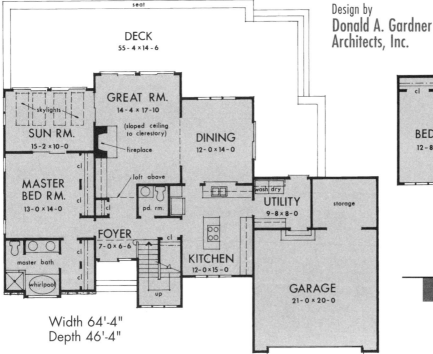

seat

DECK
55-4 × 14-6

GREAT RM.
14-4 × 17-10

(sloped ceiling
to clerestory)

skylights

SUN RM.
15-2 × 10-0

fireplace

DINING
12-0 × 14-0

loft above

MASTER
BED RM.
13-0 × 14-0

cl

pd. rm.

wash dry

UTILITY
9-8 × 8-0

storage

master bath

FOYER
7-0 × 6-6

cl

KITCHEN
12-0 × 15-0

whirlpool

up

GARAGE
21-0 × 20-0

Width 64'-4"
Depth 46'-4"

(sloped ceiling
to clerestory)

great room below

railing

cl   cl

BED RM.
12-8 × 15-0

LOFT
14-4 × 6-2

BED RM.
12-0 × 12-4

linen

cl   cl

bath

foyer
below

down

DESIGN 7627

First Floor: 1,514 square feet
Second Floor: 642 square feet
Total: 2,156 square feet

❏ Sleek contemporary lines, plenty of windows and a combination of textures give this home a lot of curb appeal. Great for entertaining, the formal dining room has a pass-through to the kitchen for ease in serving, and guests can drift into the spacious great room to gather around the cheerful fireplace for after-dinner cocktails and conversation. The large island kitchen will make meal preparations a breeze. Located on the first floor for privacy, the master bedroom suite features two walls of closets, a private bath and direct access to the sun room. Two bedrooms, a full bath and a loft complete the second floor.

Rear Elevation

DESIGN 9617

First Floor: 1,340 square feet
Second Floor: 651 square feet
Total: 1,991 square fee

❏ What a grand plan for contemporary family living! Beyond the handsome exterior are some excellent features that complement today's lifestyles. Of special note: the two-story sun room with access to the great room, the dining room, and the master bedroom; a sloped-ceilinged great room with clerestory windows; two first-floor bedrooms and a third second-floor bedroom that could double as a study; a delightful rear deck; ample storage space over the garage. If contemporary living is your style, this may be the plan for you. Please specify basement or crawlspace foundation when ordering.

Design by
Donald A. Gardner Architects, Inc.

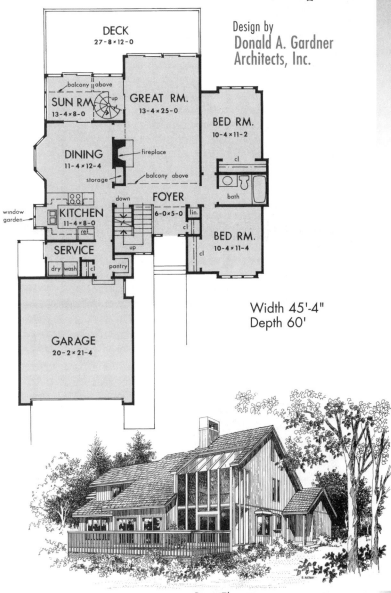

DECK
27-8 × 12-0

balcony above

SUN RM.
13-4 × 8-0

up

GREAT RM.
13-4 × 25-0

BED RM.
10-4 × 11-2

cl

DINING
11-4 × 12-4

fireplace

balcony above

bath

storage

window garden

KITCHEN
11-4 × 8-0

down

FOYER
6-0 × 5-0

lin.

ref.

cl

SERVICE

up

pantry

cl

BED RM.
10-4 × 11-4

dry wash cl

GARAGE
20-2 × 21-4

Width 45'-4"
Depth 60'

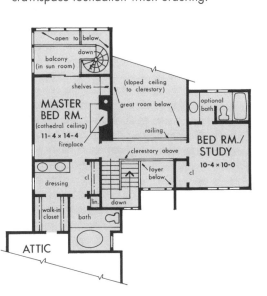

open to below

down

balcony
(in sun room)

shelves

(sloped ceiling to clerestory)

optional bath

MASTER BED RM.
(cathedral ceiling)
11-4 × 14-4
fireplace

great room below

railing

clerestory above

foyer below

BED RM./ STUDY
10-4 × 10-0

dressing

cl

lin.

down

cl

walk-in closet

bath

ATTIC

Rear Elevation

© 1986 Donald A. Gardner Architects, Inc.

Design by
Donald A. Gardner
Architects, Inc.

DECK
40-0 × 12-0

bedroom above

covered deck

SUN RM.
13-8 × 7-4

GREAT RM.
13-4 × 20-4

hot tub

fireplace

fireplace

DINING
11-8 × 12-0

MASTER
BED RM.
11-8 × 15-0

study above

breakfast bar

powder
room

FOYER
6-4 × 7-2

KITCHEN
11-8 × 12-0

window
garden

bath

walk-in
dressing

down

up

SERVICE

lin.

pantry

wash dry

GARAGE
20-2 × 21-4

Width 47'
Depth 69'-4"

BED RM
11-8 × 12-10

(sloped ceiling
to clerestory)

bath

great room below

railing

cl

bath

BED RM.
11-0 × 11-8

STUDY/PLAY
13-4 × 6-6

cl

cl

open to
below

BED RM
11-8 × 11-10

down

ATTIC

DESIGN 7626

First Floor: 1,362 square feet
Second Floor: 764 square feet
Total: 2,126 square feet

❏ This comfortable, contemporary four-bedroom home has a lot to offer an active family. The two-story foyer leads into the sloped-ceilinged great room, which is complete with a fireplace, a wall of sliding glass doors to the rear deck and direct access to the sun room. The U-shaped kitchen easily serves the dining room, with a breakfast bar for early morning meals. A first-floor master bedroom suite features a second fireplace, walk-in closet, private bath and sliding glass doors to the sun room. Three family bedrooms share two full baths and have access to a study/play area that overlooks the great room. Please specify basement or crawlspace foundation when ordering.

Rear Elevation

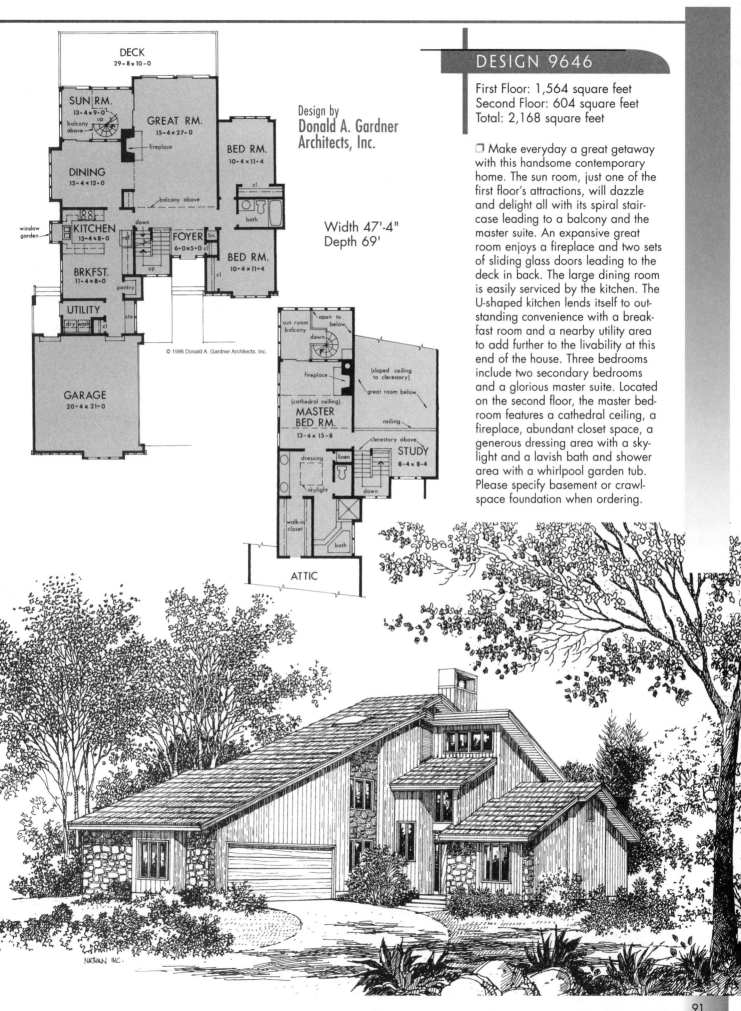

DECK
29-8 x 10-0

SUN RM.
13-4 x 9-0
balcony above

up

GREAT RM.
15-4 x 27-0

fireplace

BED RM.
10-4 x 11-4

cl

bath

DINING
13-4 x 12-0

balcony above

Design by
**Donald A. Gardner
Architects, Inc.**

window garden

KITCHEN
13-4 x 8-0

ref.

down

FOYER
6-0 x 5-0

lin.

cl

BED RM.
10-4 x 11-4

cl

BRKFST.
11-4 x 8-0

up

pantry

Width 47'-4"
Depth 69'

UTILITY
dry wash cl

sto.

© 1986 Donald A. Gardner Architects, Inc.

GARAGE
20-4 x 21-0

sun room balcony

open to below

down

fireplace

(sloped ceiling to clerestory)

great room below

(cathedral ceiling)

MASTER BED RM.
13-4 x 15-8

railing

dressing

linen

clerestory above

STUDY
8-4 x 8-4

skylight

down

walk-in closet

bath

ATTIC

NATHAN INC.

First Floor: 1,564 square feet
Second Floor: 604 square feet
Total: 2,168 square feet

❏ Make everyday a great getaway with this handsome contemporary home. The sun room, just one of the first floor's attractions, will dazzle and delight all with its spiral staircase leading to a balcony and the master suite. An expansive great room enjoys a fireplace and two sets of sliding glass doors leading to the deck in back. The large dining room is easily serviced by the kitchen. The U-shaped kitchen lends itself to outstanding convenience with a breakfast room and a nearby utility area to add further to the livability at this end of the house. Three bedrooms include two secondary bedrooms and a glorious master suite. Located on the second floor, the master bedroom features a cathedral ceiling, a fireplace, abundant closet space, a generous dressing area with a skylight and a lavish bath and shower area with a whirlpool garden tub. Please specify basement or crawlspace foundation when ordering.

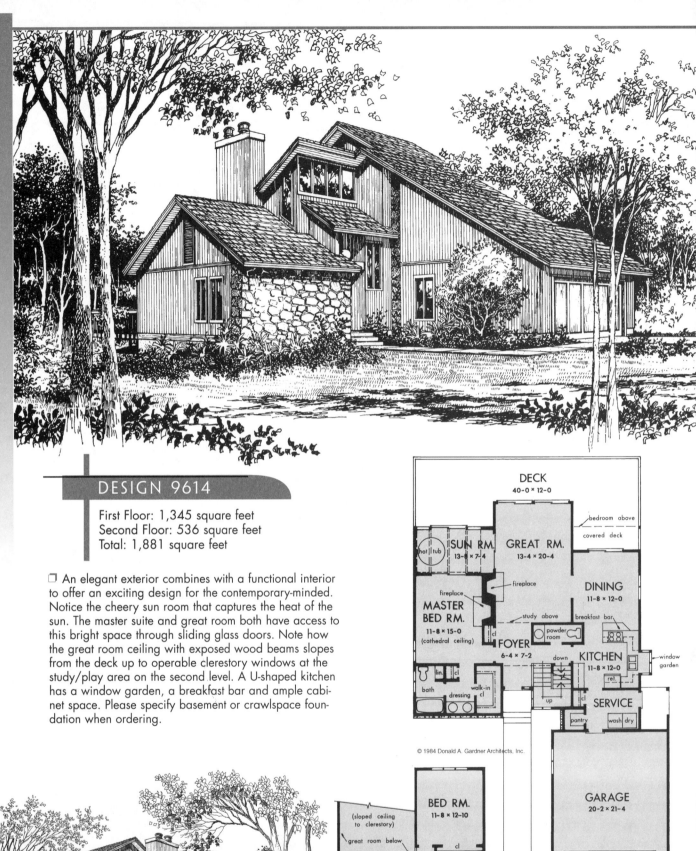

DESIGN 9614

First Floor: 1,345 square feet
Second Floor: 536 square feet
Total: 1,881 square feet

☐ An elegant exterior combines with a functional interior to offer an exciting design for the contemporary-minded. Notice the cheery sun room that captures the heat of the sun. The master suite and great room both have access to this bright space through sliding glass doors. Note how the great room ceiling with exposed wood beams slopes from the deck up to operable clerestory windows at the study/play area on the second level. A U-shaped kitchen has a window garden, a breakfast bar and ample cabinet space. Please specify basement or crawlspace foundation when ordering.

DECK
40-0 × 12-0

bedroom above

covered deck

SUN RM.
13-8 × 7-4

hot tub

GREAT RM.
13-4 × 20-4

DINING
11-8 × 12-0

fireplace

fireplace

study above

breakfast bar

MASTER
BED RM.
11-8 × 15-0
(cathedral ceiling)

powder room

FOYER
6-4 × 7-2

KITCHEN
11-8 × 12-0

window garden

down

ref.

bath

lin. cl

up

SERVICE

walk-in cl

dressing

pantry

wash dry

© 1984 Donald A. Gardner Architects, Inc.

GARAGE
20-2 × 21-4

BED RM.
11-8 × 12-10

(sloped ceiling to clerestory)

great room below

cl

railing

bath

STUDY/PLAY
13-4 × 6-6

open to below

down

cl

BED RM.
11-8 × 11-10

ATTIC

Width 45'
Depth 69'-4"

Design by
**Donald A. Gardner
Architects, Inc.**

Rear Elevation

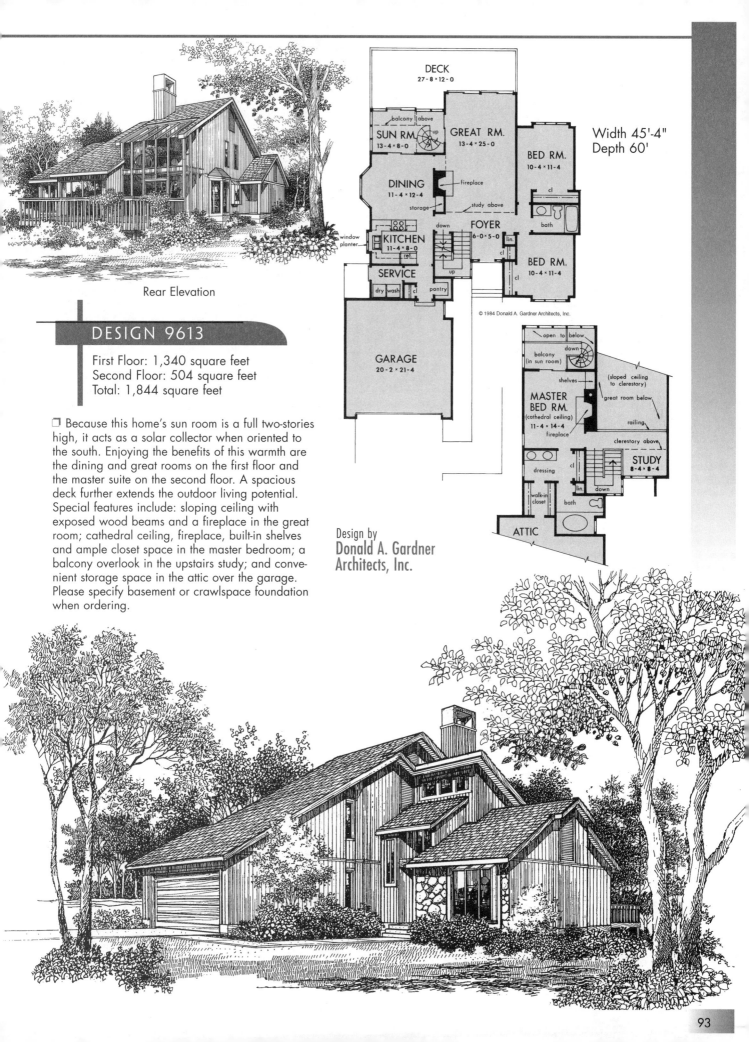

Rear Elevation

DESIGN 9613

First Floor: 1,340 square feet
Second Floor: 504 square feet
Total: 1,844 square feet

❏ Because this home's sun room is a full two-stories high, it acts as a solar collector when oriented to the south. Enjoying the benefits of this warmth are the dining and great rooms on the first floor and the master suite on the second floor. A spacious deck further extends the outdoor living potential. Special features include: sloping ceiling with exposed wood beams and a fireplace in the great room; cathedral ceiling, fireplace, built-in shelves and ample closet space in the master bedroom; a balcony overlook in the upstairs study; and convenient storage space in the attic over the garage. Please specify basement or crawlspace foundation when ordering.

DECK
27-8 × 12-0

balcony above

SUN RM.
13-4 × 8-0

GREAT RM.
13-4 × 25-0

fireplace

BED RM.
10-4 × 11-4

DINING
11-4 × 12-4

storage

study above

cl

bath

window planter

KITCHEN
11-4 × 8-0

ref.

down

FOYER
6-0 × 5-0

up

lin.

cl

BED RM.
10-4 × 11-4

SERVICE

dry | wash | cl

pantry

cl

© 1984 Donald A. Gardner Architects, Inc.

GARAGE
20-2 × 21-4

Width 45'-4"
Depth 60'

open to below

down

balcony (in sun room)

shelves

(sloped ceiling to clerestory)

great room below

MASTER BED RM.
(cathedral ceiling)
11-4 × 14-4
fireplace

railing

clerestory above

dressing

cl

STUDY
8-4 × 8-4

walk-in closet

lin.

bath

down

ATTIC

Design by
**Donald A. Gardner
Architects, Inc.**

This home, as shown in the photograph, may differ from the actual blueprints. For more detailed information, please check the floor plans carefully.

Photo by Laszlo Regos

DESIGN 2488

First Floor: 1,113 square feet
Second Floor: 543 square feet
Total: 1,656 square feet

D

❑ For a lakeside retreat or as a retirement haven, this charming design offers the best in livability. The gathering room has an oversized corner fireplace and a dramatic, full length wall of windows. The space-saving, U-shaped kitchen has a snack bar for meals on the go and an attached dining room with doors to the lovely deck. The first-floor master suite is complemented with a compartmented bath. Two bedrooms with a full bath and a balcony lounge upstairs complete the design and provide sleeping accommodations for family and guests.

QUOTE ONE®

Cost to build? See page 230 to order complete cost estimate to build this house in your area!

Design by
Home Planners

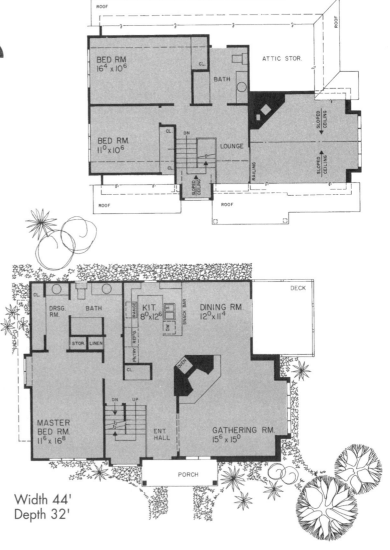

Width 44'
Depth 32'

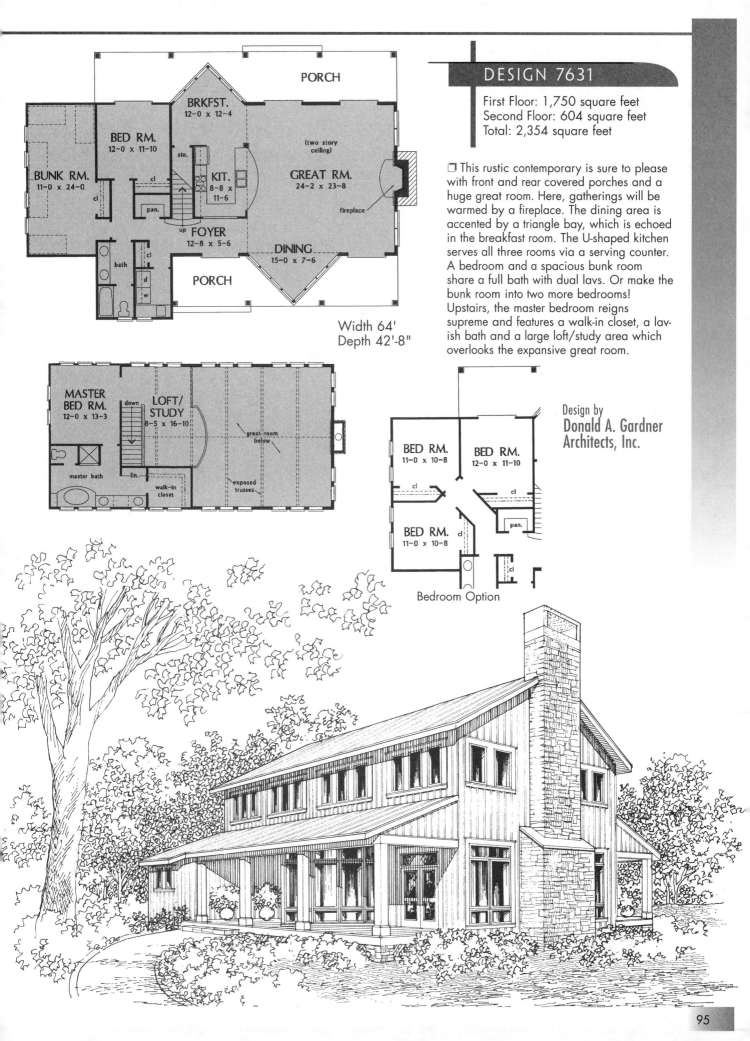

First floor plan

PORCH

BRKFST.
12-0 x 12-4

BED RM.
12-0 x 11-10

(two story ceiling)

sto.

KIT.
8-8 x 11-6

GREAT RM.
24-2 x 23-8

BUNK RM.
11-0 x 24-0

cl

cl

pan.

fireplace

up FOYER
12-8 x 5-6

bath

cl

d
w

DINING
15-0 x 7-6

PORCH

Width 64'
Depth 42'-8"

Second floor plan

MASTER
BED RM.
12-0 x 13-3

down

LOFT/
STUDY
8-5 x 16-10

great room below

master bath

lin.

walk-in
closet

exposed
trusses

Bedroom Option

BED RM.
11-0 x 10-8

BED RM.
12-0 x 11-10

cl

cl

pan.

BED RM.
11-0 x 10-8

cl

cl

Bedroom Option

DESIGN 7631

First Floor: 1,750 square feet
Second Floor: 604 square feet
Total: 2,354 square feet

☐ This rustic contemporary is sure to please with front and rear covered porches and a huge great room. Here, gatherings will be warmed by a fireplace. The dining area is accented by a triangle bay, which is echoed in the breakfast room. The U-shaped kitchen serves all three rooms via a serving counter. A bedroom and a spacious bunk room share a full bath with dual lavs. Or make the bunk room into two more bedrooms! Upstairs, the master bedroom reigns supreme and features a walk-in closet, a lavish bath and a large loft/study area which overlooks the expansive great room.

Design by
**Donald A. Gardner
Architects, Inc.**

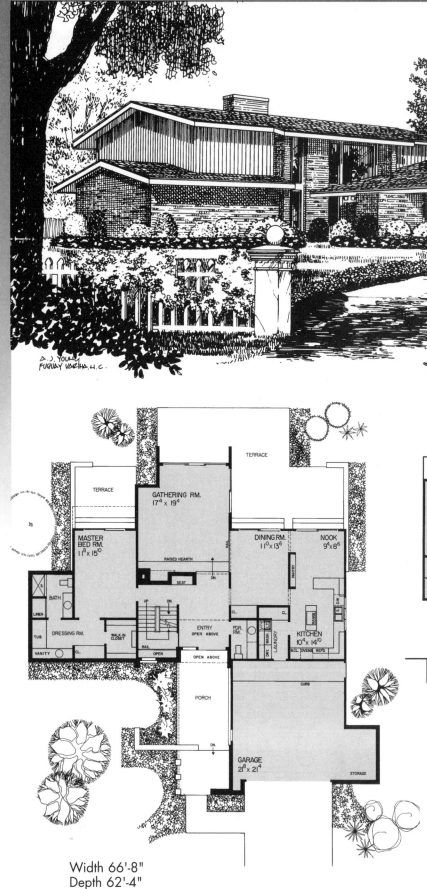

A.J. YOUNG
FUQUAY VARINA, N.C.

TERRACE

TERRACE

GATHERING RM.
17⁴ x 19⁴

MASTER BED RM.
11⁸ x 15¹⁰

DINING RM.
11⁰ x 13⁶

NOOK
9⁴ x 8⁶

RAISED HEARTH

SEAT

PANTRY

BATH

LINEN

DRESSING RM.

WALK-IN CLOSET

ENTRY
OPEN ABOVE

PDR. RM.

CL.

CL.

KITCHEN
10⁴ x 14¹⁰

TUB

VANITY

CL.

RAIL

OPEN

WASH

DRY

LAUNDRY

RANGE

DW

OVENS

REFR.

B.CL.

OPEN ABOVE

PORCH

CURB

DN.

GARAGE
21⁸ x 21⁴

STORAGE

Width 66'-8"
Depth 62'-4"

Design by
Home Planners

BALCONY

BED RM.
11⁸ x 13⁶

OPEN TO GATHERING RM. BELOW

SLOPED CEILING

BED RM.
11⁰ x 13⁶

OPEN

RAIL

CL.

DRESS. RM.

CL.

DN.

RAIL

DRESS. RM.

CL.

BATH

VANITY

OPEN TO ENTRY BELOW

BATH

RAIL

OPEN

DESIGN 2729

First Floor: 1,590 square feet
Second Floor: 756 square feet
Total: 2,346 square feet

L

❏ Entering this home will be a pleasure through the sheltered walkway to the double front doors. And the pleasure and beauty does not stop there. The entry hall and sunken gathering room are open to the upstairs for added dimension. There's even a built-in seat in the entry area. The kitchen-nook is very efficient with its many built-ins and the adjacent laundry room. The two upstairs bedrooms offer their own baths, while the first-floor master suite is designed to pamper with a lavish bath, walk-in closet and access to a private terrace. There are fine indoor/outdoor living relationships in this design. Note the spacious rear terrace with access from the gathering room, dining room and nook.

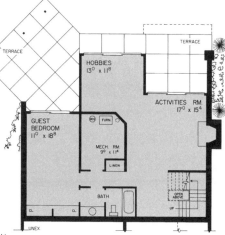

DESIGN 2937

Main Level: 1,096 square feet
Upper Level: 1,115 square feet
Lower Level: 1,104 square feet
Total: 3,315 square feet

L

❑ A splendidly symmetrical plan, this clean-lined, open-planned contemporary is a great place for the outdoor minded. A gathering room (with fireplace), dining room and breakfast room all lead out to a deck off the main level. Similarly, the lower-level activity room (another fireplace), hobby room and guest bedroom contain separate doors to the back-yard terrace. Upstairs are three bedrooms, including a suite with through-fireplace, private balcony, walk-in closet, dressing room and whirlpool.

Width 40'
Depth 58'

Design by
Home Planners

Rear Elevation

QUOTE ONE®

Cost to build? See page 230
to order complete cost estimate
to build this house in your area!

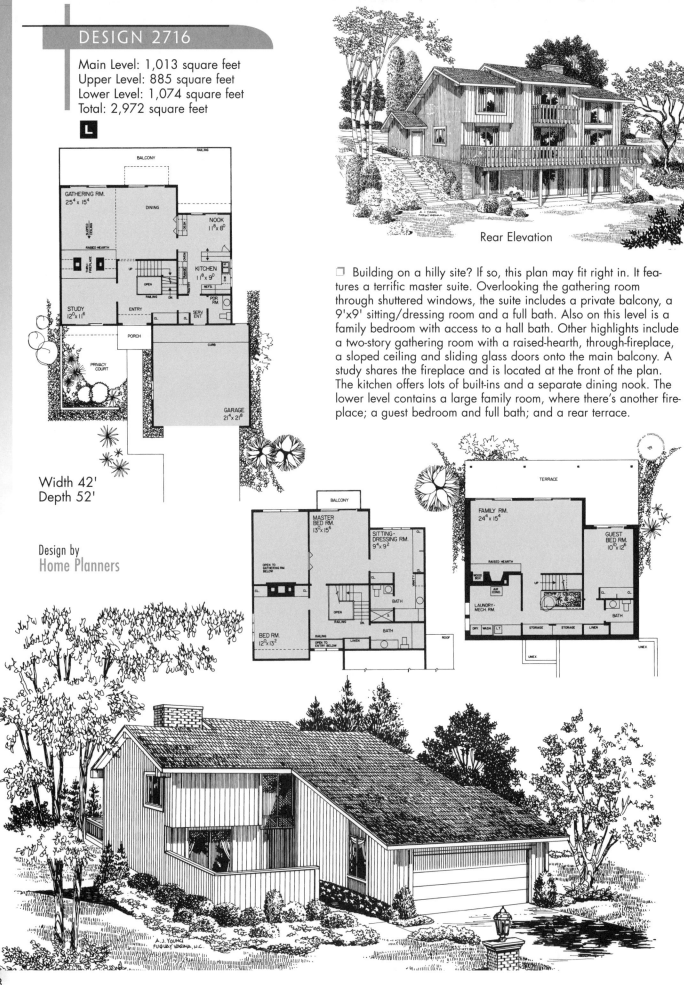

DESIGN 2716

Main Level: 1,013 square feet
Upper Level: 885 square feet
Lower Level: 1,074 square feet
Total: 2,972 square feet

L

BALCONY

RAILING

GATHERING RM.
25⁴ x 15⁴

DINING

SLOPED CEILING

NOOK
11⁸ x 8⁰

RAISED HEARTH

THRU-FIREPLACE

UP

KITCHEN
11⁸ x 9⁰

OPEN

RAILING

DN

REFS

PDR
RM.

STUDY
12⁰ x 11⁶

ENTRY

SERV.
ENT.

CL

CL

PORCH

CURB

PRIVACY
COURT

GARAGE
21⁴ x 21⁶

Width 42'
Depth 52'

Design by
Home Planners

Rear Elevation

☐ Building on a hilly site? If so, this plan may fit right in. It features a terrific master suite. Overlooking the gathering room through shuttered windows, the suite includes a private balcony, a 9'x9' sitting/dressing room and a full bath. Also on this level is a family bedroom with access to a hall bath. Other highlights include a two-story gathering room with a raised-hearth, through-fireplace, a sloped ceiling and sliding glass doors onto the main balcony. A study shares the fireplace and is located at the front of the plan. The kitchen offers lots of built-ins and a separate dining nook. The lower level contains a large family room, where there's another fireplace; a guest bedroom and full bath; and a rear terrace.

BALCONY

MASTER
BED RM.
13⁰ x 15⁶

SITTING-
DRESSING RM.
9⁴ x 9²

CL

OPEN TO
GATHERING RM.
BELOW

CL

BATH

CL

BED RM.
12⁰ x 13²

OPEN

RAILING

BATH

RAILING

OPEN TO
ENTRY BELOW

LINEN

ROOF

TERRACE

FAMILY RM.
24⁴ x 15⁴

GUEST
BED RM.
10⁴ x 12⁶

RAISED HEARTH

WOOD
BOX

UP

CL

CL

AIR
COND.

LAUNDRY-
MECH. RM.

BATH

DRY

WASH

L.T.

STORAGE

STORAGE

LINEN

UNEX.

UNEX.

DESIGN 2901

Main Level: 1,449 square feet
Upper Level: 665 square feet
Master Bedroom Level: 448 square feet
Activities Room Level: 419 square feet
Total: 2,981 square feet

L

❏ This luxurious three-bedroom home offers comfort on many levels. Its modern design incorporates a sunken rear garden room and conversation pit—with a fireplace—off a living room and dining room plus skylights in an adjacent family room with high sloped ceiling. Other features include an entrance court, activities room with a private terrace, a modern, U-shaped kitchen, an upper lounge and a lavish master bedroom suite. Two secondary bedrooms each offer plenty of storage space and share a hall bath.

Width 54'
Depth 63'-8"

Design by
Home Planners

Rear Elevation

CONTEMPORARY HOME PLANS

DESIGN 2511

Main Level: 1,043 square feet
Upper Level: 703 square feet
Lower Level: 794 square feet
Total: 2,540 square feet

L D

❑ This outstanding multi-level home comes complete with outdoor deck and balconies. The entry level provides full living space: gathering room with fireplace, study (or optional bedroom) with bath, dining room, and U-shaped kitchen. A huge deck area wraps around the gathering room and dining room for outdoor enjoyment. A bedroom and bunkroom on the upper level are joined by a wide balcony area and full bath. Lower-level space includes a large activities room with fireplace, an additional bunk room, and a full bath. Built-ins and open window areas abound throughout the plan.

Design by
Home Planners

Rear Elevation

QUOTE ONE®
Cost to build? See page 230 to order complete cost estimate to build this house in your area!

Width 40'-4"
Depth 52'

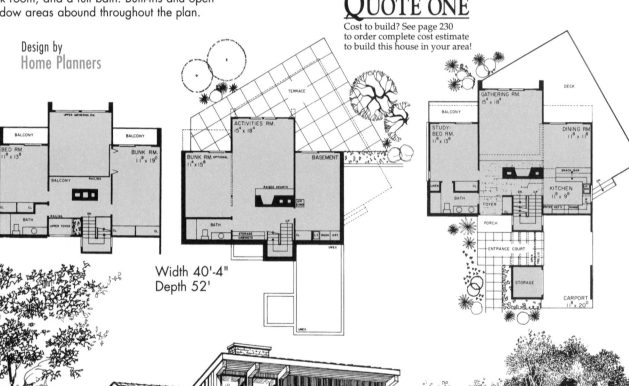

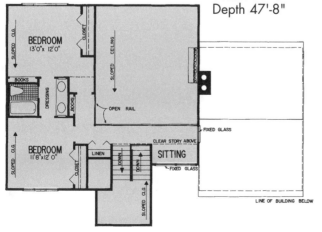

WOOD DECK

DINING
13' 4" x 13' 4"

LIVING
18' 0" x 20' 0"

B'KFAST BAR

KITCHEN
13' 4" x 10' 0"

MASTER
BEDROOM
16' 0" x 16' 0"

LAUNDRY &
STOR.

ENTRY

ENTRY
DECK

COATS

POWDER
ROOM

LINEN

DRESSING

WALK-IN
CLOSET

STONE VENEER

Width 50'-8"
Depth 47'-8"

BEDROOM
13' 0" x 12' 0"

DRESSING

OPEN RAIL

FIXED GLASS

CLEAR STORY ABOVE

BEDROOM
11' 8" x 12' 0"

LINEN

SITTING

FIXED GLASS

LINE OF BUILDING BELOW

DESIGN 4115

First Floor: 1,494 square feet
Second Floor: 597 square feet
Total: 2,091 square feet

Interior spaces are dramatically proportioned because of the long and varied rooflines of this contemporary home. The two-story living area has a sloped ceiling as does the deluxe master bedroom and two upper-level bedrooms. The U-shaped kitchen efficiently separates the dining room from the enormous workroom area. A deluxe master suite is designed to pamper the homeowner, with a warming fireplace, a large walk-in closet and a dual-bowl vanity. Two secondary bedrooms easily accommodate friends and family. A huge rear wooden deck, a small upstairs sitting room and a liberal number of windows make this a most comfortable vacation or lakeside residence.

Design by
Home Planners

DESIGN 4141

Main Level: 1,809 square feet
Upper Level: 1,293 square feet
Lower Level: 1,828 square feet
Total: 4,930 square feet

Design by
Home Planners

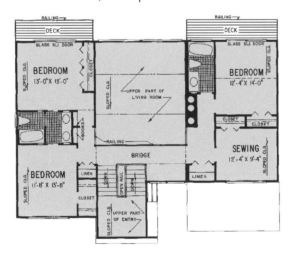

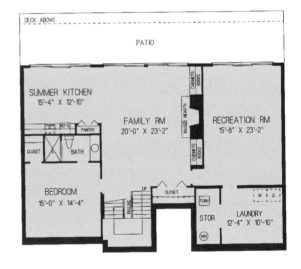

□ A spacious, two-story living room is the centerpiece of this plan with its large fireplace and access to the rear deck. Next door is the kitchen and breakfast room and adjacent formal dining room. Also on this level, an enormous master bedroom with a fireplace. Upstairs are three bedrooms and a sewing room linked by a balcony overlooking the living room. The lower level consists of a family bedroom with its own bath, a summer kitchen, a family room with a fireplace, a spacious recreation room and a large laundry room. Note that the summer kitchen, family room and recreation room all have sliding glass doors to the rear patio.

Width 82'-8"
Depth 40'

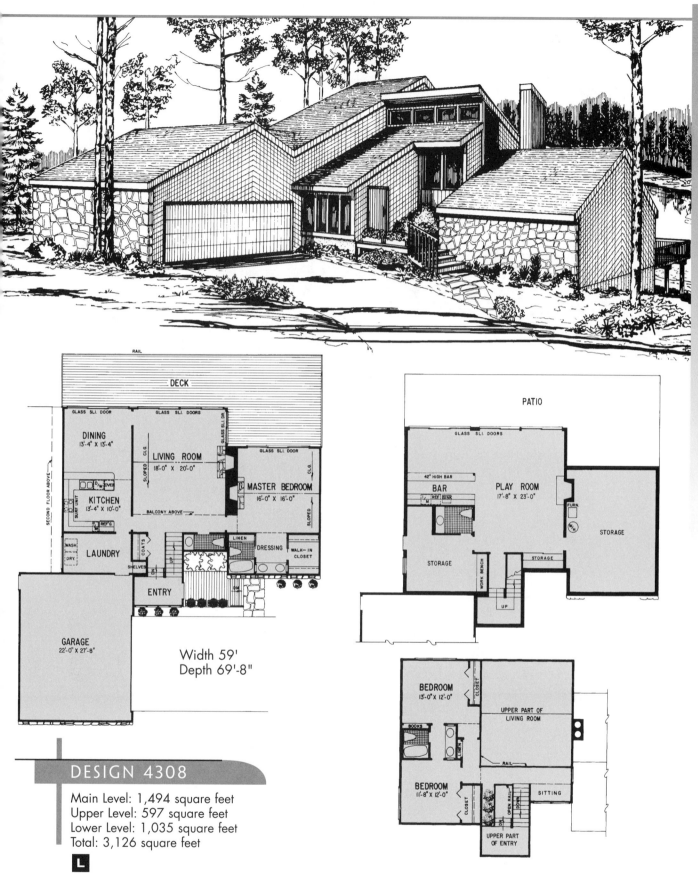

DECK

RAIL

GLASS SLI. DOOR · GLASS SLI. DOORS · GLASS SLI. DR.

DINING
13'-4" X 13'-4"

SECOND FLOOR ABOVE

SLOPED CLG.

LIVING ROOM
18'-0" X 20'-0"

GLASS SLI. DOOR

CLG.

MASTER BEDROOM
16'-0" X 16'-0"

SLOPED CLG.

KITCHEN
13'-4" X 10'-0"

SURF UNIT

D/W OVEN

REF'G.

BALCONY ABOVE

LINEN

DRESSING

WALK-IN CLOSET

WASH. DRY.

LAUNDRY

COATS

SHELVES

UP

DN

ENTRY

GARAGE
22'-0" X 27'-8"

Width 59'
Depth 69'-8"

PATIO

GLASS SLI. DOORS

42" HIGH BAR

BAR

REF SINK

PLAY ROOM
17'-8" X 23'-0"

FURN.

W/H

STORAGE

STORAGE

WORK BENCH

STORAGE

UP

BEDROOM
13'-0" X 12'-0"

CLOSET

UPPER PART OF
LIVING ROOM

BOOKS

LINEN

RAIL

BEDROOM
11'-8" X 12'-0"

CLOSET

SITTING

DN

OPEN RAIL

UPPER PART
OF ENTRY

DESIGN 4308

Main Level: 1,494 square feet
Upper Level: 597 square feet
Lower Level: 1,035 square feet
Total: 3,126 square feet

L

❏ Behind this handsome facade lies a spacious, amenity-filled plan. Downstairs from the entry is the large living room with a sloped ceiling and fireplace. Nearby is the U-shaped kitchen with a pass-through to the dining room—a convenient step-saver. Also on this level, the master suite boasts a fireplace and a sliding glass door onto the deck. The living and dining rooms also feature deck access. Upstairs are two bedrooms and a shared bath. A balcony sitting area overlooks the living room. The enormous lower-level playroom includes a fireplace, a large bar and sliding glass doors to the patio. Also notice the storage room with a built-in workbench.

Design by
Home Planners

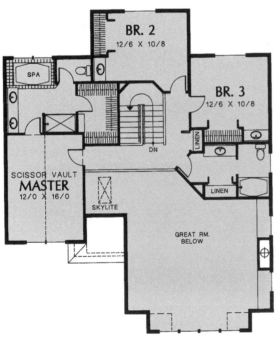

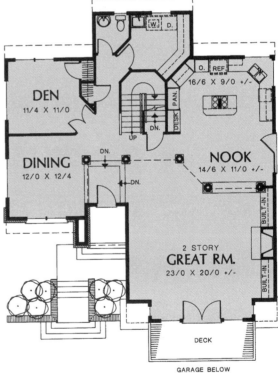

BR. 2
12/6 X 10/8

SPA

BR. 3
12/6 X 10/8

LINEN

DN

LINEN

SCISSOR VAULT
MASTER
12/0 X 16/0

SKYLITE

GREAT RM.
BELOW

DEN
11/4 X 11/0

W D

O. REF.
16/6 X 9/0 +/-

DESK PAN.

DN.

UP

DINING
12/0 X 12/4

DN.

DN.

NOOK
14/6 X 11/0 +/-

BUILT-IN

2 STORY
GREAT RM.
23/0 X 20/0 +/-

BUILT-IN

DECK

GARAGE BELOW

Width 43'-0"
Depth 50'-0"

Design by
**Alan Mascord Design
Associates, Inc.**

DESIGN 9538

First Floor: 1,538 square feet
Second Floor: 1,089 square feet
Total: 2,627 square feet

L

❏This attractive two-story home will fit a sloping lot and fulfill seaside views. The foyer opens to interior vistas through decorative columns, while the two-story great room boasts lovely French doors to a front deck. The gourmet kitchen features an island cooktop counter, a sunny corner sink and a nook with a pass-through to the great room. A formal dining room, a secluded den and a sizable laundry complete the first floor. The second-floor master suite employs a scissor-vault ceiling and a divided-light window for style, and a relaxing bath with a spa tub for comfort. Two family bedrooms, each with a private lavatory, share a full bath on this floor.

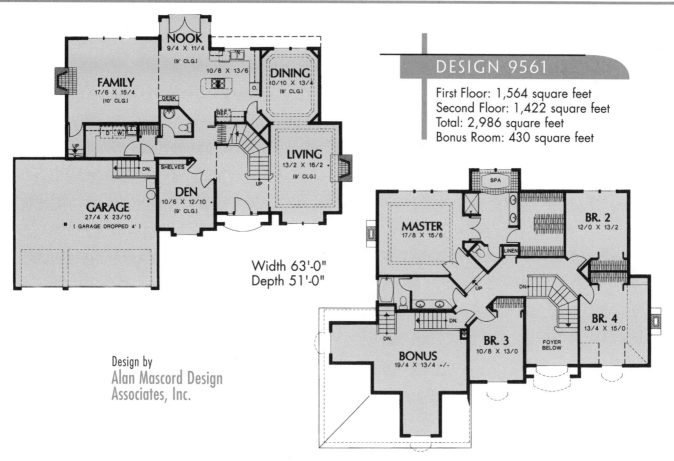

FAMILY
17/6 X 15/4
(10' CLG.)

NOOK
9/4 X 11/4
(9' CLG.)

10/8 X 13/6

DINING
10/10 X 13/4
(9' CLG.)

DESK

REF.

LIVING
13/2 X 16/2
(9' CLG.)

UP

GARAGE
27/4 X 23/10
(GARAGE DROPPED 4')

SHELVES

DN.

UP

DEN
10/6 X 12/10
(9' CLG.)

First Floor: 1,564 square feet
Second Floor: 1,422 square feet
Total: 2,986 square feet
Bonus Room: 430 square feet

Width 63'-0"
Depth 51'-0"

Design by
**Alan Mascord Design
Associates, Inc.**

SPA

MASTER
17/8 X 15/6

BR. 2
12/0 X 13/2

LINEN

UP

DN.

DN.

DN.

DN.

BR. 4
13/4 X 15/0

BONUS
19/4 X 13/4 +/-

BR. 3
10/8 X 13/0

**FOYER
BELOW**

☐ Keystones, stucco and dramatic rooflines create a stately exterior for this traditional home. The formal living and dining rooms invite elegant occasions, while the clustered family room, breakfast nook and gourmet kitchen take care of casual gatherings. A quiet study with built-in shelves opens off the foyer—perfect for a library or home office. The second-floor master suite, a few steps up from the main hallway, opens to a spa bath through French doors, a coffered ceiling and a divided walk-in closet.

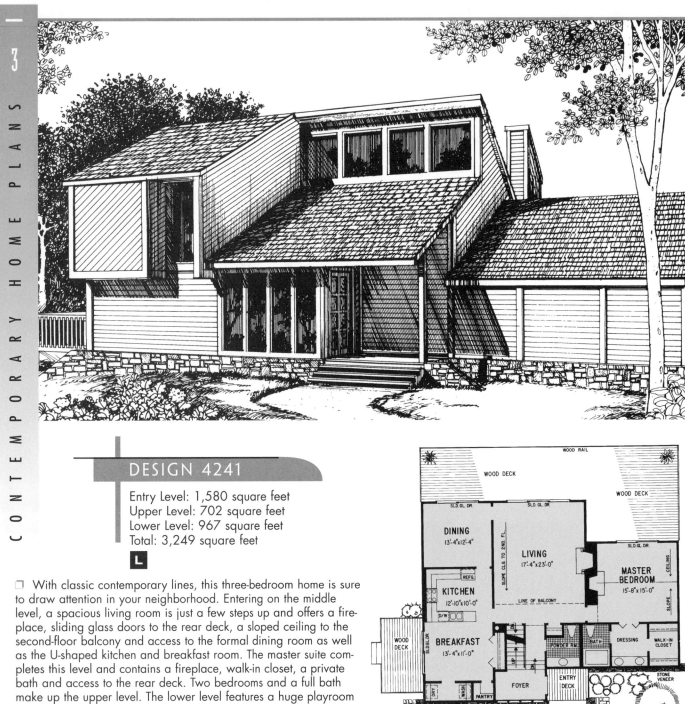

DESIGN 4241

Entry Level: 1,580 square feet
Upper Level: 702 square feet
Lower Level: 967 square feet
Total: 3,249 square feet

L

❏ With classic contemporary lines, this three-bedroom home is sure to draw attention in your neighborhood. Entering on the middle level, a spacious living room is just a few steps up and offers a fireplace, sliding glass doors to the rear deck, a sloped ceiling to the second-floor balcony and access to the formal dining room as well as the U-shaped kitchen and breakfast room. The master suite completes this level and contains a fireplace, walk-in closet, a private bath and access to the rear deck. Two bedrooms and a full bath make up the upper level. The lower level features a huge playroom and access to the garage.

Design by
Home Planners

Width 50'
Depth 38'

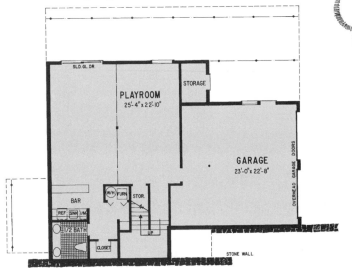

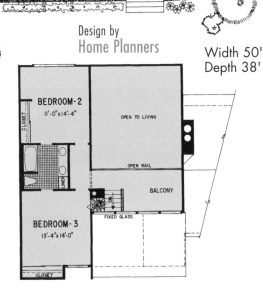

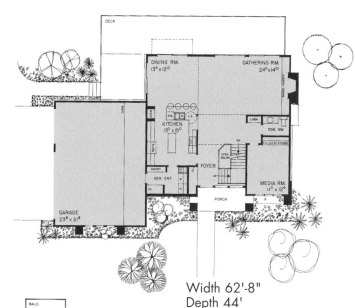

Rear Elevation

Width 62'-8"
Depth 44'

DESIGN 3362

Main Level: 1,327 square feet
Upper Level: 887 square feet
Lower Level: 1,197 square feet
Total: 3,411 square feet

☐ This attractive multi-level benefits from the comfort and ease of open planning. The entry foyer leads straight into a large gathering room with fireplace and is open to the dining room and kitchen. A perfect arrangement for the more informal demands of today! A media room features a built-in area for your TV, VCR and stereo. The sleeping area features two bedrooms on the upper level—one a master suite with His and Hers walk-in closets. The lower level includes an activities room, a wet bar and a third bedroom with a full bath.

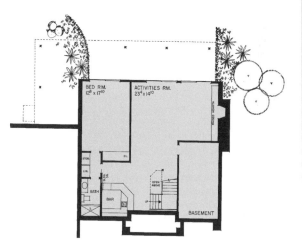

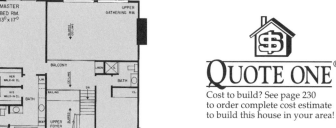

QUOTE ONE®

Cost to build? See page 230
to order complete cost estimate
to build this house in your area!

Design by
Home Planners

DESIGN 2926

Main Level: 1,570 square feet
Upper Level: 598 square feet
Lower Level: 1,080 square feet
Total: 3,248 square feet

❏ An incredible use of curving lines and circles in this modern design makes for an interesting floor plan. Balconies and overlooks highlight a main-level gathering room with a fireplace open to the study, a dining room and a kitchen with a curved breakfast room. A uniquely shaped bedroom has a balcony and full bath. Access the upper level by a curved stair to find the master suite which dominates this floor.

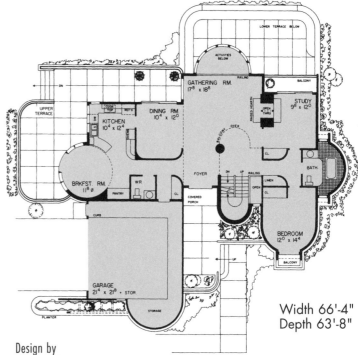

Width 66'-4"
Depth 63'-8"

Design by
Home Planners

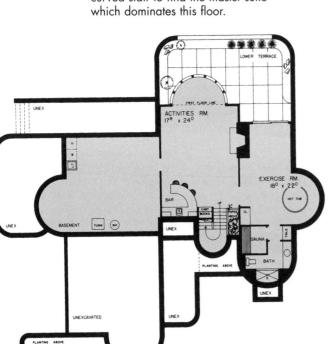

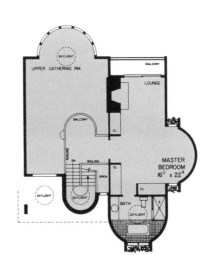

Cost to build? See page 230 to order complete cost estimate to build this house in your area!

DESIGN 7412

Main Level: 2,412 square feet
Lower Level: 130 square feet
Total: 2,542 square feet

❏ An elegant front balcony, a multitude of windows and a front-facing great room combine to give this attractive home plenty of charm. Designed to take advantage of scenic views to the front, this home puts all the gathering rooms to the fore. The spacious great room offers a fireplace, built-ins and double doors to the balcony. The island kitchen features a corner sink with a window and an adjacent nook with access to the balcony. Two bedrooms share a full bath, while the master suite is lavish with its amenities. A cozy and private den has direct access to the outdoors, making it perfect for a home business.

Design by
Home Planners

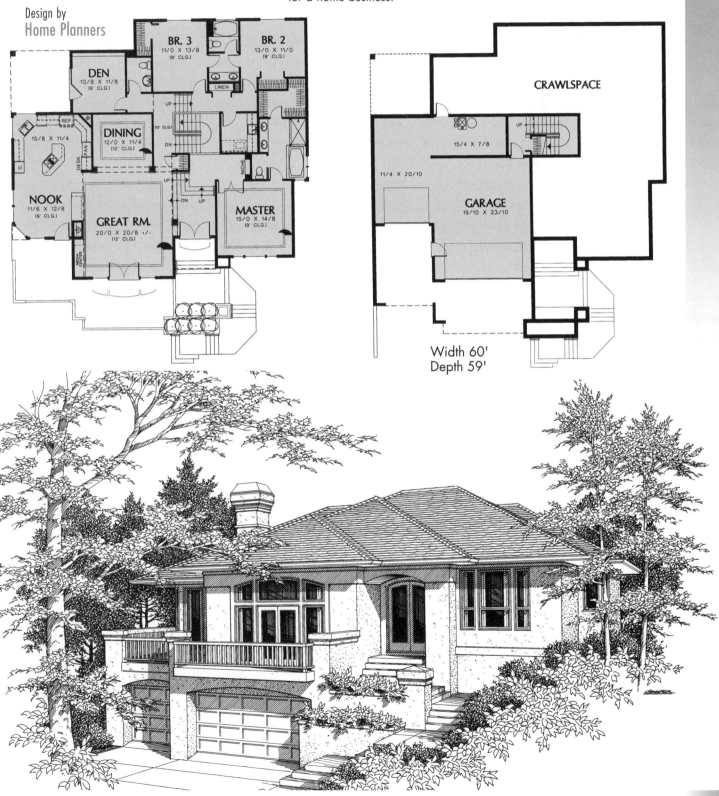

BR. 3
11/0 X 13/8
(9' CLG.)

BR. 2
13/0 X 11/0
(9' CLG.)

DEN
10/8 X 11/8
(9' CLG.)

LINEN

UP

DINING
12/0 X 11/4
(12' CLG.)

15/8 X 11/4

REF

DESK PAN

12' CLG.

DN

UP

NICHE

NOOK
11/6 X 12/8
(9' CLG.)

GREAT RM.
20/0 X 20/8 +/-
(12' CLG.)

MEDIA CENTER

DN UP

MASTER
15/0 X 14/8
(9' CLG.)

CRAWLSPACE

15/4 X 7/8

UP

11/4 X 20/10

GARAGE
19/10 X 23/10

Width 60'
Depth 59'

DESIGN 9488

Main Level: 1,713 square feet
Upper Level: 998 square feet
Lower Level: 102 square feet
Total: 2,813 square feet

Design by
**Alan Mascord Design
Associates, Inc.**

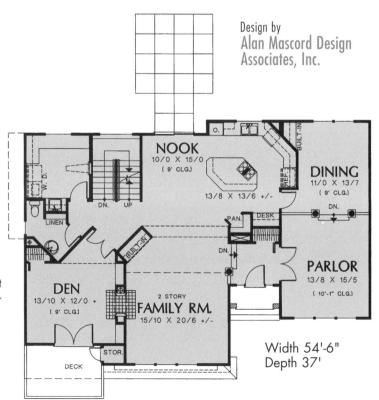

Width 54'-6"
Depth 37'

□ Designed for sloping lots, this home has much to offer in addition to its visual appeal. It is especially suited to homes that orient with a view to the front (note the decks in the master bedroom and den). The two-story family room, with through fireplace to the den, is complemented by the more formal parlor with a ten-foot ceiling. The parlor is separated from the dining room by a step with columned accents. The kitchen/nook area has an island range and is enhanced by a nine-foot ceiling. Three bedrooms upstairs include a master with lavish bath and tray ceiling. Two family bedrooms share a full bath.

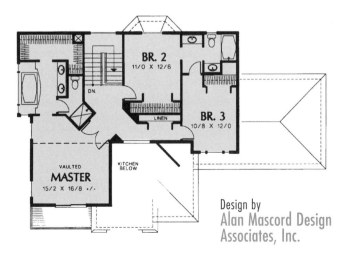

Width 59'-6"
Depth 39'

Main Level: 1,594 square feet
Upper Level: 1,038 square feet
Lower Level: 88 square feet
Total: 2,720 square feet

❏ Arched-topped, multi-pane windows, two balconies and multiple rooflines combine to create an elegant image for this multi-level home. The main level features a formal living room complete with a tray ceiling and warming fireplace, a spacious family room, an efficient island kitchen with an adjacent nook, a formal bayed dining room and a cozy den. The sleeping zone resides on the upper level and consists of two family bedrooms sharing a full bath and a master bedroom suite lavish with amenities. A fourth bedroom with its own bath, a large games room and access to the garage completes the lower level.

Design by
Alan Mascord Design
Associates, Inc.

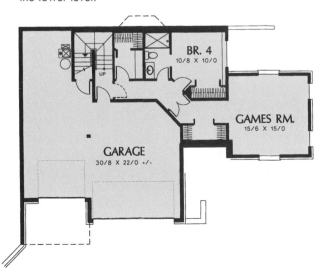

DESIGN 2608

Main Level: 728 square feet
Upper Level: 874 square feet
Lower Level: 310 square feet
Total: 1,912 square feet

L D

Tri-level living could hardly ask for more than this rustic design has to offer. Not only can you enjoy the three levels but there is also a fourth basement level for bulk storage and, perhaps, a shop area. The interior livability is outstanding. The main level has an L-shaped formal living/dining area with a fireplace in the living room, sliding glass doors in the dining room leading to the upper terrace, a U-shaped kitchen and an informal eating area. Down a few steps to the lower level is the family room with another fireplace and sliding doors to the lower terrace, a washroom and a laundry room. The upper level houses all of the sleeping facilities including three bedrooms, a bath and the master suite.

Design by
Home Planners

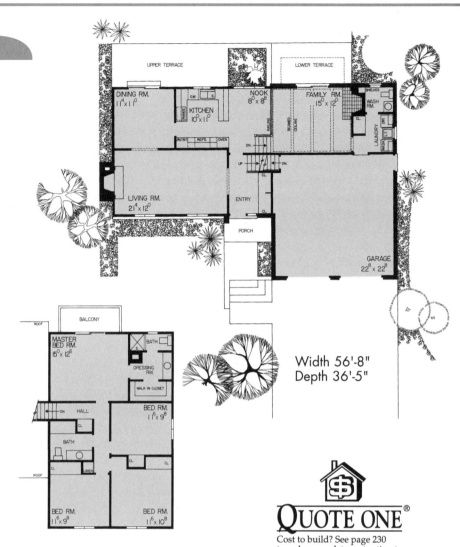

Width 56'-8"
Depth 36'-5"

QUOTE ONE®
Cost to build? See page 230
to order complete cost estimate
to build this house in your area!

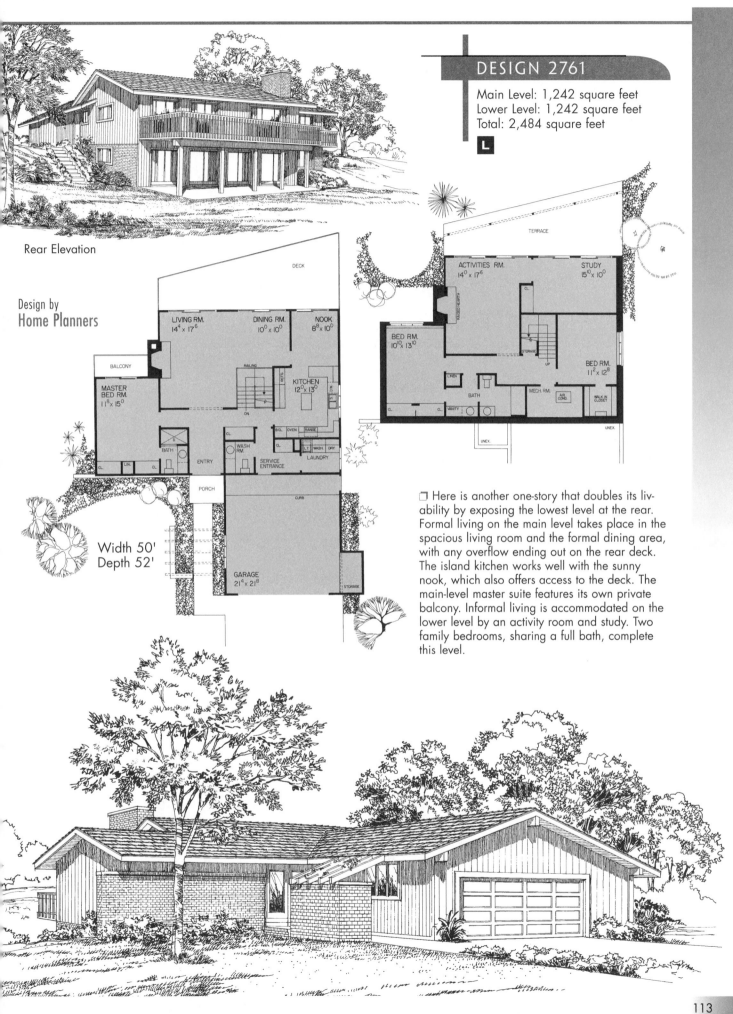

Rear Elevation

Design by
Home Planners

DESIGN 2761

Main Level: 1,242 square feet
Lower Level: 1,242 square feet
Total: 2,484 square feet

L

Main Level

DECK

LIVING RM.
14⁴ x 17⁶

DINING RM.
10⁰ x 10⁰

NOOK
8⁸ x 10⁰

BALCONY

MASTER BED RM.
11⁸ x 15⁰

RAILING

KITCHEN
12⁰ x 13⁰

BATH

WASH RM.

ENTRY

SERVICE ENTRANCE

B-Q. OVEN RANGE

LAUNDRY

LT. WASH. DRY.

CL.

DN

PORCH

CURB

Width 50'
Depth 52'

GARAGE
21⁴ x 21⁸

STORAGE

Lower Level

TERRACE

ACTIVITIES RM.
14⁰ x 17⁶

STUDY
15¹⁰ x 10⁰

CL.

BED RM.
10¹⁰ x 13¹⁰

STORAGE

UP

BED RM.
11² x 12⁸

LINEN

BATH

VANITY

MECH. RM.

AIR COND.

WALK IN CLOSET

UNEX.

UNEX.

❏ Here is another one-story that doubles its livability by exposing the lowest level at the rear. Formal living on the main level takes place in the spacious living room and the formal dining area, with any overflow ending out on the rear deck. The island kitchen works well with the sunny nook, which also offers access to the deck. The main-level master suite features its own private balcony. Informal living is accommodated on the lower level by an activity room and study. Two family bedrooms, sharing a full bath, complete this level.

DESIGN 3361

Main Level: 3,548 square feet
Lower Level: 1,036 square feet
Total: 4,584 square feet

L

❑ Here's a hillside home that can easily accommodate the largest of families and is perfect for both formal and informal entertaining. Straight back from the entry foyer is a grand gathering room/dining room combination. It is complemented by the breakfast room and a front-facing media room. The sleeping wing contains three bedrooms and two full baths. On the lower level is an activities room with summer kitchen and a fourth bedroom that makes the perfect guest room.

QUOTE ONE®

Cost to build? See page 230 to order complete cost estimate to build this house in your area!

Design by
Home Planners

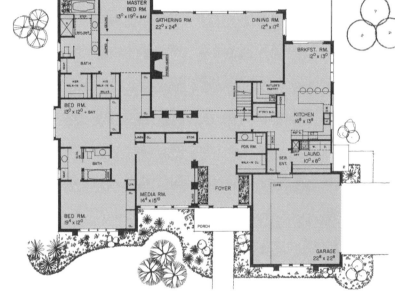

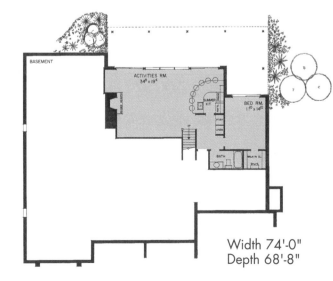

Width 74'-0"
Depth 68'-8"

Rear Elevation

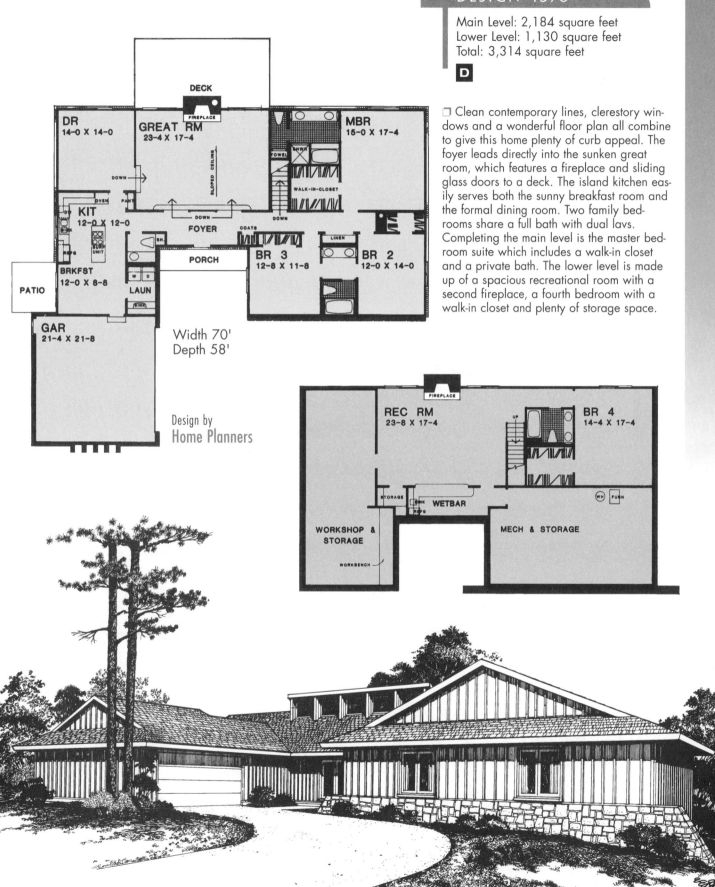

DESIGN 4376

Main Level: 2,184 square feet
Lower Level: 1,130 square feet
Total: 3,314 square feet

D

Clean contemporary lines, clerestory windows and a wonderful floor plan all combine to give this home plenty of curb appeal. The foyer leads directly into the sunken great room, which features a fireplace and sliding glass doors to a deck. The island kitchen easily serves both the sunny breakfast room and the formal dining room. Two family bedrooms share a full bath with dual lavs. Completing the main level is the master bedroom suite which includes a walk-in closet and a private bath. The lower level is made up of a spacious recreational room with a second fireplace, a fourth bedroom with a walk-in closet and plenty of storage space.

DECK

DR
14-0 X 14-0

GREAT RM
23-4 X 17-4

SLOPED CEILING

FIREPLACE

MBR
15-0 X 17-4

DOWN

TOWEL

SHWR

WALK-IN-CLOSET

DOWN

DOWN

OVEN

KIT
12-0 X 12-0

PANT

SURF UNIT

REFG

FOYER

COATS

LINEN

BR 3
12-8 X 11-8

BR 2
12-0 X 14-0

BRKFST
12-0 X 8-8

PORCH

W D

PATIO

LAUN

SINK

GAR
21-4 X 21-8

Width 70'
Depth 58'

Design by
Home Planners

FIREPLACE

REC RM
23-8 X 17-4

UP

BR 4
14-4 X 17-4

STORAGE

WETBAR

SINK REFG

WH FURN

WORKSHOP & STORAGE

MECH & STORAGE

WORKBENCH

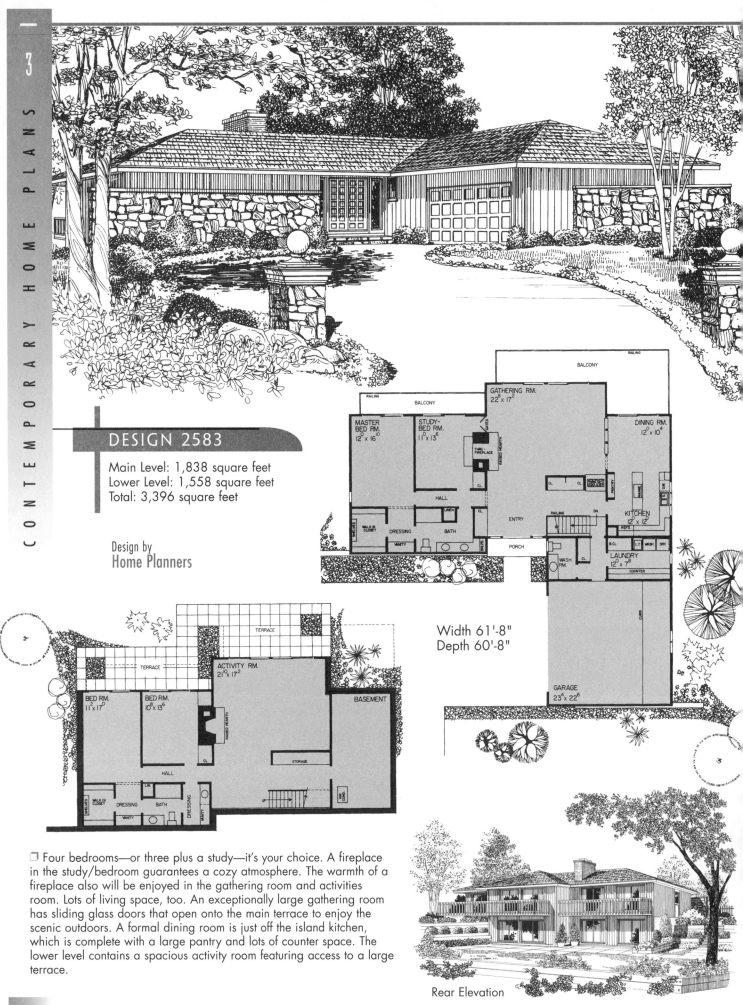

DESIGN 2583

Main Level: 1,838 square feet
Lower Level: 1,558 square feet
Total: 3,396 square feet

Design by
Home Planners

Width 61'-8"
Depth 60'-8"

❑ Four bedrooms—or three plus a study—it's your choice. A fireplace in the study/bedroom guarantees a cozy atmosphere. The warmth of a fireplace also will be enjoyed in the gathering room and activities room. Lots of living space, too. An exceptionally large gathering room has sliding glass doors that open onto the main terrace to enjoy the scenic outdoors. A formal dining room is just off the island kitchen, which is complete with a large pantry and lots of counter space. The lower level contains a spacious activity room featuring access to a large terrace.

Rear Elevation

DESIGN 2847

Main Level: 1,874 square feet
Lower Level: 1,131 square feet
Total: 3,005 square feet

L

QUOTE ONE®

Cost to build? See page 230
to order complete cost estimate
to build this house in your area!

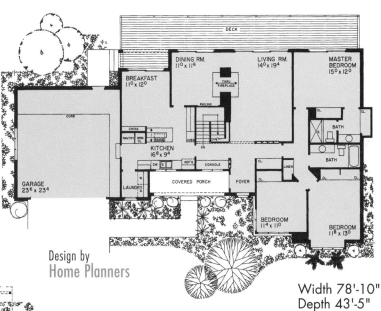

Design by
Home Planners

Width 78'-10"
Depth 43'-5"

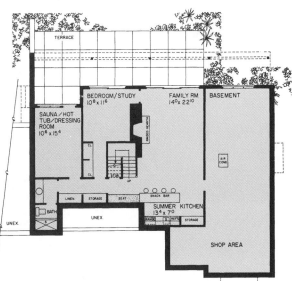

❏ Think Tudors are only two stories? Think again. This is a magnificent hillside plan, complete with first-floor fireplace, easy-to-reach rear deck (four different rooms lead out to it) and plenty of storage space. The lower level is a delight. Note the fireplace, second kitchen with snack bar, rear terrace, space for an extra bedroom (or two), built-ins galore and lots of bonus space that could easily be a workroom, exercise room or both.

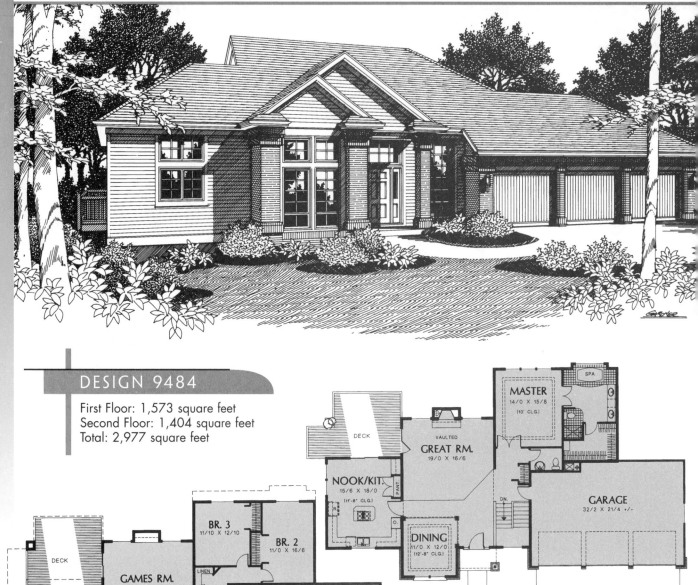

DESIGN 9484

First Floor: 1,573 square feet
Second Floor: 1,404 square feet
Total: 2,977 square feet

MASTER
14/0 X 15/8
(10' CLG.)

SPA

GREAT RM.
19/0 X 16/6

VAULTED

NOOK/KIT.
15/6 X 18/0
(11'-6" CLG.)

GARAGE
32/2 X 21/4 +/-

DN.

DINING
11/0 X 12/0
(12'-8" CLG.)

DECK

BR. 3
11/10 X 12/10

BR. 2
11/0 X 16/6

LINEN

GAMES RM.
19/0 X 16/6

DEN/BR.4
12/10 X 11/2

BUILT-IN

MECHANICAL

CRAWLSPACE

UP

STOR.

D.W.

LINEN

Width 76'
Depth 43'

Design by
**Alan Mascord Design
Associates, Inc.**

❑ There's something for every member of
the family in this captivating hillside plan.
With varied textures of brick and siding,
this home combines rustic and modern very
effectively. Inside, the first floor holds a
huge great room for family and formal
gatherings, a dining room distinguished by
columns, an island kitchen with attached
nook and outdoor deck area, and a master
suite with giant-sized bath. The games
room downstairs is joined by three bedrooms or two bedrooms and a den. Look
for another deck at this level. The three-car
garage easily shelters the family fleet.
Please specify basement or crawlspace
foundation when ordering.

Rear Elevation

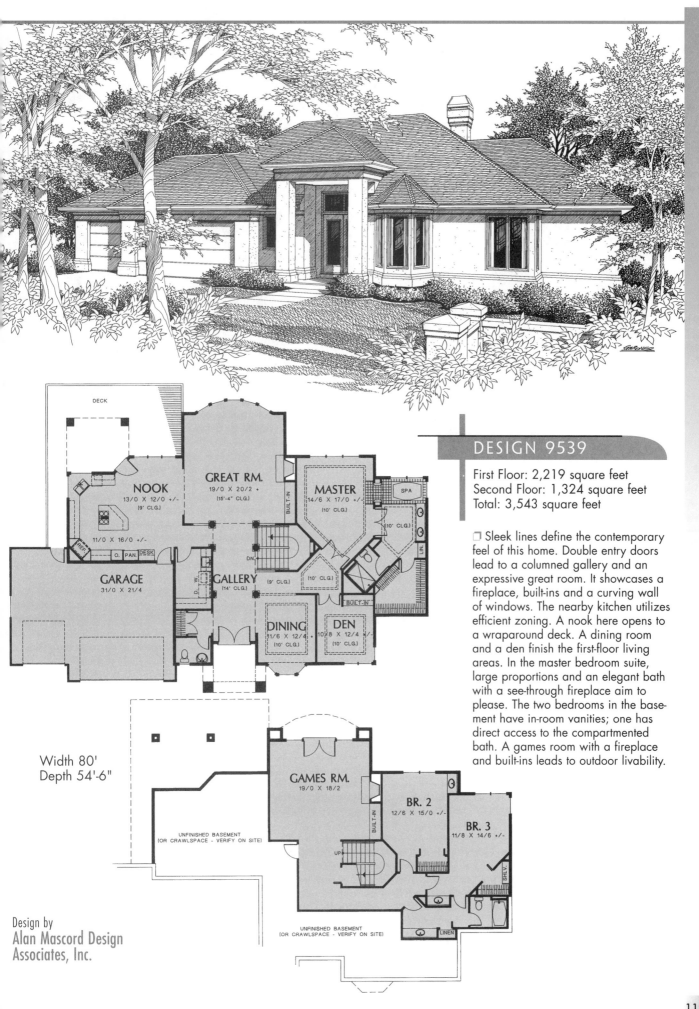

DESIGN 9539

First Floor: 2,219 square feet
Second Floor: 1,324 square feet
Total: 3,543 square feet

❒ Sleek lines define the contemporary feel of this home. Double entry doors lead to a columned gallery and an expressive great room. It showcases a fireplace, built-ins and a curving wall of windows. The nearby kitchen utilizes efficient zoning. A nook here opens to a wraparound deck. A dining room and a den finish the first-floor living areas. In the master bedroom suite, large proportions and an elegant bath with a see-through fireplace aim to please. The two bedrooms in the basement have in-room vanities; one has direct access to the compartmented bath. A games room with a fireplace and built-ins leads to outdoor livability.

Width 80'
Depth 54'-6"

Design by
**Alan Mascord Design
Associates, Inc.**

DESIGN 4391

Main Level: 1,315 square feet
Upper Level: 1,312 square feet
Lower Level: 1,273 square feet
Total: 3,900 square feet

☐ This hillside home opens with formal and informal living areas to the left of the central foyer and dining and cooking areas to the right. A large deck to the back adds outdoor enjoyment. The master bedroom, with full bath misses nothing in the way of luxury and is joined by two family bedrooms— one with a bay window—and baths. Bonus space to the front makes a perfect office or computer room. Note the recreation room with a fireplace.

Width 38'
Depth 33'

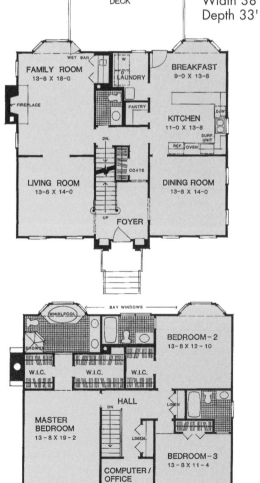

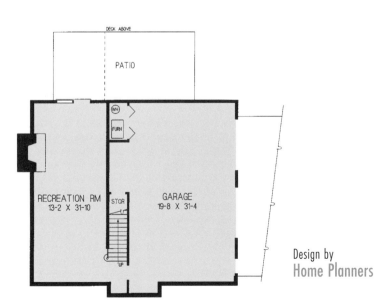

Design by
Home Planners

A BLENDING OF TRADITIONS: *Traditional and contemporary combinations*

DESIGN 7422

First Floor: 1,476 square feet
Second Floor: 886 square feet
Total: 2,362 square feet

Design by
**Alan Mascord Design
Associates, Inc.**

☐ Gabled rooflines, arched-topped windows and a three-car garage combine to give this hillside home plenty of curb appeal. The two-story foyer has a cozy den opening directly to the left, with a formal dining room nearby. The angled kitchen offers a corner sink and a snack bar into a sunny nook. A two-story great room features a wall of windows and a corner fireplace. A bedroom, full bath and laundry room inhabit the first floor. Upstairs, two family bedrooms share a full bath, while the master bedroom suite is complete with a walk-in closet, sumptuous bath and vaulted ceiling.

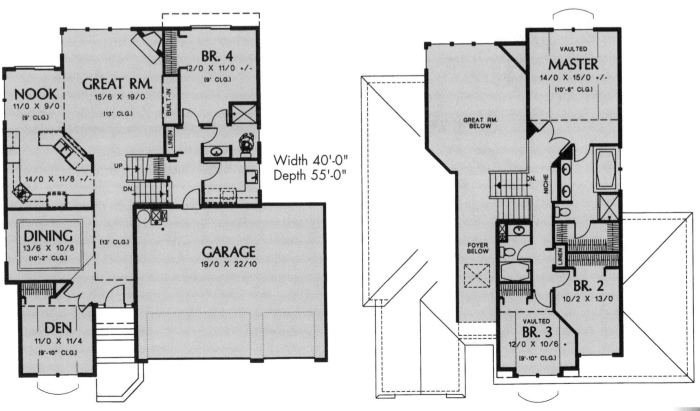

Width 40'-0"
Depth 55'-0"

DESIGN 9418

First Floor: 748 square feet
Second Floor: 720 square feet
Total: 1,468 square feet

❏ Try packing more pizazz and spaciousness into a plan of less than 1,500 square feet. Here is an ingenious solution to the problem of achieving economy without sacrificing livability. Soaring vaulted ceilings are an impressive feature of this design; they span the entire length of the adjacent living and dining rooms. The family room shares a breakfast bar with an efficiently designed kitchen. For an extra touch of class, try the optional nook with its bay window projecting into the rear yard. The master bedroom upstairs is spacious and vaulted, and boasts a walk-in wardrobe exceptionally large for a home of this size. A walk-in wardrobe and window seat enhance the second bedroom.

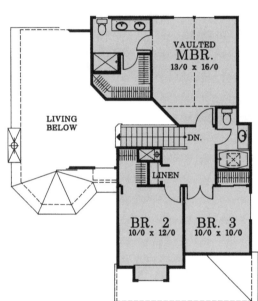

NOOK
9/0 X 9/0

KIT.
10/0 X 12/0

FAM.
12/6 x 14/0

NOOK OPTION
ADDS 87 SQ. FT.

Width 36'
Depth 43'

Design by
Alan Mascord Design Associates, Inc.

DESIGN 7405

First Floor: 1,632 square feet
Second Floor: 1,334 square feet
Total: 2,968 square feet

❏ A facade made up of brick, multi-pane windows and hipped rooflines give this home plenty of contemporary appeal. Enter through double doors to a spacious foyer which is flanked by a set of doors to the cozy den on the right and doors to the casual living areas to the left. Entertaining either formally or informally will be a breeze: the living and dining rooms flow together for dinner parties, while the large family room and sunny nook work well together for more casual gatherings. Upstairs, three family bedrooms share a full bath with dual lavs. The master bedroom suite is designed to pamper and includes a tray ceiling, huge walk-in closet and lavish bath.

Design by
Alan Mascord Design Associates, Inc.

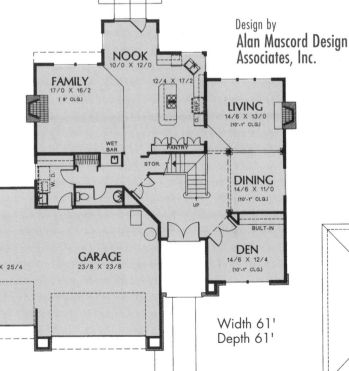

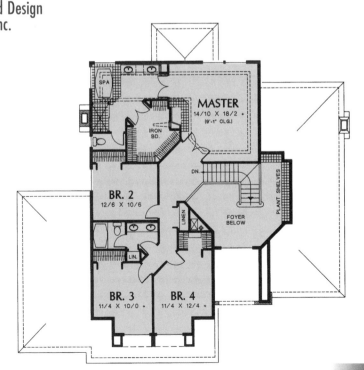

Width 61'
Depth 61'

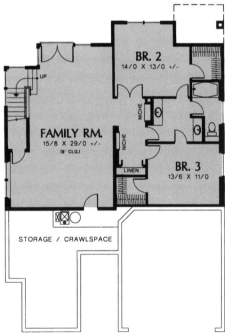

BR. 2
14/0 X 13/0 +/-

UP

FAMILY RM.
15/8 X 29/0 +/-
(9' CLG.)

NICHE

NICHE

LINEN

BR. 3
13/6 X 11/0

STORAGE / CRAWLSPACE

Design by
**Alan Mascord Design
Associates, Inc.**

DESIGN 7436

Main Floor: 1,537 square feet
Lower Floor: 1,238 square feet
Total: 2,775 square feet

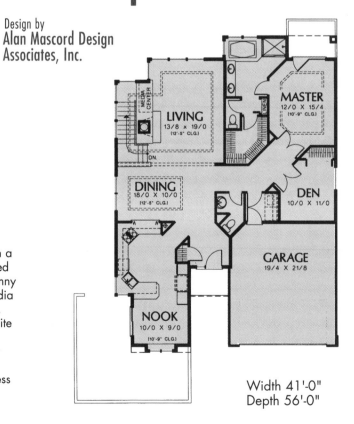

MEDIA CENTER

LIVING
13/8 X 19/0
(12'-5" CLG.)

DN.

MASTER
12/0 X 15/4
(10'-9" CLG.)

LINEN

DINING
18/0 X 10/0
(12'-5" CLG.)

DEN
10/0 X 11/0

GARAGE
19/4 X 21/8

NOOK
10/0 X 9/0
(10'-9" CLG.)

Width 41'-0"
Depth 56'-0"

❏ This stucco-and-siding exterior offers a plan with a daylight basement. On the main level, the U-shaped kitchen adjoins the formal dining room and the sunny nook. A tray ceiling, a fireplace and a built-in media center dress-up the living room. Down a short hall, the double-door den is convenient to the master suite with a walk-in closet, lavish bath and private balcony. The lower floor consists of a spacious family room with outdoor access, and two family bedrooms—each with a walk-in closet and direct access to a full bath.

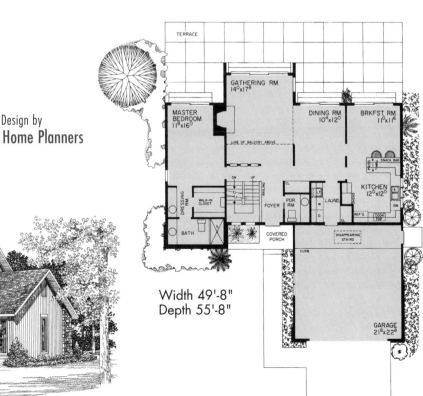

DESIGN 2905

First Floor: 1,342 square feet
Second Floor: 619 square feet
Total: 1,961 square feet

L D

▢ All of the livability in this plan is in the back! Each first-floor room, except the kitchen, has access to the rear terrace via sliding glass doors—a great way to capture an exceptional view. This plan is also ideal for a narrow lot as its width is less than 50 feet. A first-floor master suite is sure to please with a walk-in closet and many other amenities. Two bedrooms and a lounge, overlooking the gathering room, are on the second floor.

Design by
Home Planners

Width 49'-8"
Depth 55'-8"

Rear Elevation

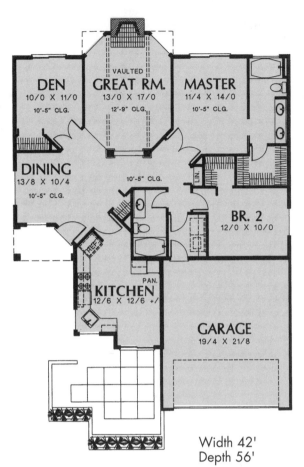

DEN
10/0 X 11/0
10'-5" CLG.

VAULTED
GREAT RM.
13/0 X 17/0
12'-9" CLG.

MASTER
11/4 X 14/0
10'-5" CLG.

DINING
13/8 X 10/4
10'-5" CLG.

10'-5" CLG.

BR. 2
12/0 X 10/0

KITCHEN
12/6 X 12/6 +/-
10'-5" CLG.

PAN.

GARAGE
19/4 X 21/8

Width 42'
Depth 56'

DESIGN 9422

Square Footage: 1,417

❏ This compact ranch leaves nothing out in the way of great features. Most rooms of the home have ten-and-a-half-foot ceilings, allowing transom windows to be used extensively. The kitchen and nook look out on a screened outdoor living area. Note the uniquely shaped great room with fireplace and vaulted ceiling. The master suite has rear-yard access and is complemented by a second smaller bedroom. Because of the narrow width of the home, it can sit comfortably on many small-sized lots.

Design by
Alan Mascord Design Associates, Inc.

This home, as shown in the photograph, may differ from the actual blueprints. For more detailed information, please check the floor plans carefully.

Photo by Bob Greenspan

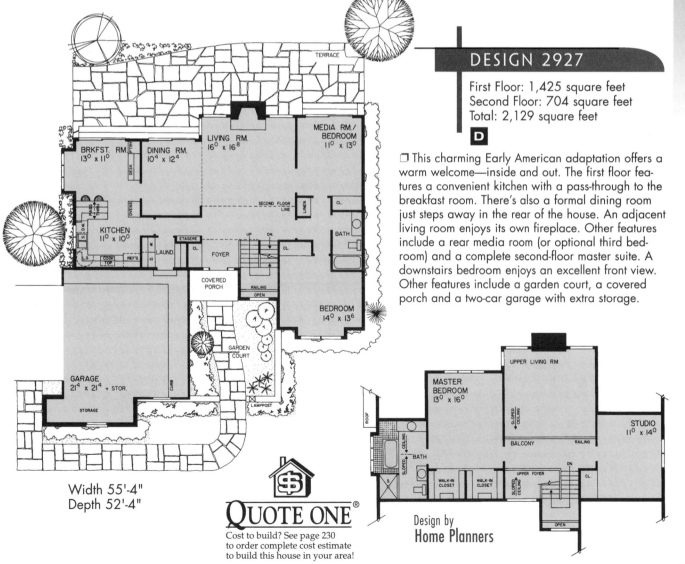

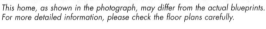

DESIGN 2927

First Floor: 1,425 square feet
Second Floor: 704 square feet
Total: 2,129 square feet

D

❏ This charming Early American adaptation offers a warm welcome—inside and out. The first floor features a convenient kitchen with a pass-through to the breakfast room. There's also a formal dining room just steps away in the rear of the house. An adjacent living room enjoys its own fireplace. Other features include a rear media room (or optional third bedroom) and a complete second-floor master suite. A downstairs bedroom enjoys an excellent front view. Other features include a garden court, a covered porch and a two-car garage with extra storage.

Width 55'-4"
Depth 52'-4"

QUOTE ONE®
Cost to build? See page 230
to order complete cost estimate
to build this house in your area!

Design by
Home Planners

DESIGN 7406

First Floor: 1,332 square feet
Second Floor: 893 square feet
Total: 2,225 square feet

❏ Multiple rooflines, vertical siding and a plentitude of windows give this two-story, hillside home a classically contemporary look. The two-story foyer is flanked by a cozy den to the left and a formal living room/dining room to the right. Casual living takes place to the rear of the home, with a spacious family room featuring a fireplace, a sunny bayed nook for tea times and an efficient island kitchen—perfect for preparation of all meals, be they a quick snack or a banquet. Upstairs, a master suite is graced with a walk-in closet and a lavish bath. Two family bedrooms share a full bath with dual lavs.

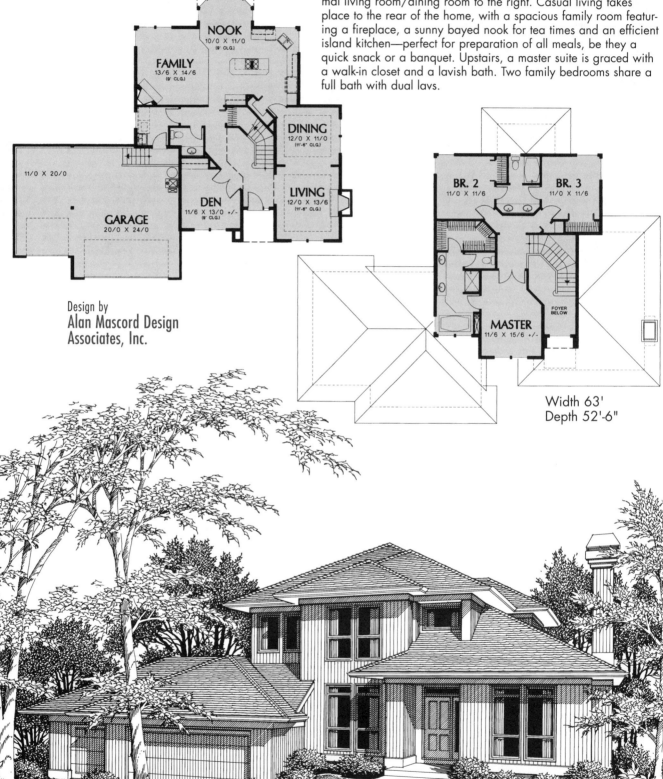

NOOK
10/0 X 11/0
(9' CLG.)

FAMILY
13/6 X 14/6
(9' CLG.)

11/0 X 20/0

GARAGE
20/0 X 24/0

DEN
11/6 X 13/0 +/-
(9' CLG.)

DINING
12/0 X 11/0
(11'-6" CLG.)

LIVING
12/0 X 13/6
(11'-6" CLG.)

Design by
**Alan Mascord Design
Associates, Inc.**

BR. 2
11/0 X 11/6

BR. 3
11/0 X 11/6

MASTER
11/6 X 15/6 +/-

FOYER
BELOW

Width 63'
Depth 52'-6"

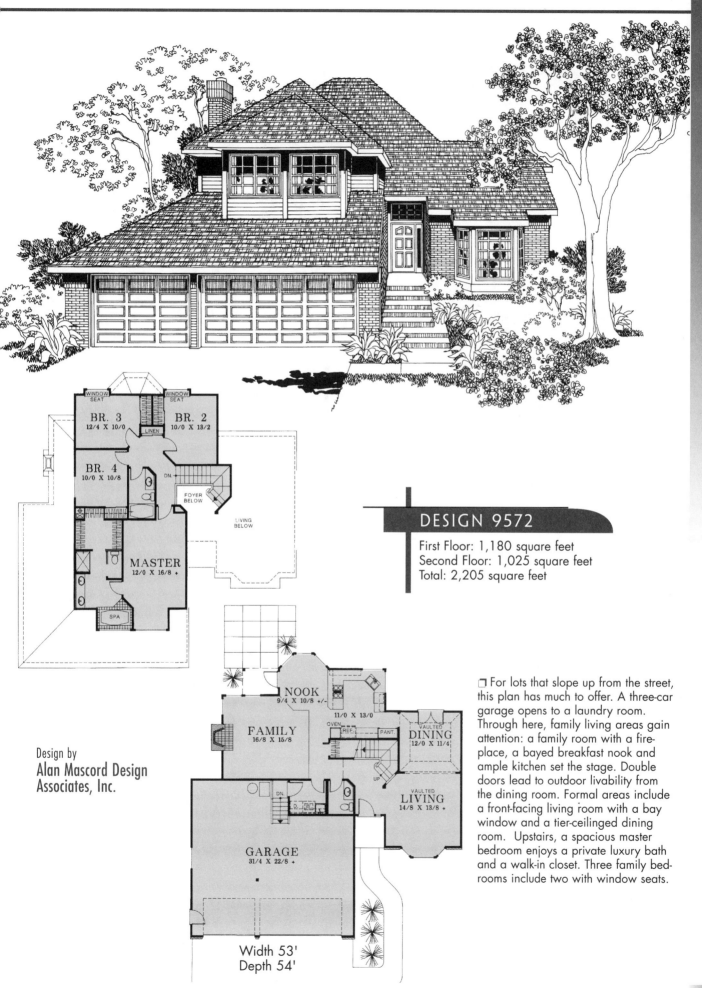

DESIGN 9572

First Floor: 1,180 square feet
Second Floor: 1,025 square feet
Total: 2,205 square feet

WINDOW SEAT

BR. 3
12/4 X 10/0

LINEN

WINDOW SEAT

BR. 2
10/0 X 13/2

BR. 4
10/0 X 10/8

DN.

FOYER BELOW

LIVING BELOW

MASTER
12/0 X 16/8 +

SPA

Design by
Alan Mascord Design Associates, Inc.

NOOK
9/4 X 10/8 +/-

11/0 X 13/0

FAMILY
16/8 X 15/8

OVEN
REF.
PANT.

VAULTED
DINING
12/0 X 11/4

UP

DN.

D.

VAULTED
LIVING
14/8 X 13/8 +

GARAGE
31/4 X 22/8 +

Width 53'
Depth 54'

❏ For lots that slope up from the street, this plan has much to offer. A three-car garage opens to a laundry room. Through here, family living areas gain attention: a family room with a fireplace, a bayed breakfast nook and ample kitchen set the stage. Double doors lead to outdoor livability from the dining room. Formal areas include a front-facing living room with a bay window and a tier-ceilinged dining room. Upstairs, a spacious master bedroom enjoys a private luxury bath and a walk-in closet. Three family bedrooms include two with window seats.

DESIGN 7416

First Floor: 1,102 square feet
Second Floor: 1,092 square feet
Total: 2,194 square feet

Design by
**Alan Mascord Design
Associates, Inc.**

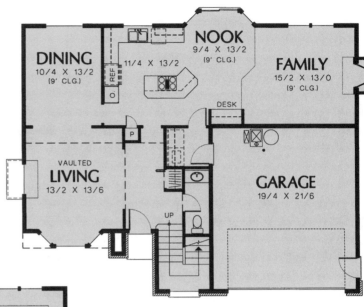

DINING
10/4 X 13/2
(9' CLG.)

NOOK
9/4 X 13/2
(9' CLG.)

FAMILY
15/2 X 13/0
(9' CLG.)

11/4 X 13/2

REF

O

DESK

P

VAULTED
LIVING
13/2 X 13/6

UP

GARAGE
19/4 X 21/6

BR. 4
10/0 X 12/8 +

BR. 3
10/0 X 11/6

SPA

MASTER
12/0 X 15/2
(9'-8" CLG)

LIVING RM.
BELOW

ENTRY
BELOW

DN.

LIN

BR. 2
11/8 X 12/2 +

Width 46'
Depth 38'

☐ A blend of textures adds class to this contemporary home. Inside, the two-story foyer leads directly to the vaulted, bayed living room. A formal dining room opens to the rear and works efficiently with the island kitchen. Casual living is a pleasure in the family room and nearby bayed nook. A fireplace awaits to add warmth and ambience to all of your gatherings. The sleeping zone is located upstairs for privacy, and consists of three secondary bedrooms sharing a full bath and a master bedroom suite rife with amenities. From a double-door entry, tray ceiling and a walk-in closet to a lavish bath, this suite is sure to please.

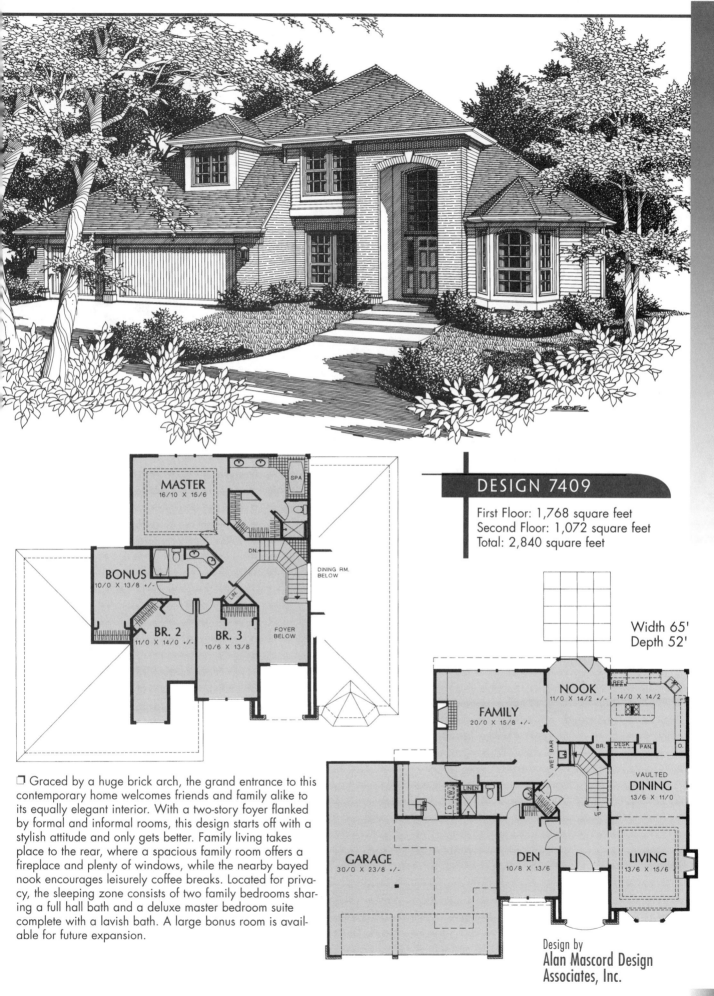

DESIGN 7409

First Floor: 1,768 square feet
Second Floor: 1,072 square feet
Total: 2,840 square feet

Width 65'
Depth 52'

MASTER
16/10 X 15/6

SPA

BONUS
10/0 X 13/8 +/-

DN.

DINING RM.
BELOW

LIN.

BR. 2
11/0 X 14/0 +/-

BR. 3
10/6 X 13/8

FOYER
BELOW

NOOK
11/0 X 14/2 +/-

FAMILY
20/0 X 15/8 +/-

REF.

14/0 X 14/2

WET BAR

BR.

DESK

PAN.

O.

VAULTED
DINING
13/6 X 11/0

UP

LINEN

D

W

GARAGE
30/0 X 23/8 +/-

DEN
10/8 X 13/6

LIVING
13/6 X 15/6

❑ Graced by a huge brick arch, the grand entrance to this contemporary home welcomes friends and family alike to its equally elegant interior. With a two-story foyer flanked by formal and informal rooms, this design starts off with a stylish attitude and only gets better. Family living takes place to the rear, where a spacious family room offers a fireplace and plenty of windows, while the nearby bayed nook encourages leisurely coffee breaks. Located for privacy, the sleeping zone consists of two family bedrooms sharing a full hall bath and a deluxe master bedroom suite complete with a lavish bath. A large bonus room is available for future expansion.

Design by
Alan Mascord Design Associates, Inc.

131

NOOK

VAULTED
FAMILY
9/8 X 13/8
17/8 X 14/0
(9' CLG.)

11/8 X 11/8

PANTRY

DINING
12/0 X 11/0 •
(9' CLG.)

10/2 X 12/0

UP

LIVING
13/0 X 13/8 •
(9' CLG.)

GARAGE
19/4 X 21/8

Width 44'
Depth 51'

DESIGN 7408

First Floor: 1,294 square feet
Second Floor: 1,414 square feet
Total: 2,709 square feet

Design by
Alan Mascord Design Associates, Inc.

BR. 3
11/8 X 12/0 +/-

VAULTED
LOFT
9/0 X 14/0

FAMILY RM.
BELOW

DN.

LINEN

LIN.

BR. 2
13/0 X 11/0 •

FOYER
BELOW

MASTER
13/6 X 14/0
(9'-8" CLG.)

❏ Stucco-and-siding and a private walled courtyard—a combination sure to provide years of pleasure. And the pleasure continues inside. The front living room opens via French doors to the walled patio while a fireplace warms cool winter evenings. The adjacent formal dining room makes dinner parties a breeze. The efficient island kitchen offers a corner sink and plenty of counter and cabinet space. The vaulted family room also has a fireplace and welcomes casual get-togethers. Three bedrooms reside up a curved staircase. Two are secondary bedrooms and share a large bath, while the third is the deluxe master bedroom suite. Here, luxuries abound, including a huge walk-in closet and a lavish bath. A vaulted loft completes this level and could be used as a study, play area or library.

DESIGN 7410

First Floor: 1,189 square feet
Second Floor: 1,030 square feet
Total: 2,219 square feet

❏ Gabled rooflines, stucco-and-siding and a grand entryway give this home a welcoming look. Inside, entertaining will be a breeze, whether its formal or informal. For those fancy dinner parties, a formal dining room with a box-bay window works well with the adjacent parlor. If a family gathering is more what you had in mind, the two-story family room complete with a fireplace and easy access to the spacious kitchen/nook area will surely please. Upstairs, a deluxe master suite shares a large loft with a secondary bedroom. The master bath is designed to pamper and leads to a huge walk-in closet.

VAULTED
MASTER
15/0 X 12/0

FAMILY RM
BELOW

LOFT
12/0 X 12/0 +/-

DN

BR. 2
13/0 X 11/0 +/-

PLANT SHELF

2 STORY
FAMILY RM.
15/6 X 16/0

Width 41'
Depth 50'

DINING
12/4 X 12/2 +/-

GARAGE
19/0 X 21/8

PARLOR
10/4 X 12/6 +/-
(11'-4" CLG.)

Design by
Alan Mascord Design Associates, Inc.

DESIGN 9551

First Floor: 1,682 square feet
Second Floor: 1,589 square feet
Total: 3,271 square feet
Bonus Room: 287 square feet

Design by
**Alan Mascord Design
Associates, Inc.**

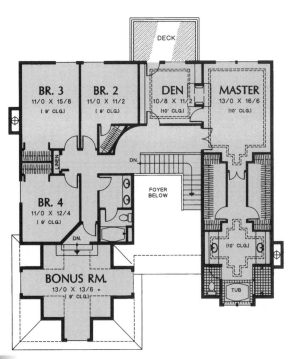

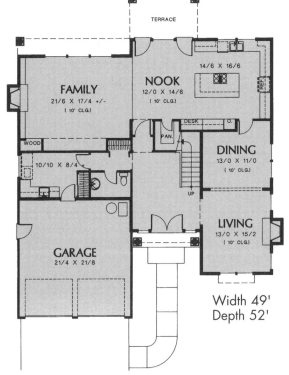

Width 49'
Depth 52'

❏ Wood shingles, a double-door glass entry and varying rooflines add a special twist to this otherwise traditional home. The plan is designed for easy living. To the right of the foyer are the formal living and dining rooms. Adjacent to the dining area is an efficient, step-saving kitchen featuring a cooktop island and a walk-in pantry. The nearby breakfast nook offers dual access to the terrace and combines well with the family room for informal gatherings. The second floor contains three bedrooms, a bath and the master suite. Two walk-in closets lead to the unique and luxurious master bath. A den, with a detailed ceiling and offering access to a private deck, and a bonus room complete the upstairs.

DESIGN 9483

First Floor: 1,697 square feet
Second Floor: 433 square feet
Total: 2,130 square feet

Design by
Alan Mascord Design Associates, Inc.

Width 42'
Depth 63'

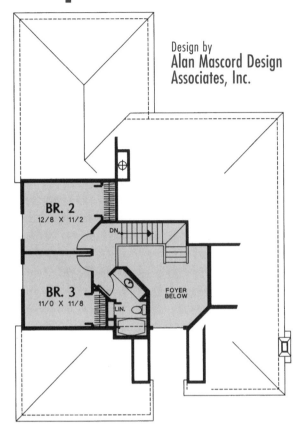

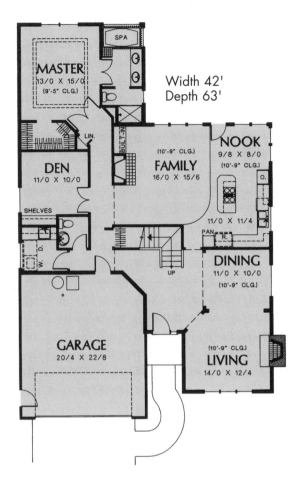

❏ High, sloping rooflines allow for a volume look with expansive windows in this 1½-story plan. The living areas are clustered on the first floor and include formal living and dining rooms, a spacious family room, a cozy den, an efficient kitchen and a private master suite tucked privately to the rear. The living room and family room both have fireplaces. Two family bedrooms are found on the second floor along with a full bath.

135

DESIGN 9642

First Floor: 1,378 square feet
Second Floor: 468 square feet
Total: 1,846 square feet

❏ This well-proportioned, compact house provides for a lifestyle that is cozy and inviting. The two-story entrance foyer has windows at the second level, allowing natural light to flood the area. Both the great room and dining room boast tray ceilings as well as round columns at their entrances. The large master suite is located on the first floor and has a gracious master bath with a double-bowl vanity, shower and whirlpool tub. Two family bedrooms share a full bath. The plan includes a crawlspace foundation.

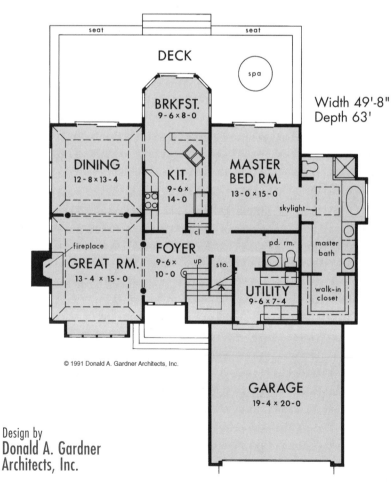

Width 49'-8"
Depth 63'

© 1991 Donald A. Gardner Architects, Inc.

Design by
**Donald A. Gardner
Architects, Inc.**

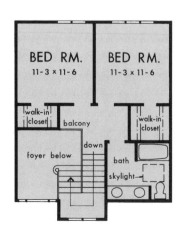

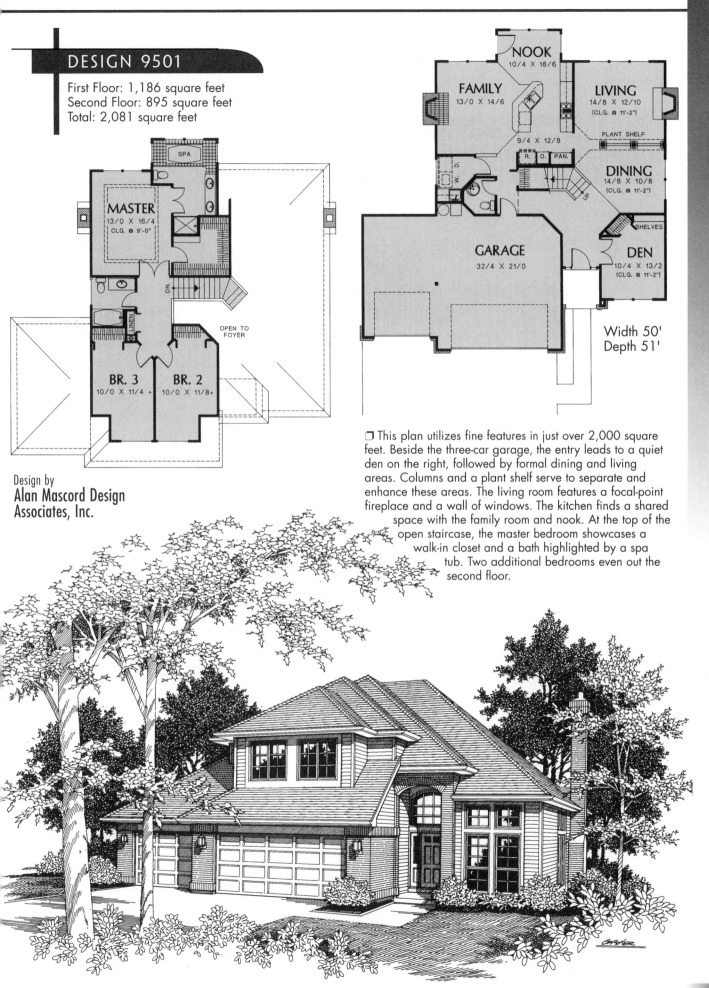

DESIGN 9501

First Floor: 1,186 square feet
Second Floor: 895 square feet
Total: 2,081 square feet

SPA

MASTER
13/0 X 16/4
CLG. 9'-0"

DN.

BR. 3
10/0 X 11/4 +

BR. 2
10/0 X 11/8+

LINEN

OPEN TO
FOYER

Design by
Alan Mascord Design Associates, Inc.

NOOK
10/4 X 18/6

FAMILY
13/0 X 14/6

LIVING
14/8 X 12/10
(CLG. 11'-2")

9/4 X 12/8

PLANT SHELF

R. O. PAN.

W. D.

DINING
14/8 X 10/8
(CLG. 11'-2")

UP

GARAGE
32/4 X 21/0

SHELVES

DEN
10/4 X 13/2
(CLG. 11'-2")

Width 50'
Depth 51'

❏ This plan utilizes fine features in just over 2,000 square feet. Beside the three-car garage, the entry leads to a quiet den on the right, followed by formal dining and living areas. Columns and a plant shelf serve to separate and enhance these areas. The living room features a focal-point fireplace and a wall of windows. The kitchen finds a shared space with the family room and nook. At the top of the open staircase, the master bedroom showcases a walk-in closet and a bath highlighted by a spa tub. Two additional bedrooms even out the second floor.

DESIGN 3454

Square Footage: 1,699

L D

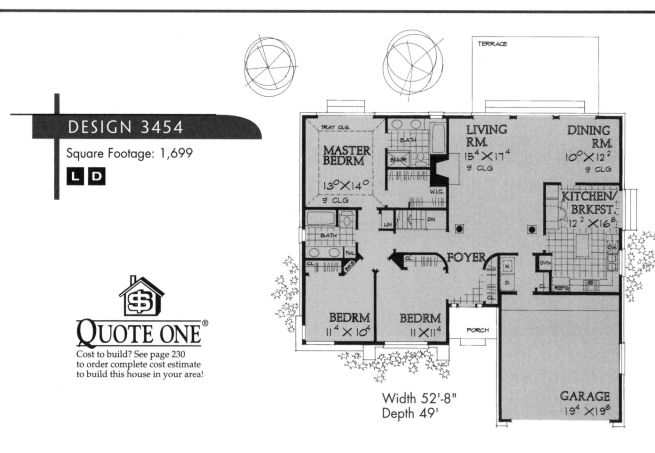

TERRACE

MASTER BEDRM
13⁰ X 14⁰
9' CLG

LIVING RM.
15⁴ X 17⁴
9' CLG

DINING RM.
10⁰ X 12²
9' CLG

KITCHEN/ BRKFST.
12² X 16⁸

FOYER

BEDRM
11⁴ X 10⁴

BEDRM
11 X 11⁴

PORCH

GARAGE
19⁴ X 19⁸

Width 52'-8"
Depth 49'

QUOTE ONE®

Cost to build? See page 230
to order complete cost estimate
to build this house in your area!

❑ Volume looks are achieved through the use of a high-pitched, hipped roof. The front gable with lower projecting brick pillars acts as a pleasing architectural feature. Another delightful architectural feature is the radial window above the front door; it brings an extra measure of natural light to the foyer. An efficient, spacious interior comes through in this compact floor plan. Through a pair of columns, an open living and dining room area creates a warm space for all sorts of living pursuits. Sliding glass doors guarantee a bright, cheerful interior while providing easy access to outdoor living. The L-shaped kitchen has an island work surface, a practical planning desk and a breakfast area with access to an outdoor living area—perfect for enjoying a morning cup of coffee. Sleeping arrangements are emphasized by the master suite with its tray ceiling and sliding glass doors to the yard.

Design by
Home Planners

DESIGN 3368

Square Footage: 2,720

L D

☐ Rooflines are the key to the interesting exterior of this design. Their configuration allows for sloped ceilings in the gathering room and large foyer. Both the gathering room and the dining room offer access to the rear terrace via sliding glass doors. The master bedroom suite has a huge walk-in closet, garden whirlpool and separate shower. Two family bedrooms share a full bath. One of these bedrooms could be used as a media room with pass-through wet bar. Note the large kitchen with conversation bay and the wide terrace to the rear.

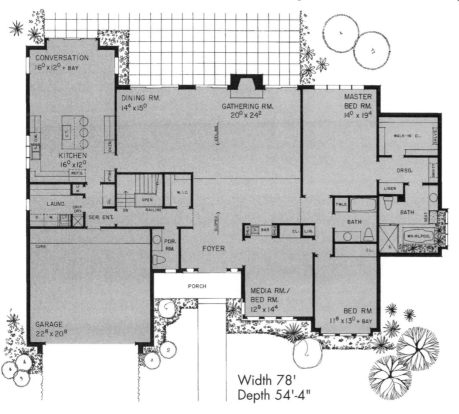

CONVERSATION
16⁰ x 12⁰ + BAY

DINING RM.
14⁴ x 15⁰

GATHERING RM.
20⁰ x 24²

MASTER
BED RM.
14⁰ x 19⁴

KITCHEN
16⁰ x 12⁰

WALK-IN CL.

OVEN

REFG.

DRSG.

LAUND.

LINEN

W.I.C.

OPEN

DN RAILING

SER. ENT.

TWLS.

BATH

BATH

WHIRLPOOL

SEAT

PDR. RM.

FOYER

BAR

CL. LIN.

PORCH

MEDIA RM./
BED RM.
12⁸ x 14⁴

BED RM.
11⁸ x 13⁰ + BAY

GARAGE
22⁸ x 20⁸

Width 78'
Depth 54'-4"

QUOTE ONE®

Cost to build? See page 230
to order complete cost estimate
to build this house in your area!

Design by
Home Planners

DESIGN 2528

Square Footage: 1,754

D

☐ This inviting, U-shaped western ranch adaptation offers outstanding living potential behind its double front doors. In only 1,754 square feet there are three bedrooms and 2½ baths. The formal living room is open to the dining area and offers a raised-hearth fireplace and a sloped ceiling. The functional kitchen features an adjacent breakfast nook and has easy access to the informal family room. A rear terrace stretches the width of the home and is accessible from the master bedroom, living room and family room. Stairs lead to a basement which may be developed at a later time.

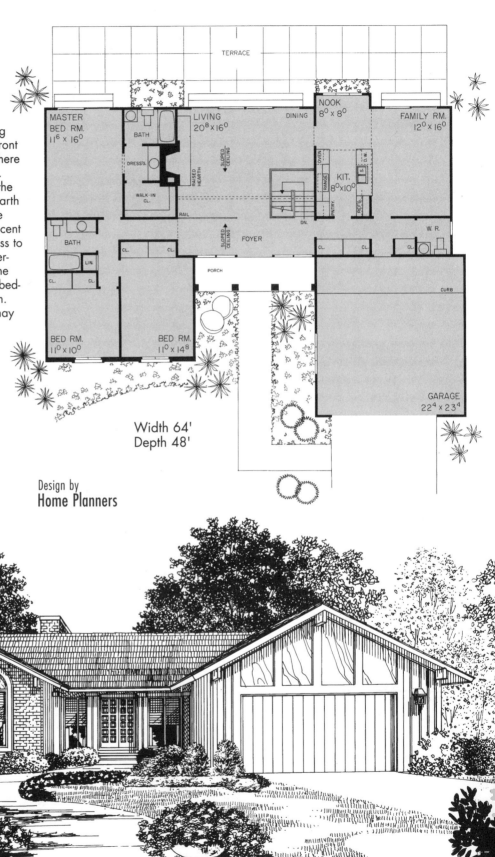

Width 64'
Depth 48'

Design by
Home Planners

Design by
Home Planners

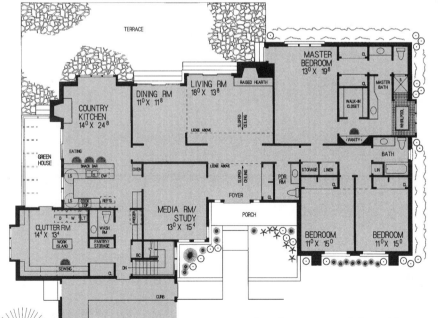

TERRACE

MASTER
BEDROOM
13⁰ X 19⁸

LIVING RM
18⁰ X 13⁸

DINING RM
11⁰ X 11⁸

RAISED HEARTH

MASTER
BATH

WALK-IN
CLOSET

W/PL/POOL

VANITY

COUNTRY
KITCHEN
14⁰ X 24⁸

GREEN
HOUSE

EATING

SNACK BAR

LS   S DW

OVEN

LEDGE ABOVE

BATH

STORAGE   LINEN

LIN

PDR
RM

FOYER

CLUTTER RM
14⁴ X 13¹

COOK
TOP

REFG

LS

FREEZER

WORK
ISLAND

PANTRY/
STORAGE

SEWING

D W LT

WASH
RM

MEDIA RM/
STUDY
13⁰ X 15⁴

PORCH

BEDROOM
11⁰ X 15⁰

BEDROOM
11⁰ X 15⁰

DN

BC

CURB

GARAGE
23⁰ X 23⁸

QUOTE ONE®
Cost to build? See page 230
to order complete cost estimate
to build this house in your area!

Width 82'-8"
Depth 74'

❏ This plan opens with formal living and dining rooms—a private media room keeps noise at bay. The greenhouse off the kitchen adds 147 square feet to the plan. It offers access to the clutter room where gardening or hobby activities may take place. At the opposite end of the house, the master bedroom and two family bedrooms make up the sleeping arrangements. The master bath creates bathing and dressing zones and is sure to delight. A wealth of built-ins throughout the home make it especially inviting.

DESIGN 4386

Square Footage: 1,811

L

❏ Empty nesters and small families will appreciate the compact design of this sharp little home. An island kitchen with breakfast nook and adjacent screened porch serves the dining room/living room. A fireplace warms the occasion. Three bedrooms, one a master suite with a full bath, allow plenty of space for a newborn's nursery or visiting grandchildren. A two-car garage fulfills all your storage needs.

Design by
Home Planners

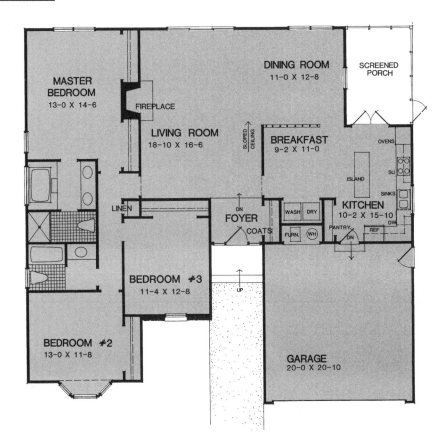

Width 53'
Depth 49'

DESIGN 2565

Square Footage: 1,540

L D

Quote One®

Cost to build? See page 230
to order complete cost estimate
to build this house in your area!

Design by
Home Planners

 This modest-sized farmhouse has much to offer in the way of livability. It may function as either a two- or three-bedroom home. The living room is huge and features a fine, raised-hearth fireplace and a beamed ceiling. The kitchen revolves around a center island cooktop and a breakfast nook. The open stairway to the basement is handy and may lead to a future recreation area. In addition to the two full baths, there is an extra wash room. Adjacent is the laundry room and the service entrance from the garage. The blueprints you order for this design will show details for three delightful elevations: the Tudor, the Colonial and the Contemporary.

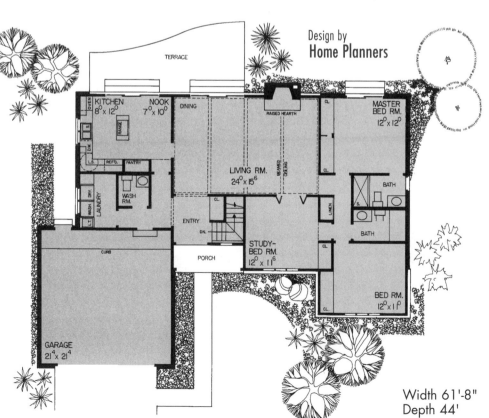

Width 61'-8"
Depth 44'

CONTEMPORARY HOME PLANS

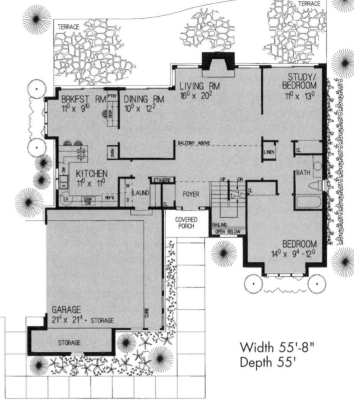

DESIGN 3342

First Floor: 1,467 square feet
Second Floor: 715 square feet
Total: 2,182 square feet

L

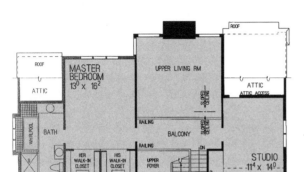

Width 55'-8"
Depth 55'

❏ Just the right amount of living space is contained in this charming traditional house and it is arranged in a great floor plan. The split-bedroom configuration, with two bedrooms (or optional study) on the first floor and the master suite on the second floor with its own studio, assures complete privacy. The living room has a second-floor balcony overlook and a warming fireplace. The full-width terrace in back is reached through sliding glass doors in each room at the rear of the house.

Design by
Home Planners

QUOTE ONE®

Cost to build? See page 230
to order complete cost estimate
to build this house in your area!

CHAPTER 5

AN AIR OF DISTINCTION: *Luxury homes with a new angle*

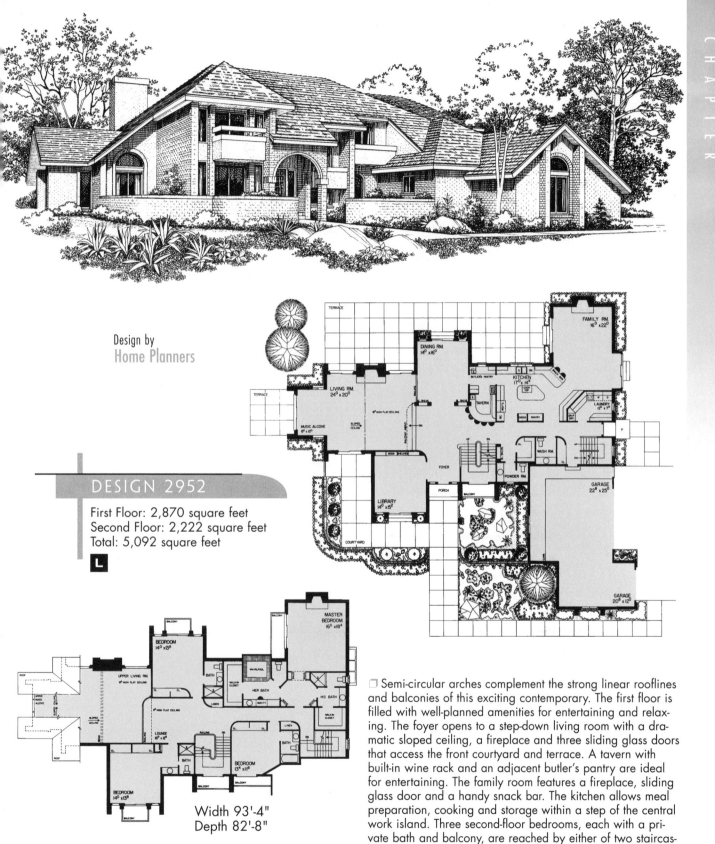

Design by
Home Planners

DESIGN 2952

First Floor: 2,870 square feet
Second Floor: 2,222 square feet
Total: 5,092 square feet

L

Width 93'-4"
Depth 82'-8"

❑ Semi-circular arches complement the strong linear rooflines and balconies of this exciting contemporary. The first floor is filled with well-planned amenities for entertaining and relaxing. The foyer opens to a step-down living room with a dramatic sloped ceiling, a fireplace and three sliding glass doors that access the front courtyard and terrace. A tavern with built-in wine rack and an adjacent butler's pantry are ideal for entertaining. The family room features a fireplace, sliding glass door and a handy snack bar. The kitchen allows meal preparation, cooking and storage within a step of the central work island. Three second-floor bedrooms, each with a private bath and balcony, are reached by either of two staircases. The master suite, with His and Hers baths and walk-in closets, whirlpool and fireplace, adds the finishing touch to this memorable home.

DESIGN 9498

First Floor: 2,270 square feet
Second Floor: 788 square feet
Total: 3,058 square feet

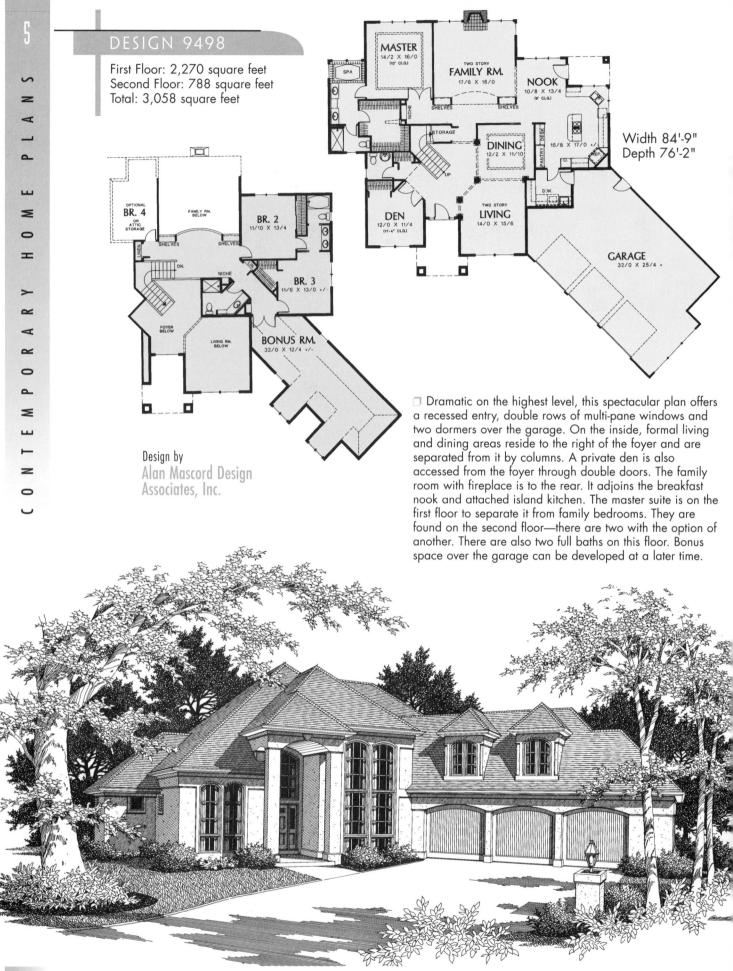

Width 84'-9"
Depth 76'-2"

Design by
Alan Mascord Design
Associates, Inc.

☐ Dramatic on the highest level, this spectacular plan offers a recessed entry, double rows of multi-pane windows and two dormers over the garage. On the inside, formal living and dining areas reside to the right of the foyer and are separated from it by columns. A private den is also accessed from the foyer through double doors. The family room with fireplace is to the rear. It adjoins the breakfast nook and attached island kitchen. The master suite is on the first floor to separate it from family bedrooms. They are found on the second floor—there are two with the option of another. There are also two full baths on this floor. Bonus space over the garage can be developed at a later time.

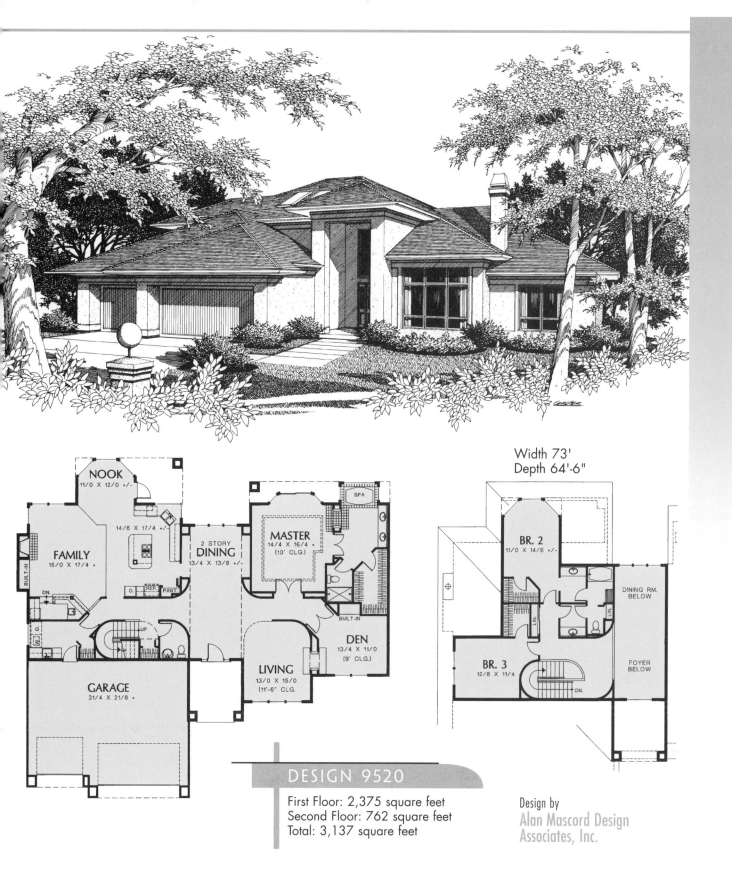

NOOK
11/0 X 12/0 +/-

14/6 X 17/4 +/-

FAMILY
15/0 X 17/4 +

BUILT-IN

DN.

W. D.

GARAGE
31/4 X 21/8 +

UP

2 STORY
DINING
13/4 X 13/8 +/-

O.

REF.

PANT.

SPA

MASTER
14/4 X 16/4 +
(10' CLG.)

BUILT-IN

DEN
13/4 X 11/0
(9' CLG.)

LIVING
13/0 X 15/0
(11'-6" CLG.)

Width 73'
Depth 64'-6"

BR. 2
11/0 X 14/6 +/-

DINING RM.
BELOW

LIN

LIN

LIN

BR. 3
12/8 X 11/4

DN.

FOYER
BELOW

DESIGN 9520

First Floor: 2,375 square feet
Second Floor: 762 square feet
Total: 3,137 square feet

Design by
Alan Mascord Design
Associates, Inc.

❑ Clean lines, a hip roof and a high, recessed entry define this sleek contemporary home. Inside, curved lines add a twist to the well-designed floor plan. For informal entertaining, gather in the multi-windowed family room with its step-down wet bar and warming fireplace. The open kitchen will delight everyone with its center cooktop island, a corner sink and an adjacent breakfast nook. A formal dining room enjoys views of the rear grounds and sepa-

rates the informal living area from the master wing. Enter the grand master suite through double doors and take special note of the see-through fireplace between the bedroom and bath. A large walk-in closet, a relaxing spa and dual vanities complete the master bath. An additional see-through fireplace is located between the living room and den. Upstairs, two family bedrooms (each with walk-in closets) share a full bath.

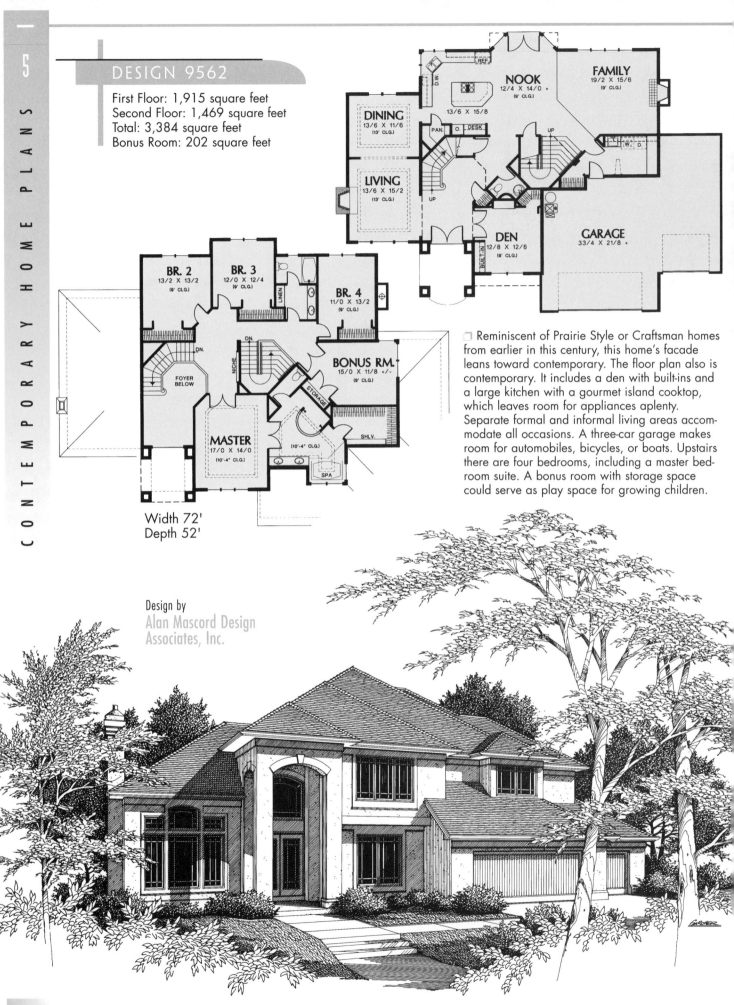

DESIGN 9562

First Floor: 1,915 square feet
Second Floor: 1,469 square feet
Total: 3,384 square feet
Bonus Room: 202 square feet

DINING
13/6 X 11/6
(13' CLG.)

LIVING
13/6 X 15/2
(13' CLG.)

NOOK
12/4 X 14/0 +
(9' CLG.)

FAMILY
19/2 X 15/6
(9' CLG.)

PAN.   O. DESK
UP
UP

DEN
12/8 X 12/6
(9' CLG.)

GARAGE
33/4 X 21/8 +

BUILT-IN

BR. 2
13/2 X 13/2
(9' CLG.)

BR. 3
12/0 X 12/4
(9' CLG.)

LINEN

BR. 4
11/0 X 13/2
(9' CLG.)

DN.
DN.

FOYER
BELOW

NICHE

BONUS RM.
15/0 X 11/8 +/-
(9' CLG.)

STORAGE

SHLV.

MASTER
17/0 X 14/0
(10'-4" CLG.)

(10'-4" CLG.)

SPA

Width 72'
Depth 52'

☐ Reminiscent of Prairie Style or Craftsman homes from earlier in this century, this home's facade leans toward contemporary. The floor plan also is contemporary. It includes a den with built-ins and a large kitchen with a gourmet island cooktop, which leaves room for appliances aplenty. Separate formal and informal living areas accommodate all occasions. A three-car garage makes room for automobiles, bicycles, or boats. Upstairs there are four bedrooms, including a master bedroom suite. A bonus room with storage space could serve as play space for growing children.

Design by
Alan Mascord Design
Associates, Inc.

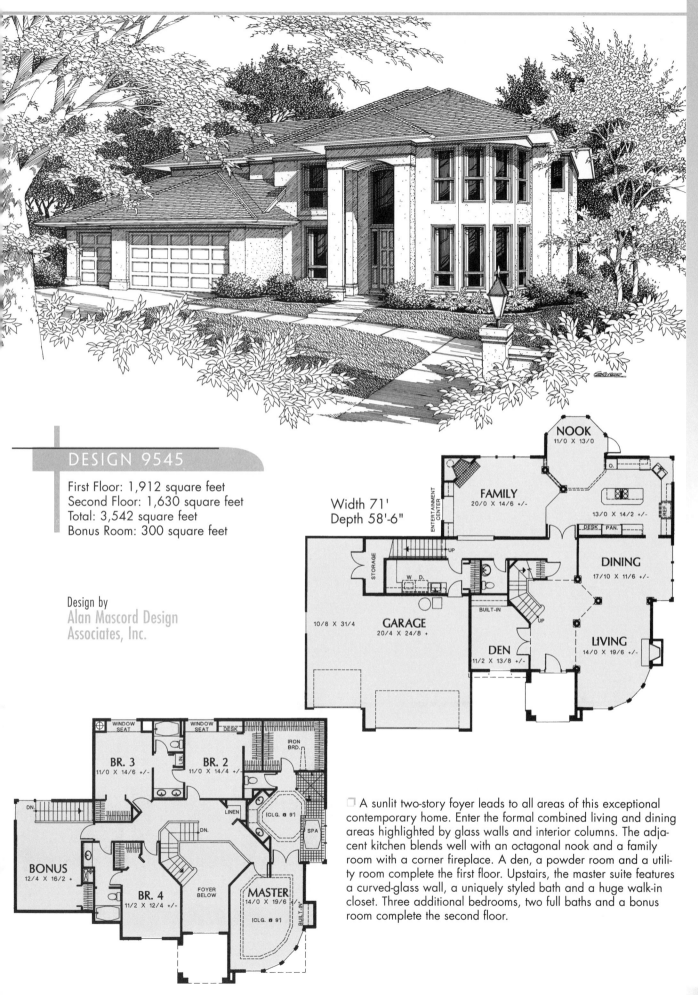

DESIGN 9545

First Floor: 1,912 square feet
Second Floor: 1,630 square feet
Total: 3,542 square feet
Bonus Room: 300 square feet

Design by
Alan Mascord Design
Associates, Inc.

Width 71'
Depth 58'-6"

A sunlit two-story foyer leads to all areas of this exceptional contemporary home. Enter the formal combined living and dining areas highlighted by glass walls and interior columns. The adjacent kitchen blends well with an octagonal nook and a family room with a corner fireplace. A den, a powder room and a utility room complete the first floor. Upstairs, the master suite features a curved-glass wall, a uniquely styled bath and a huge walk-in closet. Three additional bedrooms, two full baths and a bonus room complete the second floor.

DESIGN 9564

First Floor: 2,290 square feet
Second Floor: 2,142 square feet
Total: 4,432 square feet

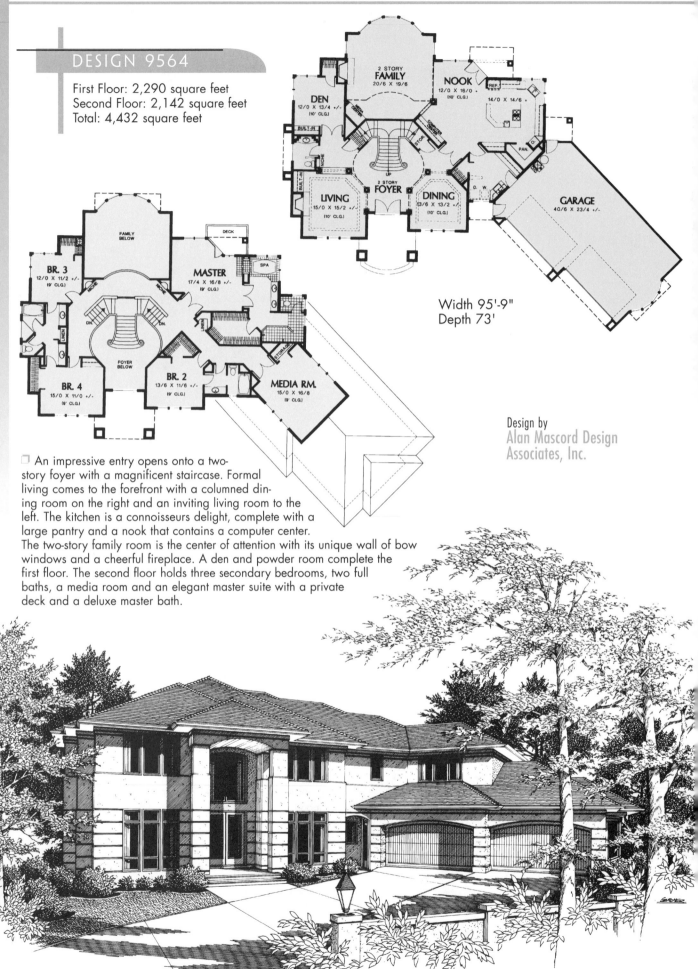

2 STORY
FAMILY
20/6 X 19/6

NOOK
12/0 X 16/0
(10' CLG.)

REF.
14/0 X 14/6

DEN
12/0 X 13/4 +/-
(10' CLG.)

PAN.

BUILT-IN

BUILT-IN

STOR.

2 STORY
FOYER

UP

LIVING
15/0 X 15/2 +/-
(10' CLG.)

DINING
13/6 X 13/2
(10' CLG.)

D. W.

GARAGE
40/6 X 23/4 +/-

FAMILY
BELOW

DECK

SPA

BR. 3
12/0 X 11/2 +/-
(9' CLG.)

MASTER
17/4 X 16/8 +/-
(9' CLG.)

LINEN

DN.

DN.

FOYER
BELOW

LINEN

STORAGE

BR. 4
15/0 X 11/0 +/-
(9' CLG.)

BR. 2
13/6 X 11/6 +/-
(9' CLG.)

MEDIA RM.
15/0 X 16/8
(9' CLG.)

Width 95'-9"
Depth 73'

Design by
Alan Mascord Design
Associates, Inc.

❏ An impressive entry opens onto a two-
story foyer with a magnificent staircase. Formal
living comes to the forefront with a columned dining room on the right and an inviting living room to the
left. The kitchen is a connoisseurs delight, complete with a
large pantry and a nook that contains a computer center.
The two-story family room is the center of attention with its unique wall of bow
windows and a cheerful fireplace. A den and powder room complete the
first floor. The second floor holds three secondary bedrooms, two full
baths, a media room and an elegant master suite with a private
deck and a deluxe master bath.

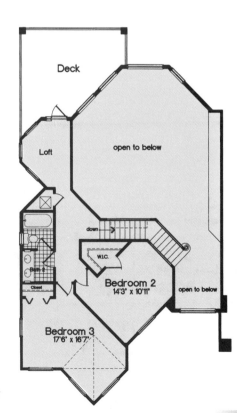

DESIGN 8698

First Floor: 2,051 square feet
Second Floor: 749 square feet
Total: 2,800 square feet

Width 50'-0"
Depth 74'-0"

Design by
Home Design
Services, Inc.

Covered Patio 17'10" x 37'0"

Master Suite 19'3" x 18'6"

Family Room 25'-0" x 21'0"

Nook 11'11" x 10'7"

Master Bath

Kitchen 14'2" x 14'8"

W.I.C.

1/2 Bath

Dining Room 12'3" x 14'3"

Foyer

Living Room 13'0" x 12'6"

Entry

Utility

up

2 Car Garage 19'3" x 19'3"

Deck

Loft

open to below

down

W.I.C.

Bedroom 2 14'3" x 10'11"

open to below

Bedroom 3 17'6" x 16'7"

At only 50 feet in width, this fabulous design will fit anywhere! From the moment you enter the home from the foyer, this floor plan explodes in every direction with huge living spaces. Flanking the foyer are the living and dining rooms, and the visual impact of the staircase is breathtaking. Two-story ceilings adorn the huge family room with double stacked glass walls. Sunlight floods the breakfast nook, and the kitchen is a gourmet's dream, complete with cooking island and loads of overhead cabinets. Tray ceilings grace the master suite, which also offers a well-designed master bath. Here, a large soaking tub, doorless shower, private toilet chamber and a huge walk-in closet are sure to please. Upstairs, two oversized bedrooms and a loft space—perfect for the home computer—share a full bath.

CONTEMPORARY HOME PLANS

Width 66'
Depth 83'

Open To
Family Room
Below

rail

down

w.i.c.

Bedroom 3
volume ceiling
13⁴ · 10⁰

lin
c.

Bath

Bedroom 4
volume ceiling
12⁴ · 11⁰

Covered Patio

Breakfast

fireplace

Master
Bedroom
volume ceiling
19⁶ · 13⁶

Bath

volume ceiling

Family Room
21² · 18⁴
volume ceiling

Living Room
volume ceiling
14⁰ · 14⁰

ref

Kitchen

dw

up

lin

closet

w.i.c.

Bath

pan

lin

Bedroom 2
13⁴ · 12⁰

Den Study
volume ceiling
13⁰ · 10⁰

Foyer

Dining
volume ceiling
13⁴ · 11¹

Utility

w
d

lin

Bath

ac

w.i.c.

Entry

lin

ac

wh

Garage

DESIGN 8655

First Floor: 2,624 square feet
Second Floor: 540 square feet
Total: 3,164 square feet

☐ This award-winning design has been recognized for its innovative use of spaces while continuing to keep family living spaces combined for maximum enjoyment. The formal spaces separate the master suite and den/study from family spaces. A convenient bath with outside access turns the den/study into a guest bedroom when needed. The master's retreat is generously supplied with space and contains a master bath with His and Hers vanities, private toilet room and walk-in closet. The perfect touch in this two-story design is the placement of two bedrooms downstairs with two extra bedrooms on the second floor. Study space on this floor overlooks the rooms below.

Design by
Home Design
Services, Inc.

J.N. HANSEN P.T.

© HOME DESIGN SERVICES, INC.

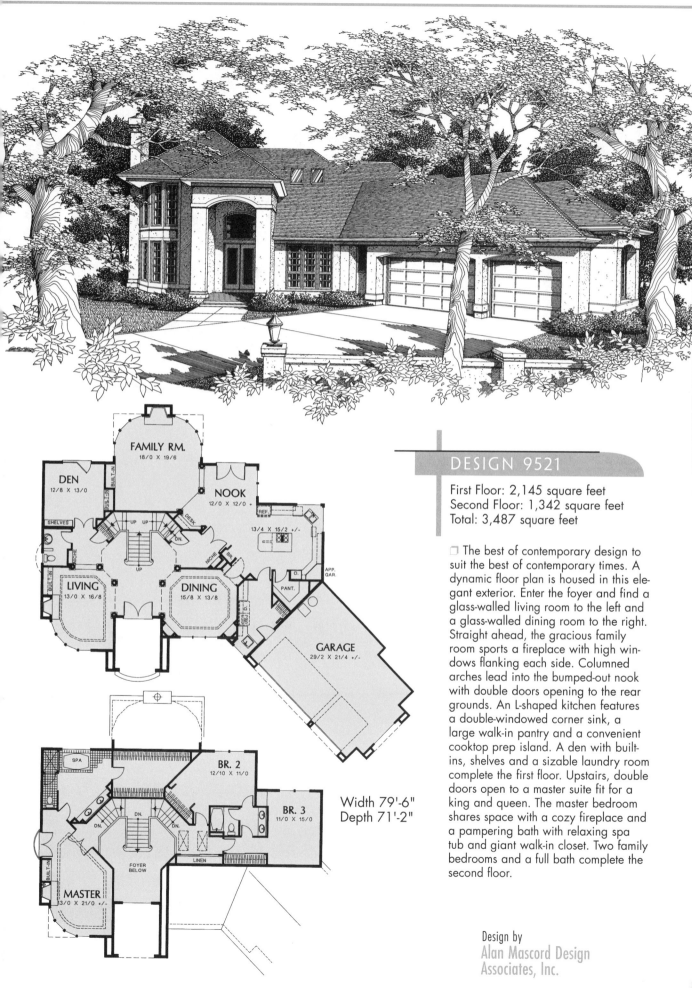

DESIGN 9521

First Floor: 2,145 square feet
Second Floor: 1,342 square feet
Total: 3,487 square feet

☐ The best of contemporary design to
suit the best of contemporary times. A
dynamic floor plan is housed in this elegant exterior. Enter the foyer and find a
glass-walled living room to the left and
a glass-walled dining room to the right.
Straight ahead, the gracious family
room sports a fireplace with high windows flanking each side. Columned
arches lead into the bumped-out nook
with double doors opening to the rear
grounds. An L-shaped kitchen features
a double-windowed corner sink, a
large walk-in pantry and a convenient
cooktop prep island. A den with built-
ins, shelves and a sizable laundry room
complete the first floor. Upstairs, double
doors open to a master suite fit for a
king and queen. The master bedroom
shares space with a cozy fireplace and
a pampering bath with relaxing spa
tub and giant walk-in closet. Two family
bedrooms and a full bath complete the
second floor.

Width 79'-6"
Depth 71'-2"

Design by
**Alan Mascord Design
Associates, Inc.**

DESIGN 8628

First Floor: 3,770 square feet
Second Floor: 634 square feet
Total: 4,404 square feet

Design by
Home Design
Services, Inc.

Width 87'
Depth 97'-6"

❑ This fresh and innovative design creates unbeatable ambience. Octagon-shaped rooms, columns and flowing spaces will delight all. The breakfast nook and family room both open onto a patio—a perfect arrangement for informal entertaining. The dining room is sure to please with elegant pillars separating it from the sunken living room. A media room delights both with its shape and by being convenient to the nearby kitchen—perfect for snack runs. A private garden surrounds the master bath and its spa tub and enormous walk-in closet. The master bedroom is enchanting with a fireplace and access to the outdoors. Additional family bedrooms come in a variety of different shapes and sizes; Bedroom 4 reigns over the second floor and features its own full bath.

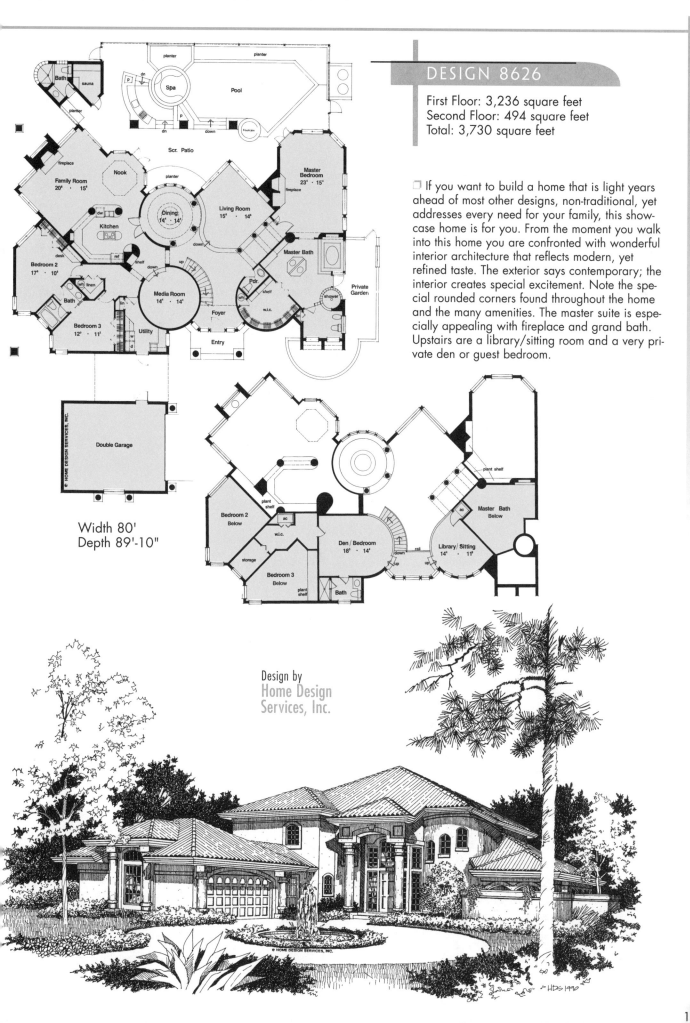

DESIGN 8626

First Floor: 3,236 square feet
Second Floor: 494 square feet
Total: 3,730 square feet

If you want to build a home that is light years ahead of most other designs, non-traditional, yet addresses every need for your family, this showcase home is for you. From the moment you walk into this home you are confronted with wonderful interior architecture that reflects modern, yet refined taste. The exterior says contemporary; the interior creates special excitement. Note the special rounded corners found throughout the home and the many amenities. The master suite is especially appealing with fireplace and grand bath. Upstairs are a library/sitting room and a very private den or guest bedroom.

First floor labels:

Bath
sauna
Family Room 20⁴ · 15⁸
Nook
Spa
Pool
Scr. Patio
planter
Living Room 15⁸ · 14⁶
Master Bedroom 23⁴ · 15⁴
fireplace
Dining 14⁴ · 14⁴
Kitchen
Master Bath
Bedroom 2 17⁴ · 10⁴
desk
Bath
Media Room 14⁴ · 14⁴
Pdr.
Private Garden
Bedroom 3 12⁶ · 11²
Utility
Foyer
w.i.c.
shower
Entry

Double Garage

Width 80'
Depth 89'-10"

Second floor labels:

Bedroom 2 Below
w.i.c.
storage
Bedroom 3 Below
Bath
Den / Bedroom 18⁶ · 14'
Library/ Sitting 14⁴ · 11⁸
Master Bath Below
plant shelf

Design by
Home Design
Services, Inc.

COPYRIGHT 1992 LARRY E. BELK

DESIGN 8035

First Floor: 3,262 square feet
Second Floor: 1,050 square feet
Total: 4,312 square feet

Design by
Larry E. Belk
Designs

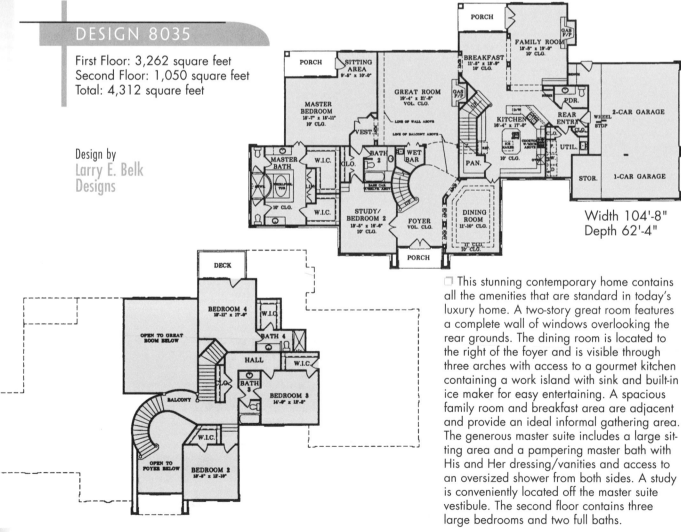

Width 104'-8"
Depth 62'-4"

☐ This stunning contemporary home contains all the amenities that are standard in today's luxury home. A two-story great room features a complete wall of windows overlooking the rear grounds. The dining room is located to the right of the foyer and is visible through three arches with access to a gourmet kitchen containing a work island with sink and built-in ice maker for easy entertaining. A spacious family room and breakfast area are adjacent and provide an ideal informal gathering area. The generous master suite includes a large sitting area and a pampering master bath with His and Her dressing/vanities and access to an oversized shower from both sides. A study is conveniently located off the master suite vestibule. The second floor contains three large bedrooms and two full baths.

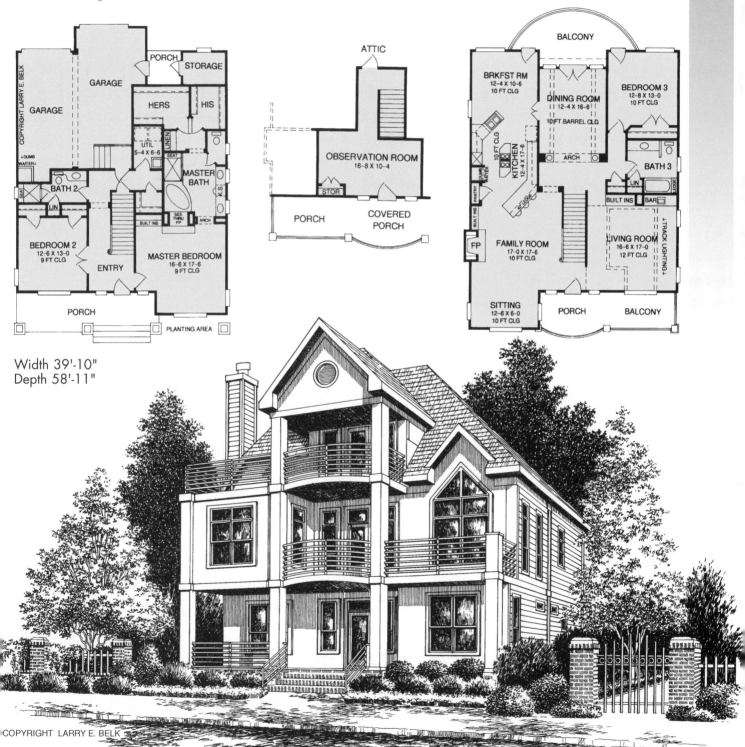

DESIGN 8119

First Floor: 1,158 square feet
Second Floor: 1,773 square feet
Third Floor: 173 square feet
Total: 3,104 square feet

Design by
**Larry E. Belk
Designs**

☐ The facade of this home is a super prelude to an equally impressive interior. The front porch provides entry to a sleeping level, with the master suite on the right and a secondary bedroom on the left. Upstairs, living areas include a family room with a sitting alcove and a living room with special ceiling treatment. The kitchen serves a breakfast room as well as a barrel-vaulted dining room. A third bedroom and two balconies further the custom nature of this home. On the third floor, an observation room with outdoor access is an extra-special touch. Please specify crawlspace or slab foundation when ordering.

Width 39'-10"
Depth 58'-11"

COPYRIGHT LARRY E. BELK

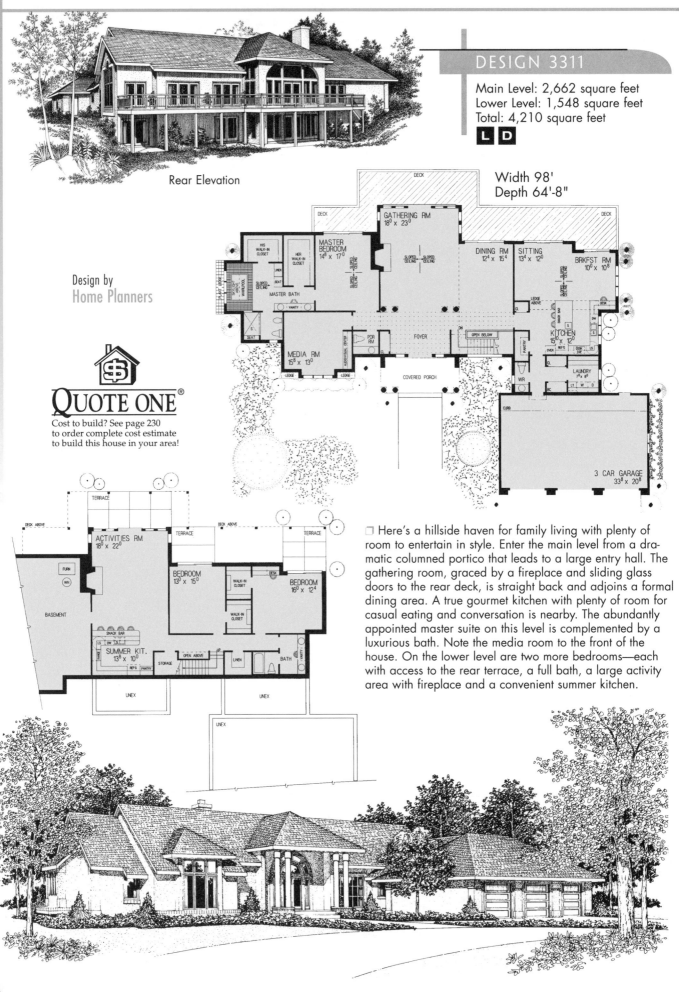

Rear Elevation

DESIGN 3311

Main Level: 2,662 square feet
Lower Level: 1,548 square feet
Total: 4,210 square feet

L **D**

Width 98'
Depth 64'-8"

Design by
Home Planners

QUOTE ONE®

Cost to build? See page 230
to order complete cost estimate
to build this house in your area!

Here's a hillside haven for family living with plenty of room to entertain in style. Enter the main level from a dramatic columned portico that leads to a large entry hall. The gathering room, graced by a fireplace and sliding glass doors to the rear deck, is straight back and adjoins a formal dining area. A true gourmet kitchen with plenty of room for casual eating and conversation is nearby. The abundantly appointed master suite on this level is complemented by a luxurious bath. Note the media room to the front of the house. On the lower level are two more bedrooms—each with access to the rear terrace, a full bath, a large activity area with fireplace and a convenient summer kitchen.

DESIGN 8683

First Floor: 2,254 square feet
Second Floor: 608 square feet
Total: 2,862 square feet

Design by
**Home Design
Services, Inc.**

☐ Indoor/outdoor relationships are enhanced by the beautiful courtyard that decorates the center of this home. A gallery provides views of the courtyard and leads to a kitchen featuring a center work island and an adjacent breakfast room offering easy access to the back yard. Combined with the family room, this space will be a favorite for informal gatherings. To the left, the gallery leads to the formal living room and master suite. The secluded master bedroom features a tray ceiling and double doors that lead to a covered patio. Retreat to the master bath, where a relaxing tub awaits to pamper and enjoy. The second floor contains a full bath shared by Bedrooms 3 and 4 and a loft with its own balcony that provides flexible space for an additional bedroom.

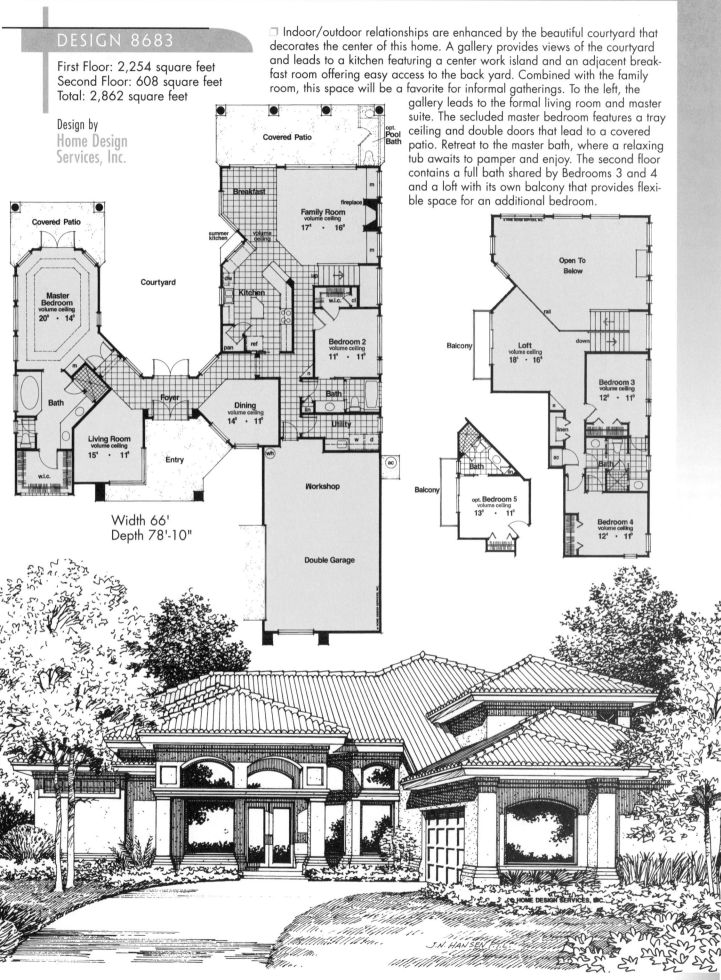

Width 66'
Depth 78'-10"

J.N. HANSEN

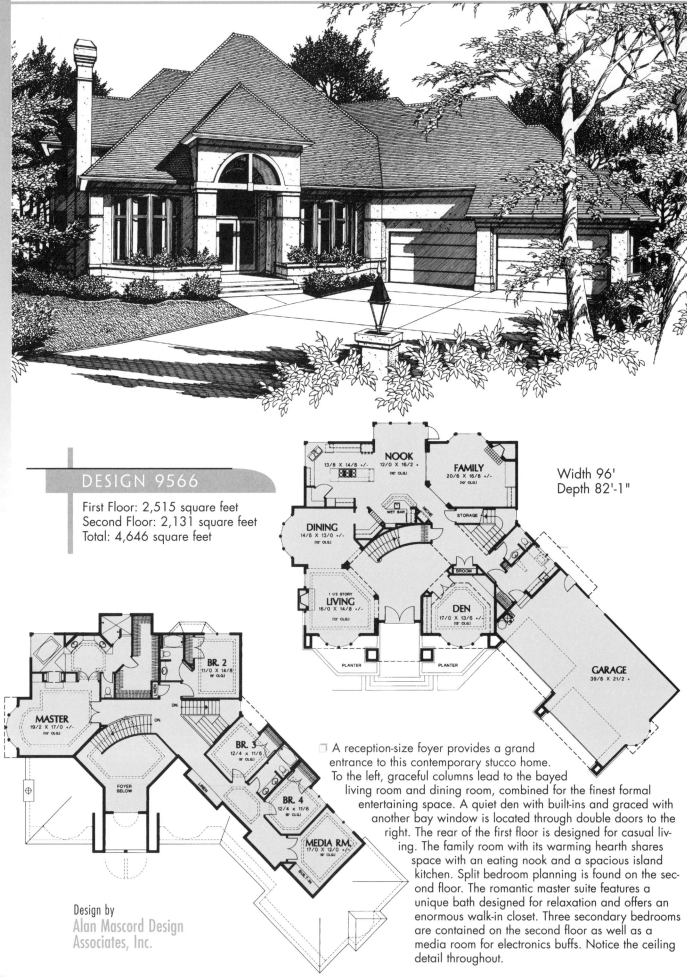

DESIGN 9566

First Floor: 2,515 square feet
Second Floor: 2,131 square feet
Total: 4,646 square feet

Width 96'
Depth 82'-1"

NOOK
12/0 X 16/2 +
(10' CLG.)

FAMILY
20/6 X 16/8 +/-
(10' CLG.)

13/8 X 14/8 +/-

DINING
14/6 X 13/0 +/-
(10' CLG.)

WET BAR

NICHE

STORAGE

BROOM

1 1/2 STORY LIVING
16/0 X 14/8 +/-
(13' CLG.)

DEN
17/0 X 13/6 +/-
(13' CLG.)

PLANTER   PLANTER

GARAGE
39/8 X 21/2 +

BR. 2
11/0 X 14/8
(9' CLG.)

DN.

DN.

MASTER
19/2 X 17/0 +/-
(10' CLG.)

BR. 3
12/4 x 11/6
(9' CLG.)

LINEN

FOYER BELOW

BR. 4
12/4 x 11/6
(9' CLG.)

MEDIA RM.
17/0 X 12/0
(9' CLG.)

BUILT-IN

❑ A reception-size foyer provides a grand entrance to this contemporary stucco home. To the left, graceful columns lead to the bayed living room and dining room, combined for the finest formal entertaining space. A quiet den with built-ins and graced with another bay window is located through double doors to the right. The rear of the first floor is designed for casual living. The family room with its warming hearth shares space with an eating nook and a spacious island kitchen. Split bedroom planning is found on the second floor. The romantic master suite features a unique bath designed for relaxation and offers an enormous walk-in closet. Three secondary bedrooms are contained on the second floor as well as a media room for electronics buffs. Notice the ceiling detail throughout.

Design by
Alan Mascord Design
Associates, Inc.

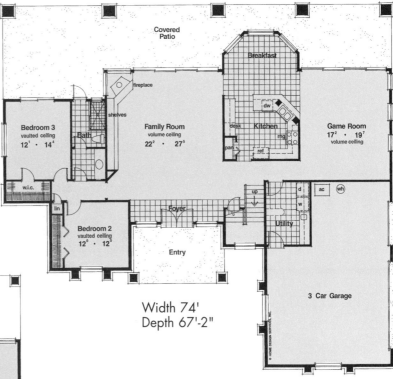

DESIGN 8643

First Floor: 2,136 square feet
Second Floor: 1,046 square feet
Total: 3,182 square feet

Design by
**Home Design
Services, Inc.**

Width 74'
Depth 67'-2"

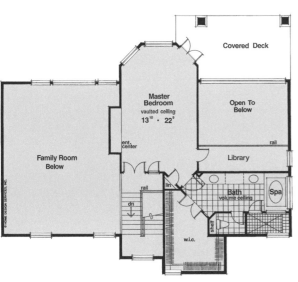

Varied textures and rooflines, combined with a grand entrance, give this contemporary home plenty of curb appeal. Inside, the foyer opens directly into the family room, which is graced by a corner fireplace, built-in shelves and a wall of sliding glass doors. The efficient kitchen and oversized nook conveniently separate the family room from the game room, providing ease in serving either room. Two family bedrooms share a pool bath and complete this level. Upstairs, privacy is insured with the master suite reigning supreme and enjoying a private covered deck. The master bath features a huge walk-in closet, a spa tub, a large separate shower and a dual-bowl vanity. A loft library is a fine finishing touch to this level.

Photos by Bob Greenspan

This home, as shown in the photograph, may differ from the actual blueprints.
For more detailed information, please check the floor plans carefully.

DESIGN 3558

First Floor: 2,328 square feet
Second Floor: 603 square feet
Total: 2,931 square feet

L D

Even the most active family will be comfortable with the spaciousness this plan offers. A broad foyer leads back to a living room that measures a full 24 feet across and features a breathtaking window view of the rear yard and doors to the covered porch. Adjacent to the gourmet island kitchen is a conversation area where the family is sure to gather, complete with doors to the porch, snack bar and a cozy fireplace. A butler's pantry leads to the formal dining room. Placed conveniently on the first floor, the master suite features a roomy bath with a huge walk-in closet and dual vanities. A library with plenty of wall space for custom bookcases completes this level. Two large bedrooms are found on the second floor and share a full hall bath.

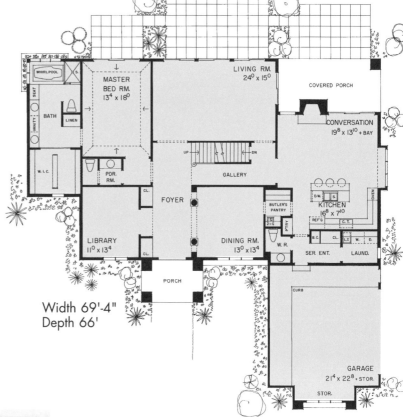

Width 69'-4"
Depth 66'

Cost to build? See page 230 to order complete cost estimate to build this house in your area!

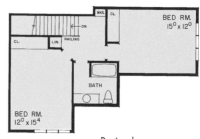

Rear Elevation

Design by
Home Planners

Width 82'-4"
Depth 72'

Design by
Home Design
Services, Inc.

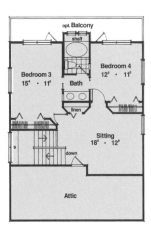

DESIGN 8679

First Floor: 2,531 square feet
Second Floor: 669 square feet
Total: 3,200 square feet

This exquisite brick and stucco contemporary takes its cue from the tradition of Frank Lloyd Wright. The formal living and dining area combine to provide a spectacular view of the rear grounds. Unique best describes the private master suite, highlighted by a mitered bow window, a raised sitting area complete with a wet bar, oversized His and Hers walk-in closets and a lavish master bath complete with a relaxing corner tub, a separate shower and twin vanities. The family living area encompasses the left portion of the plan, featuring a spacious family room with a corner fireplace, access to the covered patio from the breakfast area and a step-saving kitchen. Bedroom 2 connects to a private bath. Upstairs, two bedrooms share a balcony, a sitting room and full bath.

DESIGN 6635

First Floor: 4,760 square feet
Second Floor: 1,552 square feet
Total: 6,312 square feet

Design by
**The Sater
Design Collection**

Rear Elevation

☐ As beautiful from the rear as from the front, this home features a spectacular blend of arch-top windows, French doors and balusters. Dramatic two-story ceilings and tray details add custom spaciousness. An impressive, informal leisure room has a sixteen-foot-high tray ceiling, an entertainment center and a grand ale bar. The large, gourmet kitchen is well appointed and easily serves the nook and formal dining room. The master suite has a large bedroom and a bayed sitting area. His and Hers vanities and walk-in closets and a curved, glass-block shower are highlights in the bath. The staircase leads to the deluxe secondary guest suites, two of which have observation decks to the rear and each with their own full baths.

QUOTE ONE®

Cost to build? See page 230
to order complete cost estimate
to build this house in your area!

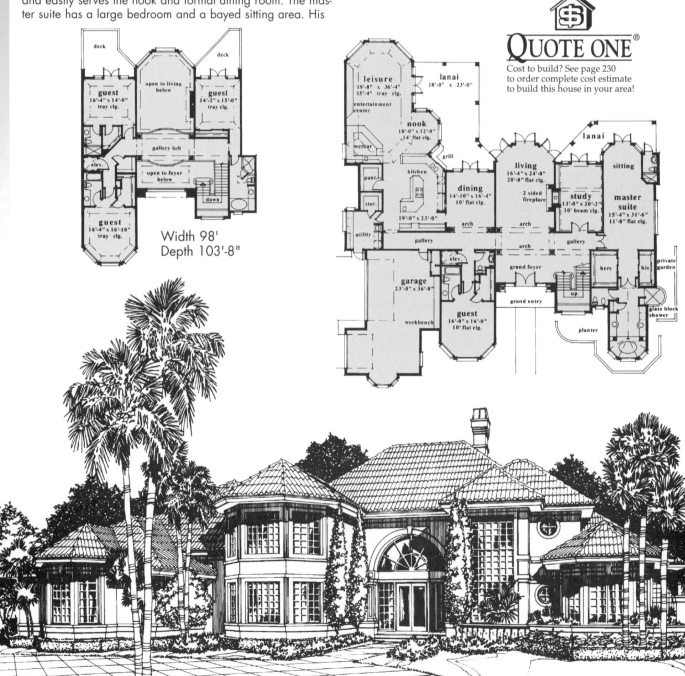

Width 98'
Depth 103'-8"

© The Sater Group, Inc.

HOLZHAUER INC. 94

DESIGN 6648

First Floor: 2,618 square feet
Second Floor: 1,945 square feet
Total: 4,563 square feet

Double doors open to a grand foyer with a formal dining room to the left. The nearby kitchen and nook combine with a multi-windowed two-story leisure room for more casual living, and an adjacent two-story living room for more formal pursuits. The first-floor master suite features a large walk-in closet, a luxurious bath and access to the rear veranda. The second floor contains a guest suite with a private bath and balcony, a bedroom/bonus room with its own balcony and a second master suite. This second master bedroom is highlighted by double doors opening onto a private deck. A walk-in closet, a spacious bath with a bumped-out tub and a separate shower provide finishing touches to this private suite.

deck
40'-0" x 10'-0"

open to leisure room below

balcony

open to living room below

master suite
16'-8" x 19'-4"
11' clg.

guest
15'-4" x 12'-8"
9'-4" clg.

overlook

open to below

loft

down

open to below

br. / bonus
12'-0" x 21'-8"
vault. clg.

balcony

© The Sater Group, Inc.

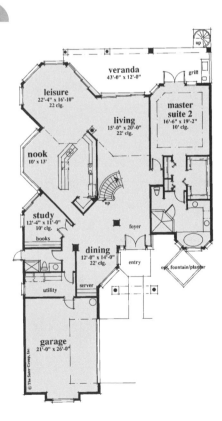

veranda
43'-0" x 12'-0"

grill

leisure
22'-4" x 16'-10"
22 clg.

living
15'-0" x 20'-0"
22' clg.

master suite 2
16'-6" x 19'-2"
10' clg.

nook
10' x 13'

up

study
12'-4" x 11'-0"
10' clg.

books

foyer

open fountain/planter

dining
12'-0" x 14'-0"
22' clg.

entry

server

utility

garage
21'-0" x 26'-0"

© The Sater Group, Inc.

Width 54'-8"
Depth 97'-4"

DESIGN 9554

Main Level: 1,989 square feet
Upper Level: 1,349 square feet
Total: 3,338 square feet
Lower Level: 592 square feet

❒ Dramatic balconies and spectacular window treatment enhance this stunning luxury home. Inside, a through-fireplace warms the formal living room and a restful den. Both living spaces open onto a balcony that invites quiet reflection on starry nights. The banquet-sized dining room is easily served from the adjacent kitchen. Here, space is shared with an eating nook that provides access to the rear grounds and a family room with a corner fireplace perfect for casual gatherings. The upper level contains two family bedrooms and a luxurious master suite that enjoys its own private balcony. The lower level accommodates a shop and a bonus room for future development.

QUOTE ONE®

Cost to build? See page 230
to order complete cost estimate
to build this house in your area!

NOOK
10/0 X 17/0

FAMILY
18/0 X 16/0

12/0 + X 16/0

GALLERY

DINING
13/6 X 14/8

10' CLG.

VAULTED
LIVING
16/0 X 15/0

DEN
15/6 X 12/8 +/-

Width 63'
Depth 48'

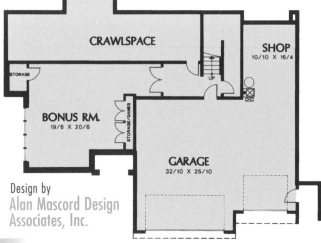

CRAWLSPACE

SHOP
10/10 X 16/4

STORAGE

UP

STORAGE/GAMES

BONUS RM.
19/6 X 20/6

GARAGE
32/10 X 25/10

Design by
**Alan Mascord Design
Associates, Inc.**

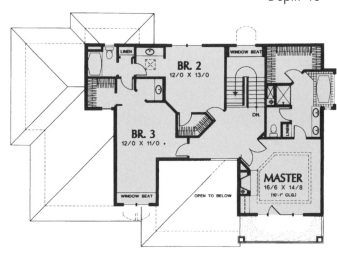

LINEN

BR. 2
12/0 X 13/0

WINDOW SEAT

DN.

BR. 3
12/0 X 11/0 +

LINEN

MASTER
16/6 X 14/8
(10'-1" CLG.)

WINDOW SEAT

OPEN TO BELOW

DESIGN 8703

First Floor: 3,395 square feet
Second Floor: 757 square feet
Total: 4,152 square feet

☐ Old World Mediterranean flavor spills over and combines with classic contemporary lines through the courtyard and at the double door entry to this three-bedroom home. The formal living room is defined by columns and a glass wall that looks out over the rear patio. The formal dining room offers access to the front courtyard with French doors. A den/library also has French doors to the courtyard and accesses the pool bath for the occasional guest. Double doors bring you into the world of the master suite and sumptuous luxury. A lavish bath features a soaking tub, glass enclosed shower and His and Hers walk-in closets. Two large family bedrooms, both with bay windows, share a full bath. A spectacular loft awaits upstairs to accommodate a home theater, game room or bedroom areas.

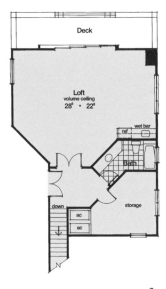

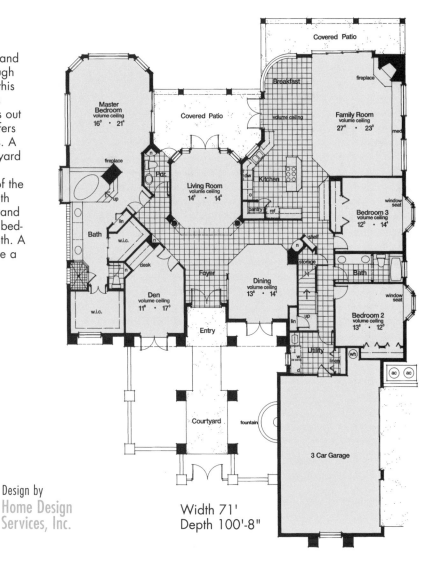

Design by
Home Design
Services, Inc.

Width 71'
Depth 100'-8"

J.N. HANSEN P.T.L

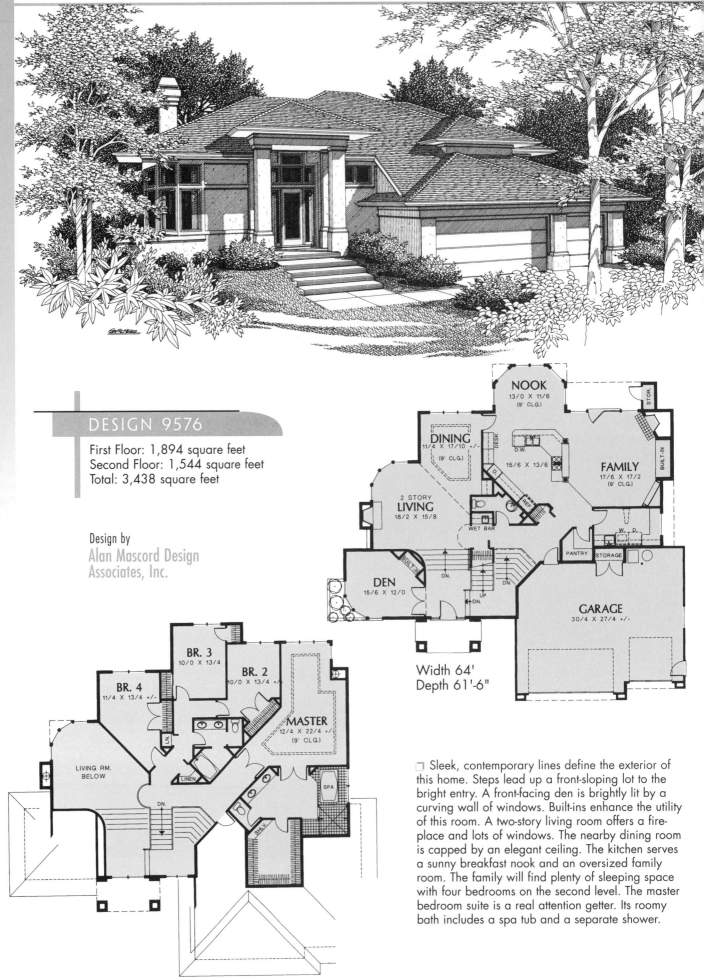

DESIGN 9576

First Floor: 1,894 square feet
Second Floor: 1,544 square feet
Total: 3,438 square feet

Design by
Alan Mascord Design
Associates, Inc.

NOOK
13/0 X 11/6
(9' CLG.)

DINING
11/4 X 17/10 +/-
(9' CLG.)

DESK

D.W.

15/6 X 13/6

STOR.

BUILT-IN

FAMILY
17/6 X 17/2
(9' CLG.)

2 STORY
LIVING
18/2 X 15/8

REF.

WET BAR

W. D.

DEN
15/6 X 12/0

BUILT-IN

DN.

DN.

UP

DN.

PANTRY

STORAGE

GARAGE
30/4 X 27/4 +/-

Width 64'
Depth 61'-6"

BR. 3
10/0 X 13/4

BR. 2
10/0 X 13/4 +/-

BR. 4
11/4 X 13/4 +/-

MASTER
12/4 X 22/4 +/-
(9' CLG.)

LIN.

LINEN

SPA

LIVING RM.
BELOW

DN.

SHLV.

☐ Sleek, contemporary lines define the exterior of
this home. Steps lead up a front-sloping lot to the
bright entry. A front-facing den is brightly lit by a
curving wall of windows. Built-ins enhance the utility
of this room. A two-story living room offers a fireplace and lots of windows. The nearby dining room
is capped by an elegant ceiling. The kitchen serves
a sunny breakfast nook and an oversized family
room. The family will find plenty of sleeping space
with four bedrooms on the second level. The master
bedroom suite is a real attention getter. Its roomy
bath includes a spa tub and a separate shower.

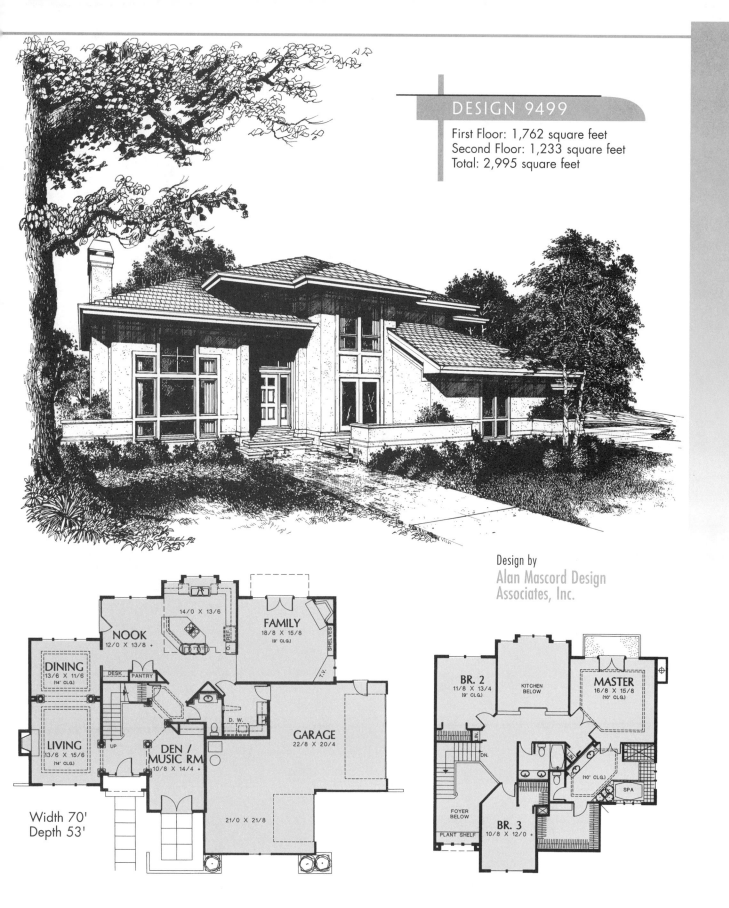

DESIGN 9499

First Floor: 1,762 square feet
Second Floor: 1,233 square feet
Total: 2,995 square feet

Design by
Alan Mascord Design
Associates, Inc.

DINING
13/6 X 11/6
(14' CLG.)

NOOK
12/0 X 13/8 +

14/0 X 13/6

FAMILY
18/8 X 15/8
(9' CLG.)

REF.

DESK PANTRY

SHELVES

T.V.

LIVING
13/6 X 15/6
(14' CLG.)

UP

**DEN /
MUSIC RM.**
10/8 X 14/4 +

D. W.

GARAGE
22/8 X 20/4

21/0 X 21/8

Width 70'
Depth 53'

BR. 2
11/8 X 13/4
(9' CLG.)

KITCHEN
BELOW

MASTER
16/8 X 15/8
(10' CLG.)

DN.

IN.

(10' CLG.)

SPA

FOYER
BELOW

BR. 3
10/8 X 12/0 +

PLANT SHELF

This stucco contemporary plan is resplendent and quite distinct with wide eaves and inventive window design. The floor plan adds some unique touches as well. The entry foyer leads to a formal living room and dining room on the left and a den or music room on the right. The family room is to the back of the plan and contains a warming corner fireplace. The kitchen is quite differ-

ent—it boasts a two-story ceiling and is overlooked by the balcony upstairs. Bedrooms include two family bedrooms with a shared bath and a master suite. The master suite includes a private balcony and pampering bath. Cove ceilings can be found in the master suite and also in the dining room and living room.

DESIGN 8131

First Floor: 2,772 square feet
Second Floor: 933 square feet
Total: 3,705 square feet
Bonus Room: 310 square feet

Design by
**Larry E. Belk
Designs**

Width 74'-8"
Depth 61'-10"

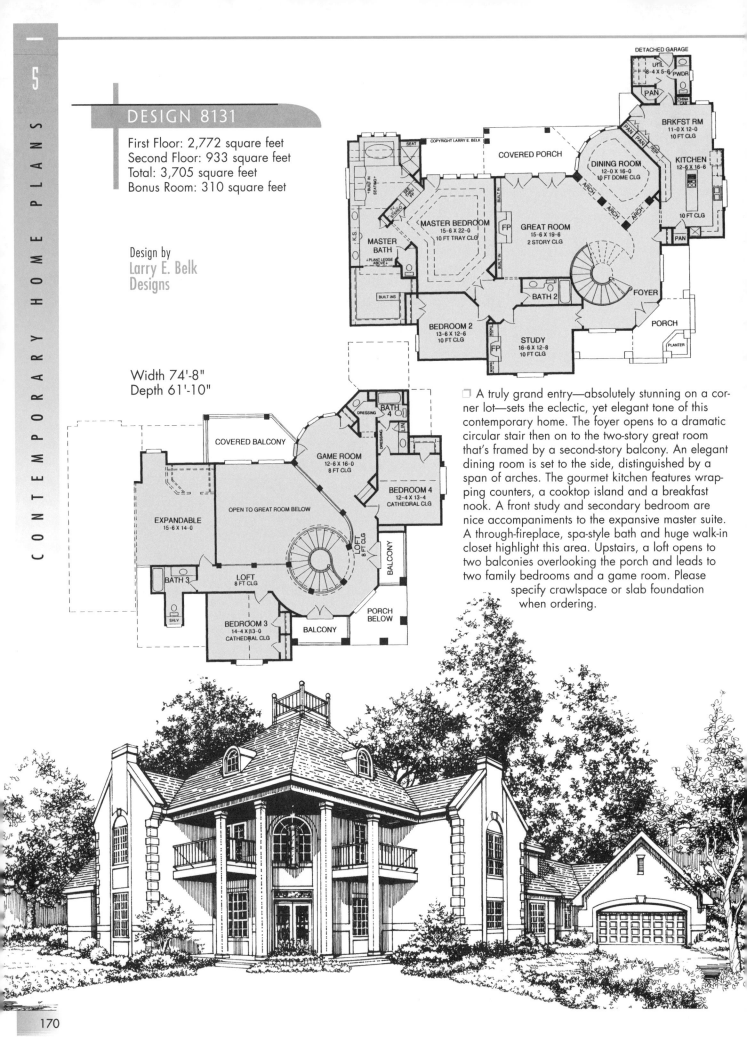

COPYRIGHT LARRY E. BELK

DETACHED GARAGE

UTIL
8-4 X 5-6

PWDR

PAN

CHINA CABI

BRKFST RM
11-0 X 12-0
10 FT CLG

KITCHEN
12-6 X 16-6

COVERED PORCH

DINING ROOM
12-0 X 16-0
10 FT DOME CLG

10 FT CLG

SEAT

MASTER BEDROOM
15-6 X 22-0
10 FT TRAY CLG

FP

GREAT ROOM
15-6 X 19-6
2 STORY CLG

MASTER
BATH

PLANT LEDGE
ABOVE

K.S.

BUILT INS

BATH 2

FOYER

BEDROOM 2
13-6 X 12-6
10 FT CLG

STUDY
16-6 X 12-8
10 FT CLG

FP

PORCH

PLANTER

COVERED BALCONY

BATH 4

DRESSING

LIN

GAME ROOM
12-6 X 16-0
8 FT CLG

DRESSING

BEDROOM 4
12-4 X 13-4
CATHEDRAL CLG

EXPANDABLE
15-6 X 14-0

OPEN TO GREAT ROOM BELOW

LOFT
8 FT CLG

BALCONY

BATH 3

LOFT
8 FT CLG

SHLV

BEDROOM 3
14-4 X 13-0
CATHEDRAL CLG

BALCONY

PORCH
BELOW

□ A truly grand entry—absolutely stunning on a corner lot—sets the eclectic, yet elegant tone of this contemporary home. The foyer opens to a dramatic circular stair then on to the two-story great room that's framed by a second-story balcony. An elegant dining room is set to the side, distinguished by a span of arches. The gourmet kitchen features wrapping counters, a cooktop island and a breakfast nook. A front study and secondary bedroom are nice accompaniments to the expansive master suite. A through-fireplace, spa-style bath and huge walk-in closet highlight this area. Upstairs, a loft opens to two balconies overlooking the porch and leads to two family bedrooms and a game room. Please specify crawlspace or slab foundation when ordering.

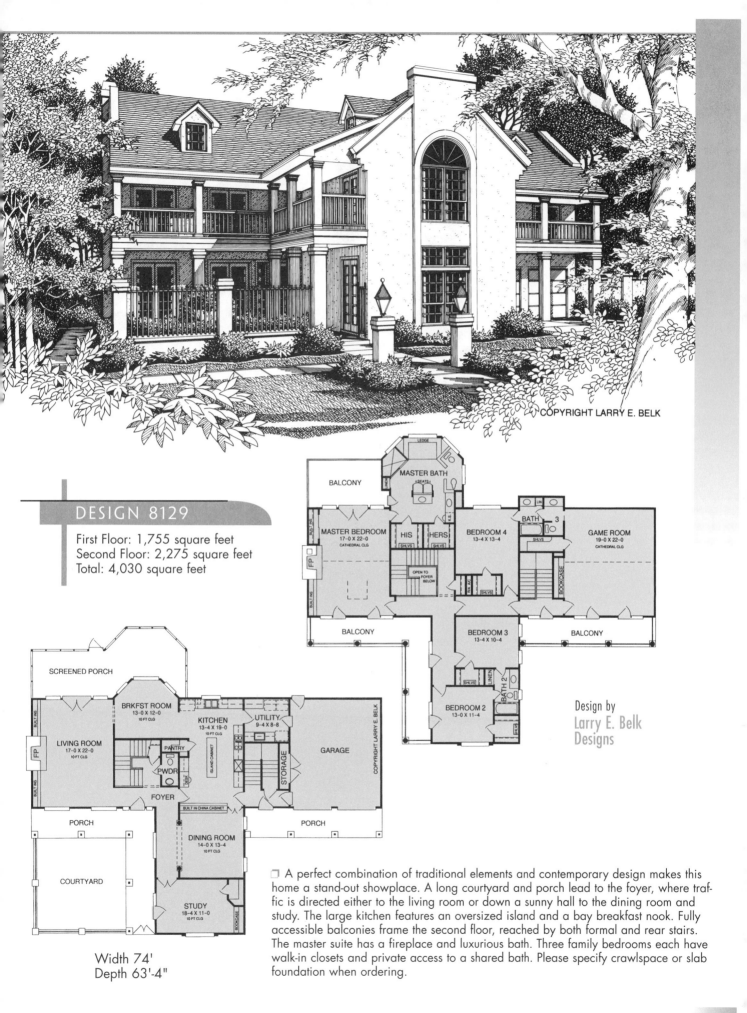

COPYRIGHT LARRY E. BELK

DESIGN 8129

First Floor: 1,755 square feet
Second Floor: 2,275 square feet
Total: 4,030 square feet

LEDGE

MASTER BATH

BALCONY

BATH 3

MASTER BEDROOM
17-0 X 22-0
CATHEDRAL CLG

HIS   HERS

BEDROOM 4
13-4 X 13-4

GAME ROOM
19-0 X 22-0
CATHEDRAL CLG

OPEN TO FOYER BELOW

BOOKCASE

BALCONY

BEDROOM 3
13-4 X 10-4

BALCONY

SCREENED PORCH

BRKFST ROOM
13-0 X 12-0
10 FT CLG

KITCHEN
13-4 X 19-0
10 FT CLG

UTILITY
9-4 X 8-8

BEDROOM 2
13-0 X 11-4

BATH 2

Design by
Larry E. Belk
Designs

LIVING ROOM
17-0 X 22-0
10 FT CLG

PANTRY

ISLAND CABINET

STORAGE

GARAGE

PWDR

FOYER

BUILT IN CHINA CABINET

COPYRIGHT LARRY E. BELK

PORCH

PORCH

DINING ROOM
14-0 X 13-4
10 FT CLG

COURTYARD

STUDY
18-4 X 11-0
10 FT CLG

BOOKCASE

❏ A perfect combination of traditional elements and contemporary design makes this home a stand-out showplace. A long courtyard and porch lead to the foyer, where traffic is directed either to the living room or down a sunny hall to the dining room and study. The large kitchen features an oversized island and a bay breakfast nook. Fully accessible balconies frame the second floor, reached by both formal and rear stairs. The master suite has a fireplace and luxurious bath. Three family bedrooms each have walk-in closets and private access to a shared bath. Please specify crawlspace or slab foundation when ordering.

Width 74'
Depth 63'-4"

171

Design by
Home Planners

Width 90'
Depth 46'

DESIGN 2781

First Floor: 2,132 square feet
Second Floor: 1,156 square feet
Total: 3,288 square feet

L D

☐ This beautifully designed two-story provides an eye-catching exterior. The floor plan is a perfect complement. The front kitchen features an island range, adjacent breakfast nook and pass-through to a formal dining room. The master suite offers a spacious walk-in closet and dressing room. The side terrace can be reached from the master suite, the gathering room and the study. The second floor contains three bedrooms and storage space galore. The center lounge offers a sloped ceiling and skylight.

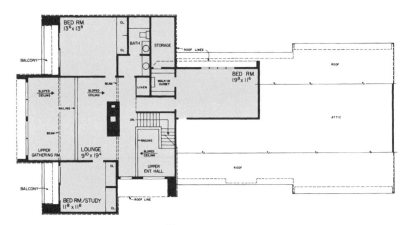

QUOTE ONE®
Cost to build? See page 230
to order complete cost estimate
to build this house in your area!

DESIGN 3364

First Floor: 2,861 square feet
Second Floor: 1,859 square feet
Total: 4,720 square feet

Design by
Home Planners

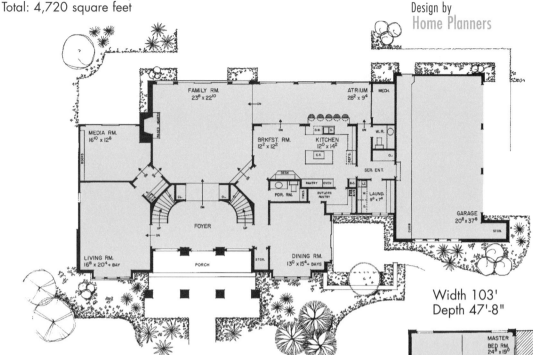

Width 103'
Depth 47'-8"

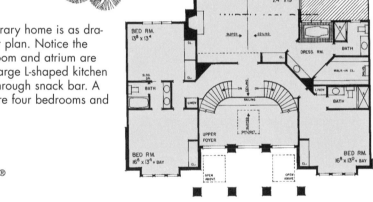

❒ The impressive stonework facade of this contemporary home is as dramatic as it is practical—and it contains a grand floor plan. Notice the varying levels—a family room, living room, media room and atrium are down a few steps from the elegant entry foyer. The large L-shaped kitchen is highlighted by an island work center and a pass-through snack bar. A double curved staircase leads to a second floor where four bedrooms and three full baths are found.

QUOTE ONE®

Cost to build? See page 230
to order complete cost estimate
to build this house in your area!

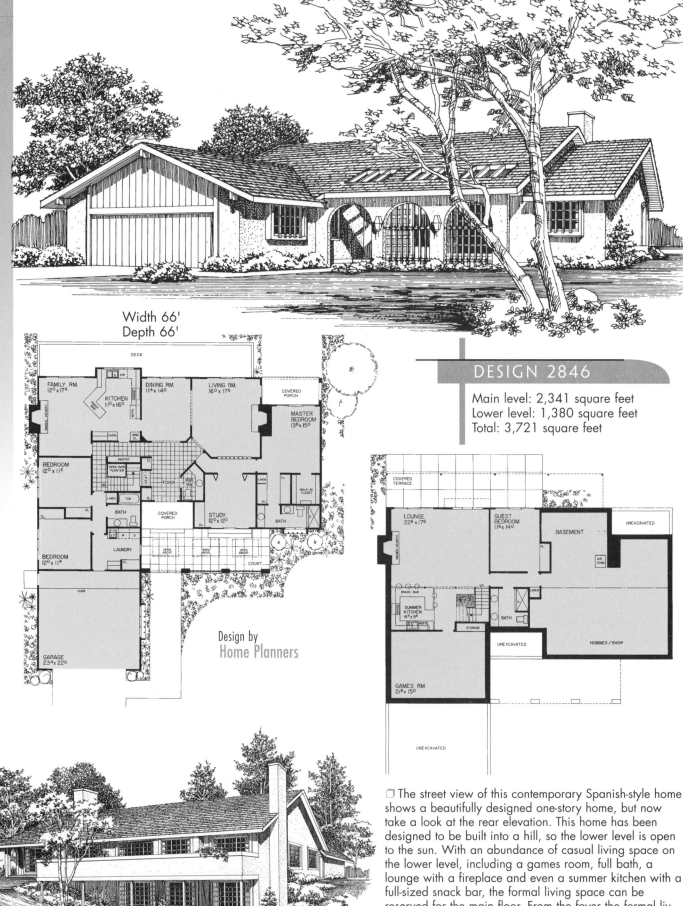

Width 66'
Depth 66'

FAMILY RM. 12⁰×17⁶

KITCHEN 11⁰×16⁰

DINING RM. 11⁴×14⁰

LIVING RM. 16⁰×17⁶

DECK

COVERED PORCH

MASTER BEDROOM 13⁸×15⁰

BEDROOM 12⁰×11²

OVEN

PANTRY

OPEN OVER PLANTER

FOYER

WALK-IN CLOSET

BATH

CL

LINEN TUB

COVERED PORCH

STUDY 12⁰×12⁰

BATH

BEDROOM 12⁰×11⁴

LAUNDRY

OPEN ABOVE

OPEN ABOVE

OPEN ABOVE

COURT

CURB

GARAGE 23⁴×22⁰

Design by
Home Planners

DESIGN 2846

Main level: 2,341 square feet
Lower level: 1,380 square feet
Total: 3,721 square feet

COVERED TERRACE

LOUNGE 22⁶×17⁶

GUEST BEDROOM 11⁶×14⁰

BASEMENT

UNEXCAVATED

AIR COND.

SNACK BAR

SUMMER KITCHEN 14⁸×9⁸

BATH

LINEN

STORAGE

UNEXCAVATED

HOBBIES / SHOP

GAMES RM. 21⁸×15⁰

UNEXCAVATED

Rear Elevation

☐ The street view of this contemporary Spanish-style home shows a beautifully designed one-story home, but now take a look at the rear elevation. This home has been designed to be built into a hill, so the lower level is open to the sun. With an abundance of casual living space on the lower level, including a games room, full bath, a lounge with a fireplace and even a summer kitchen with a full-sized snack bar, the formal living space can be reserved for the main floor. From the foyer the formal living room and dining room take center stage. The large kitchen has an angled snack bar that is open to the family room. The master suite has a covered porch and split-vanity bath. Two family bedrooms share a full hall bath.

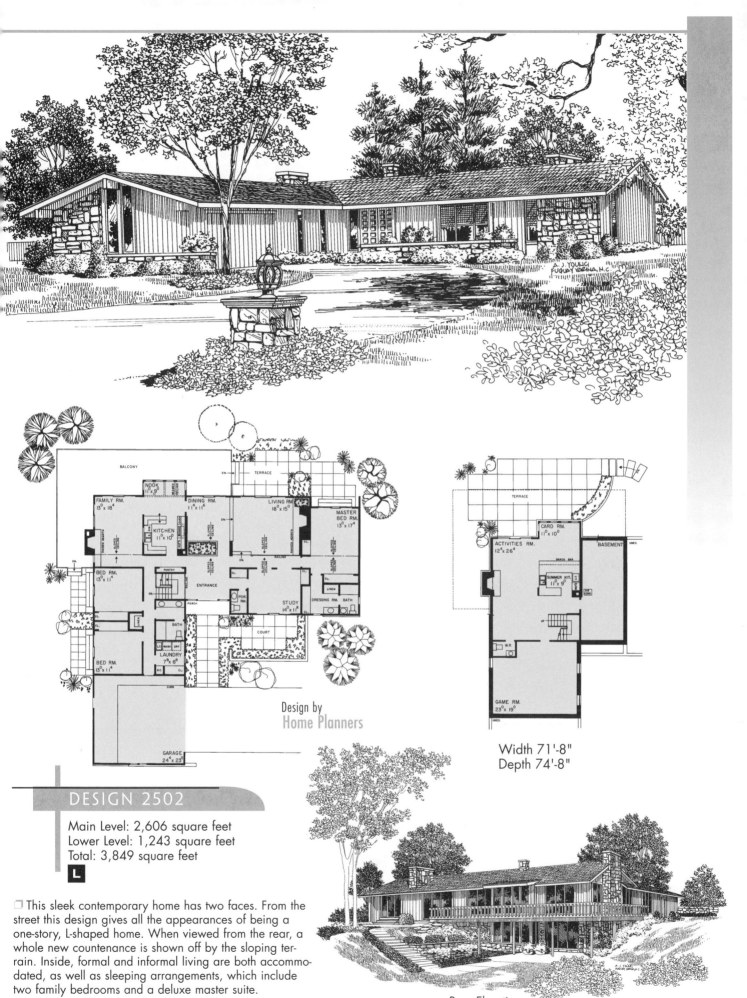

Design by
Home Planners

Width 71'-8"
Depth 74'-8"

DESIGN 2502

Main Level: 2,606 square feet
Lower Level: 1,243 square feet
Total: 3,849 square feet

L

☐ This sleek contemporary home has two faces. From the street this design gives all the appearances of being a one-story, L-shaped home. When viewed from the rear, a whole new countenance is shown off by the sloping terrain. Inside, formal and informal living are both accommodated, as well as sleeping arrangements, which include two family bedrooms and a deluxe master suite.

Rear Elevation

Width 97'
Depth 102'-8"

SUN RM.
20⁰x14⁰
SLOPED CEILING

TERRACE

LIVING RM.
21⁰x14⁰

MEDIA RM.
15⁰x11⁸

MASTER BEDROOM
16⁰x22⁰

WHIRLPOOL
SKYLIGHT ABOVE

BATH

COUNTRY KITCHEN
18⁰x30⁰

OPEN THRU FIREPLACE
RAISED HEARTH

DRESSING/ EXERCISE RM.
16⁸x12⁴

SKYLIGHT ABOVE

LINEN SEAT

DINING RM.
14⁰x12⁰

SNACK BAR

BALCONY OVER

OPEN

WALK-IN CLOSET

CHINA SHELVES

FOYER

POWDER RM.

COVERED PORCH

REFG.

WASH RM.

PANTRY

SHELVES
WORK BENCH

CL.

FREEZER

COVERED PORCH

WORK ISLAND

SEWING

CLUTTER RM.
17⁶x14⁰

COVERED PORCH

2 CAR GARAGE
22⁸x22⁸

Design by
Home Planners

1 CAR GARAGE
20⁸x11⁴

BEDROOM
13⁶x14⁰

BEDROOM
13⁸x14⁰

BATH

BALCONY

RAILING

UPPER FOYER

Quote One®

Cost to build? See page 230
to order complete cost estimate
to build this house in your area!

DESIGN 2920

First Floor: 3,067 square feet
Second Floor: 648 square feet
Total: 3,715 square feet

L **D**

This contemporary design has a great deal to offer. A fireplace opens up to both the living room and country kitchen. The kitchen is a gourmets' delight, with a huge walk-in pantry, a deluxe work island which includes a snack bar, and easy access to the formal dining room. A media room has plenty of storage and offers access to the rear terrace. Privacy is the key word when describing the sleeping areas. The first-floor master bedroom is away from the traffic of the house and features a dressing/exercise room, a whirlpool tub and shower and a spacious walk-in closet. Two more bedrooms and a full bath are on the second floor. The three-car garage is arranged so that the owners have use of a double-garage with an attached single on reserve for guests. The cheerful sun room adds 296 square feet to the total.

Photo by Bob Greenspan

*This home, as shown in the photograph, may differ from the actual blueprints.
For more detailed information, please check the floor plans carefully.*

DESIGN 2679

Main Level: 1,179 square feet
Upper Level: 681 square feet
Lower Level: 680 square feet
Family Room Level: 643 square feet
Total: 3,183 square feet

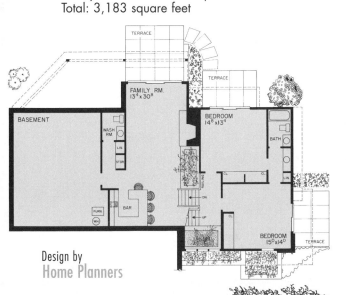

Design by
Home Planners

Width 65'
Depth 57'

Rear Elevation

☐ This spacious modern contemporary home offers plenty of livability on many levels. The main level includes a breakfast room in addition to a dining room. Adjacent is a sloped-ceilinged living room with raised hearth. The upper level features an isolated master bedroom suite with adjoining study or sitting room and a balcony. The family room level includes a long rectangular family room with an adjoining terrace on one end and a bar with a washroom at the other end. A spacious basement is included. Two other bedrooms are positioned in the lower level with their own view of the terrace. The rear deck provides lots of space for outdoor entertaining and relaxation.

J.N. HANSEN

DESIGN 8702

Square Footage: 2,397

Width 73'-2"
Depth 73'-2"

Floor plan labels:

Master Bedroom 16⁸ · 13⁰
Covered Patio
Family Room 19⁴ · 15¹⁰ fireplace
Breakfast
summer kitchen
Electric Clothes Carousel
w.i.c.
Pdr.
Living Room 15⁸ · 12⁰
dw Kitchen
Bath
shelf
ref
Bedroom 2 11⁰ · 11⁰
Bath
Den / Study 11⁴ · 11⁰
Foyer
Dining 14⁰ · 11⁰
Utility
Bedroom 3 11⁰ · 11⁰
Entry
shelf
wh ac
ac
Fountain
Garden
3 Car Garage

☐ Dramatic rooflines and a unique entrance set the mood of this contemporary home from curbside. Double doors lead into the foyer, which opens directly to the formal living/dining rooms. A den/study is adjacent to this area and offers a quiet retreat. The spacious kitchen is sure to please the gourmet of the family with a large cooktop work island, plenty of counter and cabinet space and an adjoining breakfast nook. The spacious family room expands this area and features a wall of windows and a warming fireplace. Two secondary bedrooms share a full bath. Located away from them for privacy, the master bedroom suite is designed with pleasure in mind. Included in the suite is a lavish bath and a deluxe walk-in closet, as well as access to the covered patio.

Design by
Home Design
Services, Inc.

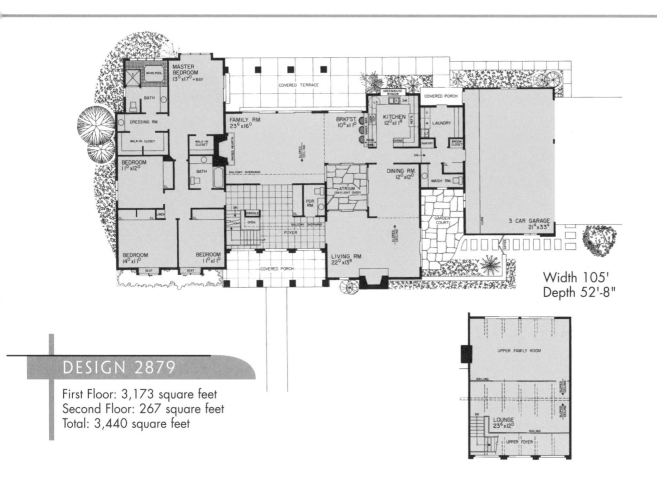

Width 105'
Depth 52'-8"

DESIGN 2879

First Floor: 3,173 square feet
Second Floor: 267 square feet
Total: 3,440 square feet

This lavish modern design has it all, including an upper lounge, family room and foyer. A centrally located atrium with skylight provides focal interest downstairs. A large, efficient kitchen with snack bar service to the breakfast room enjoys its own greenhouse window. The spacious family room shares a warming fireplace and a view of the rear covered terrace. To the front, a living room with fireplace delights in a view of the garden court as well as the atrium. The deluxe master suite features a relaxing whirlpool, dressing area and an abundance of walk-in closets. Three secondary bedrooms, two with window seats, share a full bath.

QUOTE ONE®

Cost to build? See page 230
to order complete cost estimate
to build this house in your area!

Design by
Home Planners

Family Room
22'0" x 16'0"

Kitchen
19'0" x 14'8"

Covered Patio
44'0" x 24'10"

Sitting Area
10'11" x 15'2"

Master Suite
13'7" x 18'0"

Nook
11'4 x 12'0"

Living Room
14'8 x 13'3"

Bedroom 2
12'0" x 12'10"

W.I.C.

Master Bath

Bath 2

Utility

Dining Room
13'2" x 12'8"

Foyer

Den / Library
13'4" x 13'4"

Bedroom 3
12'0" x 13'0"

Entry

Covered Walk

2 Car Garage
20'8" x 20'10"

2 Car Garage
20'8" x 20'8"

Width 85'-4"
Depth 89'-4"

DESIGN 8700

Square Footage: 3,506

Have a lot of cars in your family? If so, this house is perfect for you. The master and family garages celebrate the passion for automobiles in a sensible way. No more dents from the kids' bikes and toys. The house itself breaks new design ground and addresses many concerns for the large family. A grand foyer leads to the invitingly large living room, which is dramatic with a view through a wall of glass to the rear. Columns flank the formal dining room and help define the large nook across the hall. Family space abounds with a true informal dining room and a gourmet kitchen, which overlooks the glass walled family room. The master wing is lavishly designed with a sitting room, private sleeping chamber and ultra-deluxe bath. Two large secondary bedrooms reside on the opposite side of the home and share a full bath with dual lavs.

Design by
Home Design
Services, Inc.

Width 62'
Depth 83'-8"

Pool

planter   closet   planter

Bedroom 3
volume ceiling
12⁰ • 12⁰

Bath

Covered
Patio

steps

Master
Bath

planter

plant
shelf

summer
kitchen

Bedroom 4
volume ceiling
12⁰ • 12⁰

Family Room
volume ceiling
17⁸ • 29⁰

Master
Bedroom
volume ceiling
15⁸ • 19⁸

fireplace

Living Room
volume ceiling
14⁴ • 20⁰

Breakfast
volume ceiling

linen

w.i.c.

ac

w
d

dw

Utility   rpf   Kitchen

rng

o.

pantry

Dining
14⁰ • 14⁰

Bath

ac

wh

Foyer

Bedroom 2
volume ceiling
13⁴ • 12⁰

3 Car
Garage

planter

planter

Entry

DESIGN 8678

Square Footage: 3,091

❏ With elegantly formal columns standing at attention around the entryway, this design starts off as impressive and only gets better. Inside, ceiling detail in the foyer and the formal dining room immediately reinforces the graceful qualities of this beautiful home. A large and airy living room awaits to accommodate any entertaining you might have in mind, while the spacious family room encourages more casual encounters with a warming fireplace and access to the covered patio. An angled kitchen is nearby and offers a sunny breakfast room for early morning risers. Three secondary bedrooms accommodate both family and friends, while a lavish master bedroom suite promises pampering for the fortunate homeowner.

Design by
Home Design
Services, Inc.

DESIGN 8690

Square Footage: 3,556

Width 85'
Depth 85'

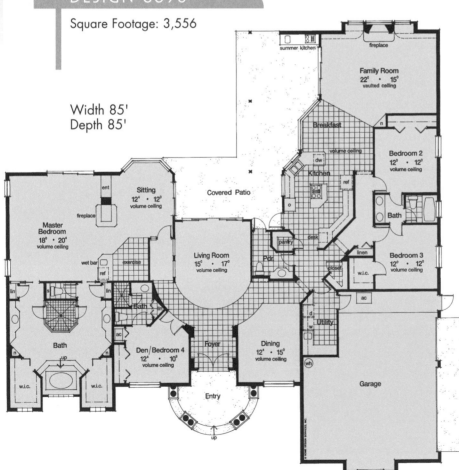

A beautiful curved portico provides a majestic entrance to this one-story home. Curved ceilings in the formal living and dining rooms continue the extraordinary style. To the left of the foyer is a den/bedroom with a private bath, ideal for use as a guest suite. The exquisite master suite features a see-through fireplace and an exercise area with a wet bar. A sumptuous soaking tub and island shower in the master bath invite relaxation. The family wing is geared for casual living with a powder room/patio bath, a huge island kitchen with a walk-in pantry, a glass-walled breakfast nook and a grand family room with a fireplace and media wall. Two family bedrooms share a private bath.

Design by
**Home Design
Services, Inc.**

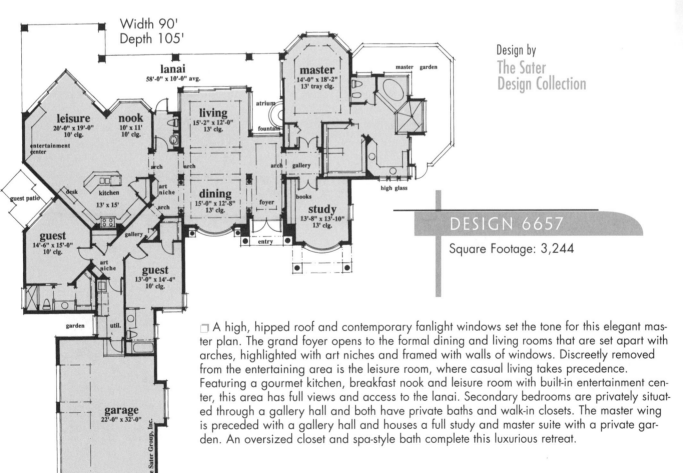

Width 90'
Depth 105'

lanai
58'-0" x 10'-0" avg.

master
14'-0" x 18'-2"
13' tray clg.

master garden

leisure
20'-0" x 19'-0"
10' clg.

nook
10' x 11'
10' clg.

living
15'-2" x 12'-0"
13' clg.

atrium

fountain

entertainment center

Design by
**The Sater
Design Collection**

guest patio

desk

kitchen
13' x 15'

art niche

arch

arch

arch

gallery

dining
15'-0" x 12'-8"
13' clg.

foyer

books

high glass

guest
14'-6" x 15'-0"
10' clg.

gallery

art niche

study
13'-8" x 13'-10"
13' clg.

entry

DESIGN 6657

Square Footage: 3,244

art niche

guest
13'-0" x 14'-4"
10' clg.

garden

util.

garage
22'-0" x 32'-0"

☐ A high, hipped roof and contemporary fanlight windows set the tone for this elegant master plan. The grand foyer opens to the formal dining and living rooms that are set apart with arches, highlighted with art niches and framed with walls of windows. Discreetly removed from the entertaining area is the leisure room, where casual living takes precedence. Featuring a gourmet kitchen, breakfast nook and leisure room with built-in entertainment center, this area has full views and access to the lanai. Secondary bedrooms are privately situated through a gallery hall and both have private baths and walk-in closets. The master wing is preceded with a gallery hall and houses a full study and master suite with a private garden. An oversized closet and spa-style bath complete this luxurious retreat.

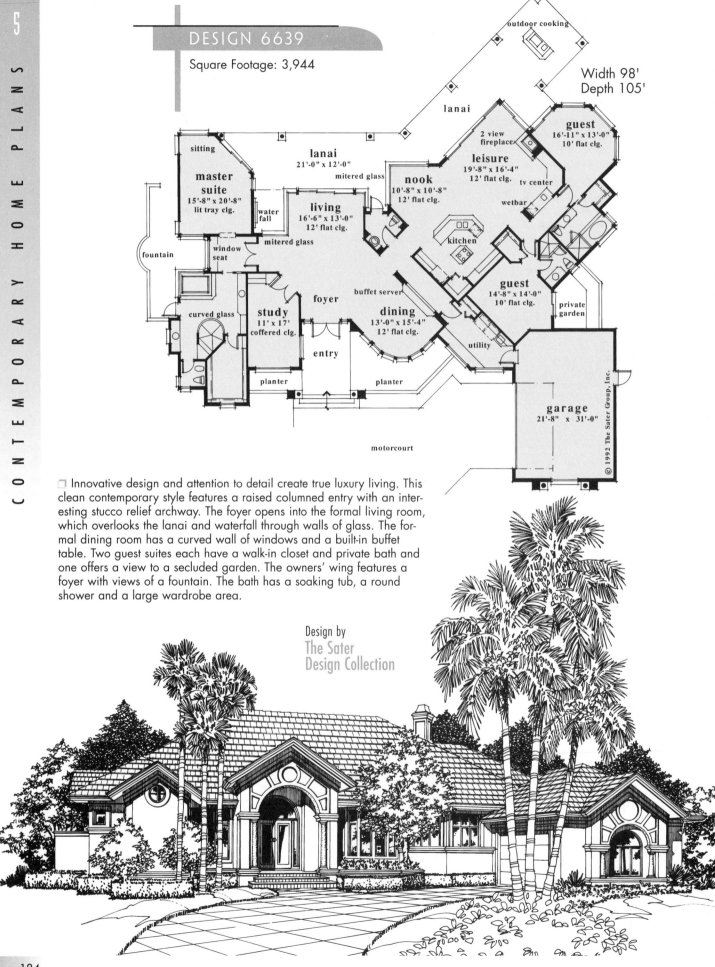

DESIGN 6639

Square Footage: 3,944

Width 98'
Depth 105'

outdoor cooking

lanai

sitting

master suite
15'-8" x 20'-8"
lit tray clg.

lanai
21'-0" x 12'-0"

mitered glass

water fall

living
16'-6" x 13'-0"
12' flat clg.

nook
10'-8" x 10'-8"
12' flat clg.

leisure
19'-8" x 16'-4"
12' flat clg.

2 view fireplace

guest
16'-11" x 13'-0"
10' flat clg.

tv center

wetbar

fountain

window seat

mitered glass

foyer

kitchen

curved glass

study
11' x 17'
coffered clg.

buffet server

dining
13'-0" x 15'-4"
12' flat clg.

guest
14'-8" x 14'-0"
10' flat clg.

private garden

entry

utility

planter

planter

motorcourt

garage
21'-8" x 31'-0"

© 1992 The Sater Group, Inc.

⬔ Innovative design and attention to detail create true luxury living. This clean contemporary style features a raised columned entry with an interesting stucco relief archway. The foyer opens into the formal living room, which overlooks the lanai and waterfall through walls of glass. The formal dining room has a curved wall of windows and a built-in buffet table. Two guest suites each have a walk-in closet and private bath and one offers a view to a secluded garden. The owners' wing features a foyer with views of a fountain. The bath has a soaking tub, a round shower and a large wardrobe area.

Design by
The Sater
Design Collection

DESIGN 6637

Square Footage: 4,187

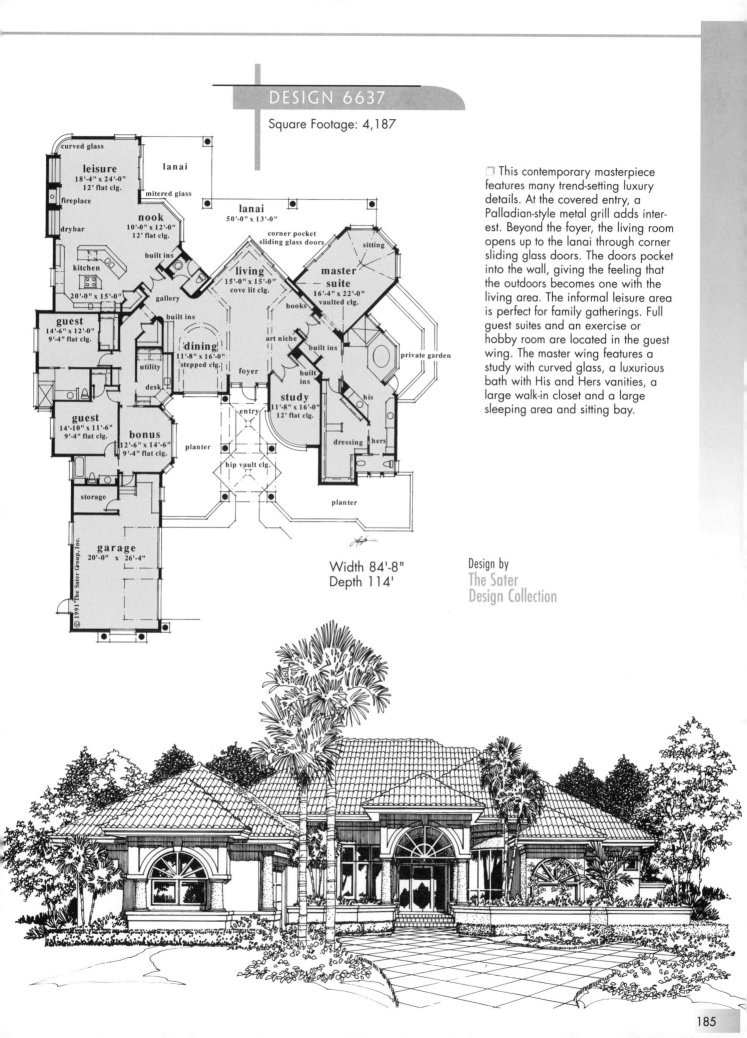

Floor plan labels:

curved glass

leisure
18'-4" x 24'-0"
12' flat clg.

lanai

fireplace

mitered glass

drybar

lanai
50'-0" x 13'-0"

nook
10'-0" x 12'-0"
12' flat clg.

corner pocket
sliding glass doors

built ins

sitting

kitchen
20'-0" x 15'-0"

living
15'-0" x 15'-0"
cove lit clg.

master
suite
16'-4" x 22'-0"
vaulted clg.

gallery

books

guest
14'-6" x 12'-0"
9'-4" flat clg.

built ins

art niche

built ins

dining
11'-8" x 16'-0"
stepped clg.

private garden

utility

foyer

built
ins

desk

his

guest
14'-10" x 11'-6"
9'-4" flat clg.

study
11'-8" x 16'-0"
12' flat clg.

entry

bonus
12'-6" x 14'-6"
9'-4" flat clg.

planter

dressing

hers

hip vault clg.

storage

planter

garage
20'-0" x 26'-4"

© 1991 The Sater Group, Inc.

Width 84'-8"
Depth 114'

□ This contemporary masterpiece features many trend-setting luxury details. At the covered entry, a Palladian-style metal grill adds interest. Beyond the foyer, the living room opens up to the lanai through corner sliding glass doors. The doors pocket into the wall, giving the feeling that the outdoors becomes one with the living area. The informal leisure area is perfect for family gatherings. Full guest suites and an exercise or hobby room are located in the guest wing. The master wing features a study with curved glass, a luxurious bath with His and Hers vanities, a large walk-in closet and a large sleeping area and sitting bay.

Design by
The Sater
Design Collection

DESIGN 8688

Square Footage: 2,636

A towering entry welcomes you into the foyer of this soaring contemporary design. Interior glass walls supply openness to the den/study and mirror the arches to the formal dining room. The sunken living room has a bay-windowed wall that provides expansive views of the rear yard. Located to the rear, the master suite accesses the powder room/patio bath. Sliding glass doors from the suite open onto the patio. The master bath features His and Hers walk-in closets, a sunken vanity/bath area and a doorless shower. Casual living takes place in the family wing, which holds the gourmet kitchen, the nook and a family room with a fireplace. Two secondary bedrooms share a private bath.

Design by
Home Design
Services, Inc.

Width 71'-8"
Depth 71'-4"

DESIGN 8087

First Floor: 5,183 square feet
Second Floor: 238 square feet
Total: 5,421 square feet

❏ Contemporary styling coupled with traditional finishes of brick and stucco make this home a stand-out that caters to the discriminating few. The entry, with a two-story ceiling, steps down into an enormous great room with a see-through fireplace. A formal living room is open from the entry and begins one wing of the home. The bedroom wing provides three bedrooms, each with a large amenity-filled bath, as well as a study area and a recreation room. The opposite wing houses the dining room, kitchen, breakfast room and two more bedrooms. The kitchen offers a curved window overlooking the side yard and a cooktop island with a vegetable sink. A stair leads to a loft overlooking the great room and entry.

Design by
Larry E. Belk
Designs

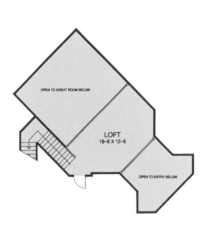

Width 93'-5"
Depth 113'

DESIGN 8706

Square Footage: 2,636

Design by
Home Design
Services, Inc.

Master Bedroom 18⁰ • 15⁰ volume ceiling

Living Room 16² • 16⁰ volume ceiling

Covered Patio

Family Room 18⁸ • 16⁴ volume ceiling

Breakfast

Kitchen

Bedroom 2 11¹⁰ • 11⁰ volume ceiling

Den Study 14⁰ • 11² volume ceiling

Foyer

Dining 13⁰ • 12⁰ volume ceiling

Bedroom 3 13⁰ • 11⁰ volume ceiling

Entry

Double Garage

☐ A towering entry welcomes you in the foyer of this soaring contemporary design. Interior glass walls give openness to the den/study, and mirror the arches to the formal dining room. The sunken living room has a bayed window wall, which views the patio. The master suite wing also holds the den/study, which can access the powder room/patio bath. Sliding glass doors from the master suite access the patio. The master bath features dual closets, a sunken vanity/bath area and a doorless shower. The family wing holds the gourmet kitchen, nook and family room with a fireplace.

Width 68'-8"
Depth 76'

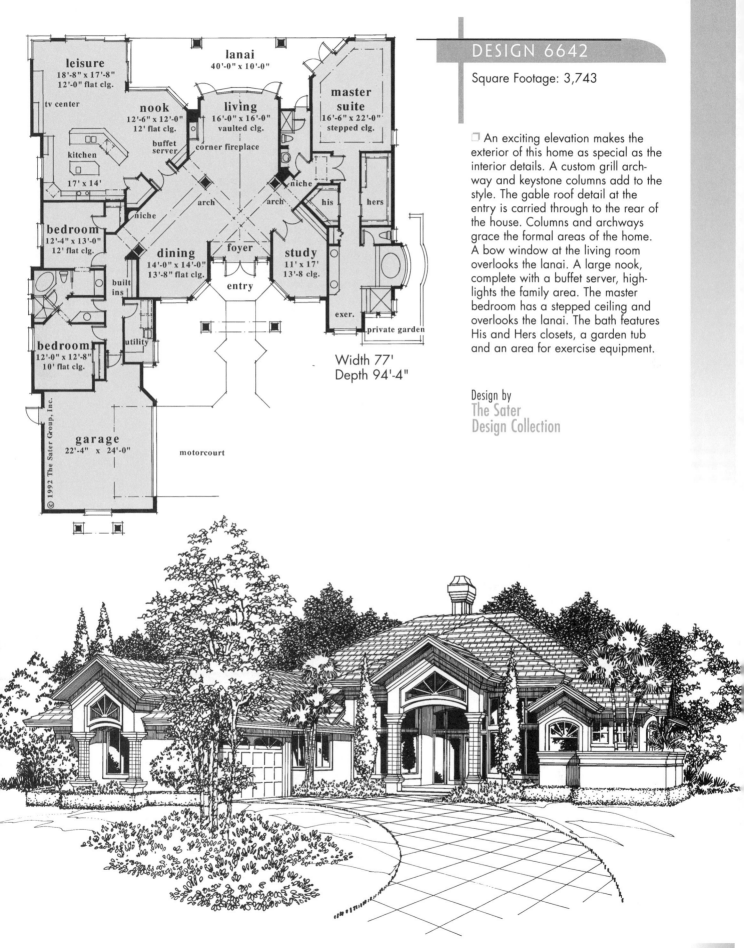

leisure
18'-8" x 17'-8"
12'-0" flat clg.

tv center

lanai
40'-0" x 10'-0"

nook
12'-6" x 12'-0"
12' flat clg.

living
16'-0" x 16'-0"
vaulted clg.

master
suite
16'-6" x 22'-0"
stepped clg.

kitchen
17' x 14'

buffet
server

corner fireplace

niche

his

hers

arch

arch

niche

bedroom
12'-4" x 13'-0"
12' flat clg.

dining
14'-0" x 14'-0"
13'-8" flat clg.

foyer

study
11' x 17'
13'-8 clg.

niche

built
ins

entry

bedroom
12'-0" x 12'-8"
10' flat clg.

utility

exer.

private garden

Width 77'
Depth 94'-4"

garage
22'-4" x 24'-0"

motorcourt

© 1992 The Sater Group, Inc.

DESIGN 6642

Square Footage: 3,743

❑ An exciting elevation makes the exterior of this home as special as the interior details. A custom grill archway and keystone columns add to the style. The gable roof detail at the entry is carried through to the rear of the house. Columns and archways grace the formal areas of the home. A bow window at the living room overlooks the lanai. A large nook, complete with a buffet server, highlights the family area. The master bedroom has a stepped ceiling and overlooks the lanai. The bath features His and Hers closets, a garden tub and an area for exercise equipment.

Design by
The Sater
Design Collection

DESIGN 6636

Square Footage: 4,565

❏ There is plenty to love about this home—4,565 square feet to love, to be exact. It combines luxurious and leisurely living in a perfect design for families or empty nesters. A freestanding entryway leads straight ahead to the living room, with the informal areas to the left and the private master suite to the right. The leisure room, with fireplace and built-in entertainment center, is the focal point of the informal area. It is within steps of the wraparound island kitchen and breakfast nook. Another highlight of the home is the luxurious master bedroom suite. The suite's deluxe bath has a freestanding double vanity, raised soaking tub, sauna, exercise room and two walk-in closets.

Design by
**The Sater
Design Collection**

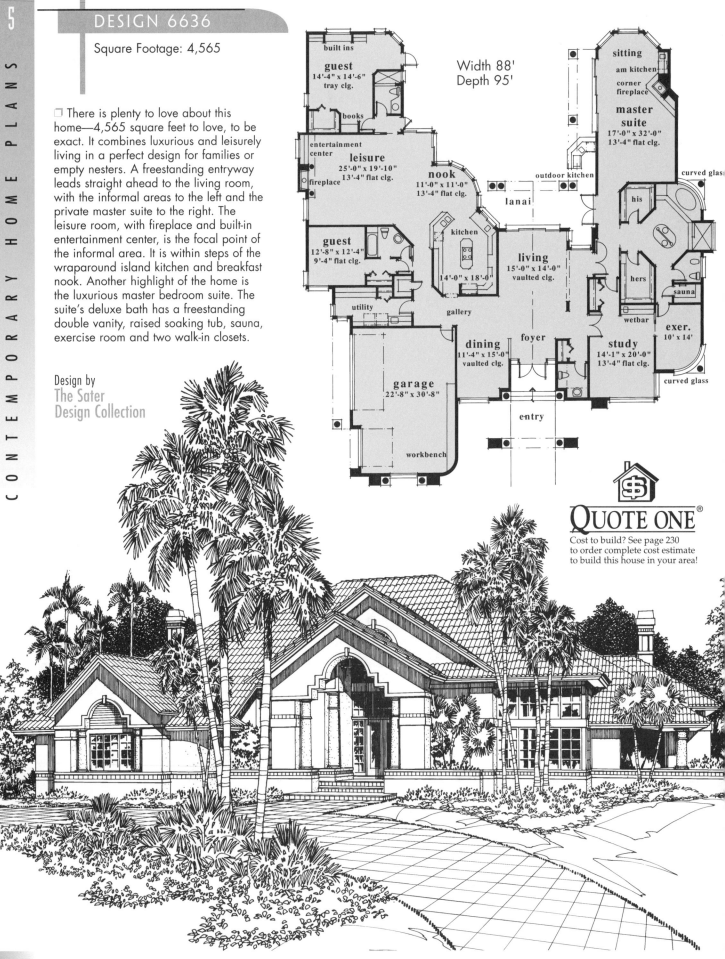

Width 88'
Depth 95'

QUOTE ONE®
Cost to build? See page 230
to order complete cost estimate
to build this house in your area!

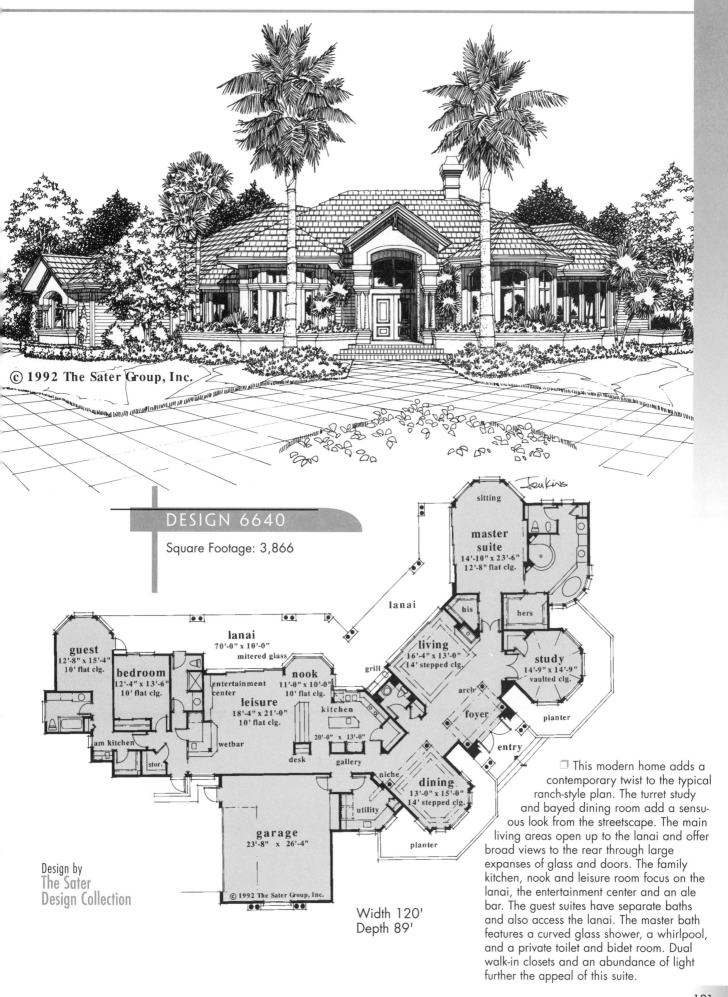

© 1992 The Sater Group, Inc.

DESIGN 6640

Square Footage: 3,866

master suite
14'-10" x 23'-6"
12'-8" flat clg.

sitting

his

hers

living
16'-4" x 13'-0"
14' stepped clg.

study
14'-9" x 14'-9"
vaulted clg.

lanai

grill

arch

planter

foyer

entry

guest
12'-8" x 15'-4"
10' flat clg.

bedroom
12'-4" x 13'-6"
10' flat clg.

lanai
70'-0" x 10'-0"
mitered glass

entertainment center

nook
11'-0" x 10'-0"
10' flat clg.

leisure
18'-4" x 21'-0"
10' flat clg.

kitchen
20'-0" x 13'-0"

am kitchen

wetbar

desk

gallery

stor.

niche

dining
13'-0" x 15'-0"
14' stepped clg.

planter

utility

garage
23'-8" x 26'-4"

© 1992 The Sater Group, Inc.

Design by
**The Sater
Design Collection**

Width 120'
Depth 89'

This modern home adds a contemporary twist to the typical ranch-style plan. The turret study and bayed dining room add a sensuous look from the streetscape. The main living areas open up to the lanai and offer broad views to the rear through large expanses of glass and doors. The family kitchen, nook and leisure room focus on the lanai, the entertainment center and an ale bar. The guest suites have separate baths and also access the lanai. The master bath features a curved glass shower, a whirlpool, and a private toilet and bidet room. Dual walk-in closets and an abundance of light further the appeal of this suite.

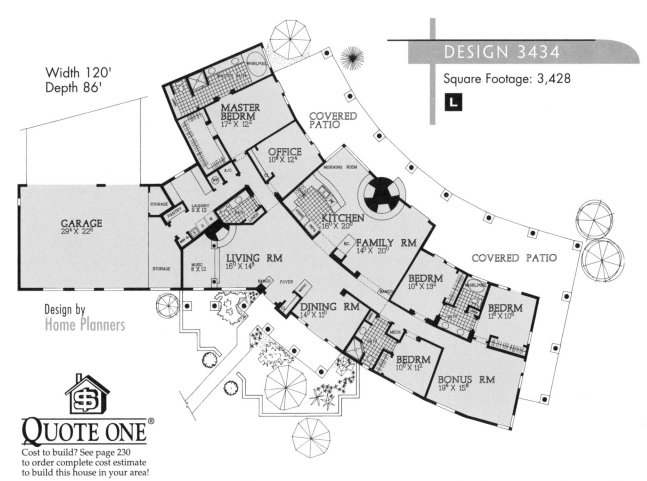

Width 120'
Depth 86'

MASTER BEDRM
17² X 12²

OFFICE
10⁶ X 12⁴

COVERED PATIO

MORNING ROOM

GARAGE
29⁴ X 22⁶

STORAGE

PANTRY

LAUNDRY
9 X 12

KITCHEN
16⁰ X 20⁰

FAMILY RM
14⁰ X 20⁰

STORAGE

MUSIC
8 X 12

LIVING RM
16⁰ X 14⁸

COVERED PATIO

BEDRM
10⁴ X 13²

BEDRM
11⁸ X 10⁶

BANCO FOYER

DINING RM
14⁰ X 11⁰

BEDRM
10⁰ X 11²

BONUS RM
19⁴ X 15⁸

DESIGN 3434

Square Footage: 3,428

L

Design by
Home Planners

QUOTE ONE®
Cost to build? See page 230
to order complete cost estimate
to build this house in your area!

☐ An in-line floor plan follows the tradition of the original Santa Fe-style homes. The slight curve to the overall configuration lends an interesting touch. From the front courtyard, the plan opens to a formal living room and dining room complemented by a family room and a kitchen with an adjoining morning room. The master bedroom is found to one side of the plan while family bedrooms share space at the opposite end. There's also a huge office and a bonus/study area for private times. With 3½ baths, a workshop garage, full laundry/sewing area, and three courtyards, this plan adds up to great livability.

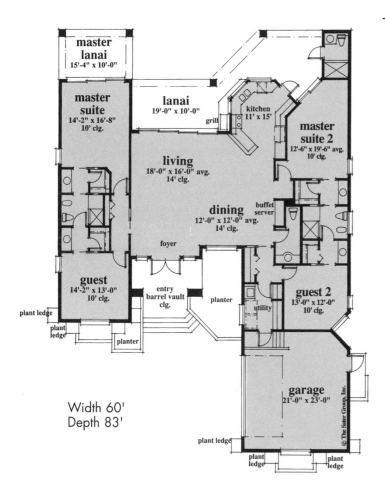

master
lanai
15'-4" x 10'-0"

master
suite
14'-2" x 16'-8"
10' clg.

lanai
19'-0" x 10'-0"

kitchen
11' x 15'

grill

master
suite 2
12'-6" x 19'-6" avg.
10' clg.

living
18'-0" x 16'-0" avg.
14' clg.

dining
12'-0" x 12'-0" avg.
14' clg.

buffet
server

foyer

guest
14'-2" x 13'-0"
10' clg.

plant ledge

plant
ledge

planter

entry
barrel vault
clg.

planter

utility

guest 2
13'-0" x 12'-0"
10' clg.

© The Sater Group, Inc.

garage
21'-0" x 23'-0"

plant ledge

plant
ledge

plant
ledge

Width 60'
Depth 83'

DESIGN 6645

Square Footage: 2,473

❏ Luxurious living begins as soon as you step into the entryway of this home. With columns and a barrel-vaulted ceiling, it opens through double doors to the foyer and combined living and dining rooms. The octagonal kitchen serves this area with a pass-through counter. Two master suites characterize this plan as the perfect vacation retreat. Two guest rooms enjoy quiet locales and direct access to the master baths. Outdoor living areas include a master lanai and another that stretches around the back of the house. A pool bath is easily accessible from the lanai. A two-car garage and a utility room finish off the plan.

Design by
**The Sater
Design Collection**

DESIGN 2948

Square Footage: 1,830

❑ Originally styled for Southwest living, this home is a good choice in any region where casual elegance is desired. Easy living is the focus of the large gathering room, apparent in its open relationship to the dining room and kitchen via a snack bar. The long galley kitchen is designed for work efficiency and has a planning desk, service entrance and a beautiful breakfast room framed with windows. The master bedroom and bath have a dramatic sloped ceiling and are joined by a traditional dressing room. Two secondary bedrooms—the front facing one would make a nice study—share a hall bath.

QUOTE ONE®

Cost to build? See page 230 to order complete cost estimate to build this house in your area!

Design by
Home Planners

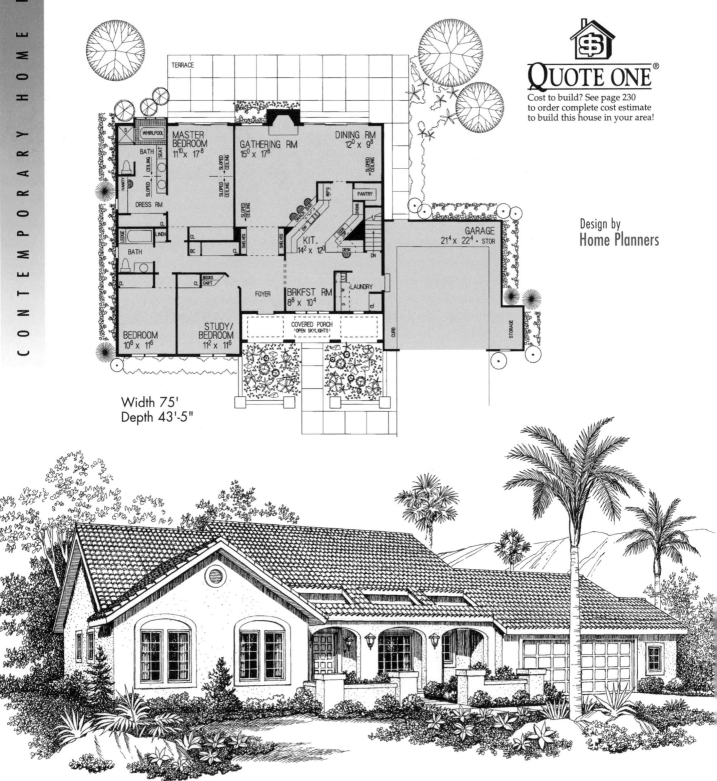

Width 75'
Depth 43'-5"

DESIGN 2912

Square Footage: 1,864

❏ This contemporary design with smart Spanish styling incorporates careful zoning by room functions with lifestyle comfort. All three bedrooms, including a master bedroom suite with a large dressing area and lavish bath, are isolated at one end of the home. Entry to a breakfast room and kitchen is possible through a mud room off the garage. That's good news for carrying groceries from car to kitchen or slipping off muddy shoes. The efficient kitchen includes a snack bar and a convenient cooktop with easy service to the breakfast room, dining room and gathering room. A large rear gathering room features a sloped ceiling and a fireplace. A covered porch just off the dining room furthers living potential.

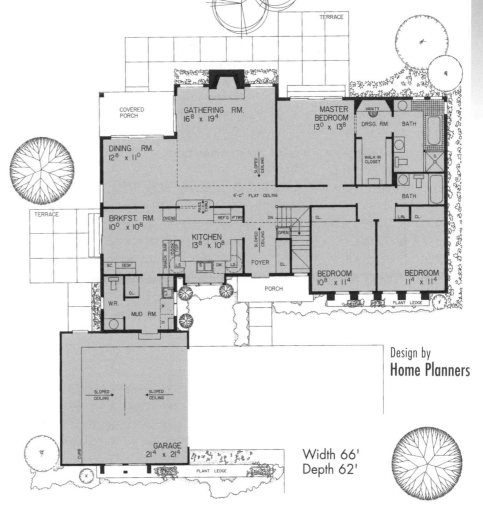

Design by
Home Planners

Width 66'
Depth 62'

Cost to build? See page 230 to order complete cost estimate to build this house in your area!

DESIGN 2875

Square Footage: 1,913

L D

❏ This elegant Spanish design incorporates excellent indoor/outdoor living relationships for families who enjoy the sun. Note the overhead openings for rain and sun to fall upon a front garden, while a twin-arched entry leads to the front porch and foyer. Inside, the floor plan features a modern kitchen with pass-through to a large gathering room with fireplace. Other features include a dining room, laundry room, a study off the foyer, plus three bedrooms including a master bedroom with its own whirlpool tub.

Design by
Home Planners

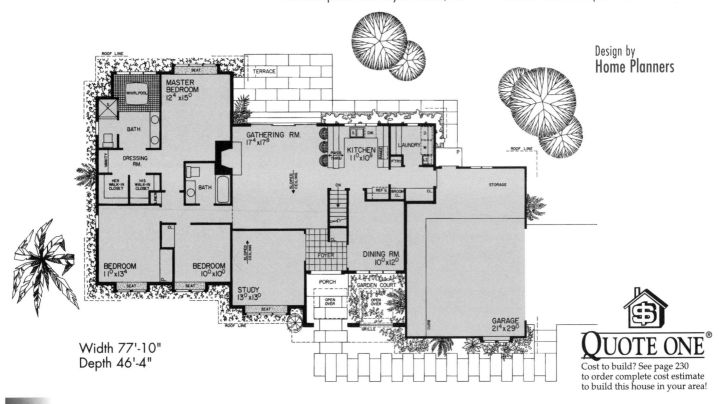

Width 77'-10"
Depth 46'-4"

Quote One®

Cost to build? See page 230
to order complete cost estimate
to build this house in your area!

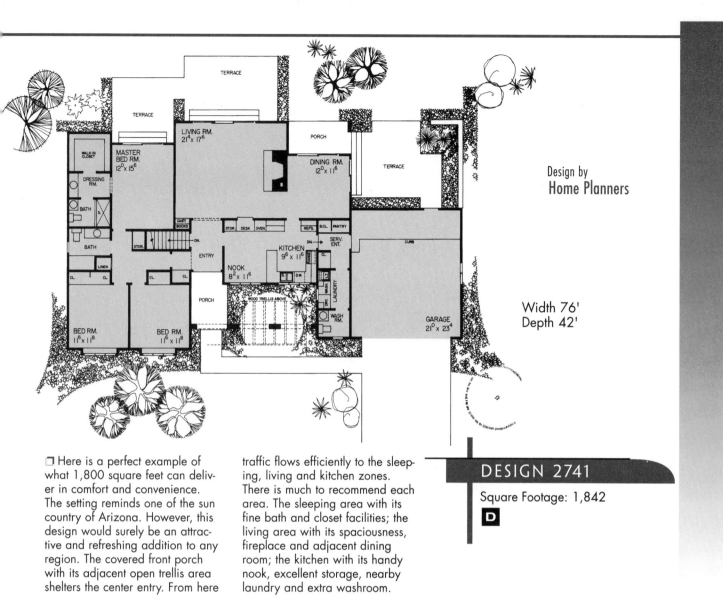

Design by
Home Planners

Width 76'
Depth 42'

□ Here is a perfect example of what 1,800 square feet can deliver in comfort and convenience. The setting reminds one of the sun country of Arizona. However, this design would surely be an attractive and refreshing addition to any region. The covered front porch with its adjacent open trellis area shelters the center entry. From here traffic flows efficiently to the sleeping, living and kitchen zones. There is much to recommend each area. The sleeping area with its fine bath and closet facilities; the living area with its spaciousness, fireplace and adjacent dining room; the kitchen with its handy nook, excellent storage, nearby laundry and extra washroom.

DESIGN 2741

Square Footage: 1,842

D

E. REINKE

DESIGN 3344

Square Footage: 3,054

L

❐ This home features interior planning for today's active family. Living areas include a living room with a fireplace, a cozy study and a family room with a wet bar. Convenient to the kitchen is the formal dining room with an attractive bay window overlooking the back yard. The four-bedroom sleeping area contains a sumptuous master suite, complete with His and Hers walk-in closets and baths. A cheerful flower porch is accessed from the master suite, living room and dining room.

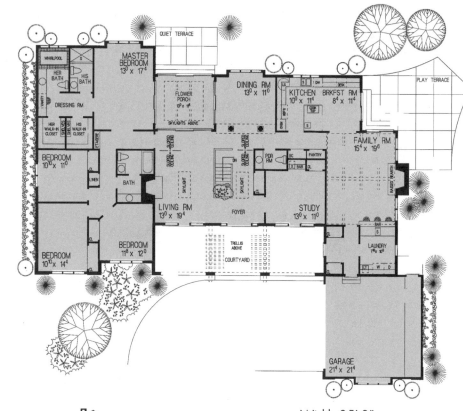

Design by
Home Planners

QUOTE ONE®

Cost to build? See page 230
to order complete cost estimate
to build this house in your area!

Width 85'-8"
Depth 70'-2"

DESIGN 9740

Square Footage: 1,838

❑ Arched windows and a dramatic arched entry enhance this exciting Southwestern home. The expansive great room, highlighted by a cathedral ceiling and a fireplace, offers direct access to the rear patio and the formal dining room—a winning combination for both formal and informal get-togethers. An efficient U-shaped kitchen provides plenty of counter space and easily serves both the dining room and the great room. Sunlight fills the master bedroom through a wall of windows which affords views of the rear grounds. The master bath invites relaxation with its soothing corner tub and separate shower. Two secondary bedrooms (one serves as an optional study) share an adjacent bath.

Design by
Donald A. Gardner
Architects, Inc.

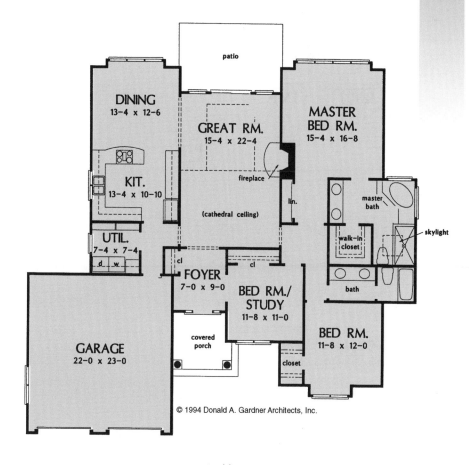

© 1994 Donald A. Gardner Architects, Inc.

Width 60'
Depth 55'

Quote One®

Cost to build? See page 230
to order complete cost estimate
to build this house in your area!

Design by
Home Planners

DESIGN 2950

Square Footage: 2,559

Width 74'
Depth 66'-10"

❏ A natural desert dweller, this stucco, tile-roofed beauty is equally comfortable in any clime. Inside, there's a well-planned design. Common living areas— gathering room, formal dining room and breakfast room—are offset by a quiet study that could be used as a bedroom or guest room. A master suite features two walk-in closets, a double vanity and whirlpool spa. The two-car garage provides a service entrance; close by is an adequate laundry area and a pantry. A lovely hearth warms the gathering room and complements the snack bar area.

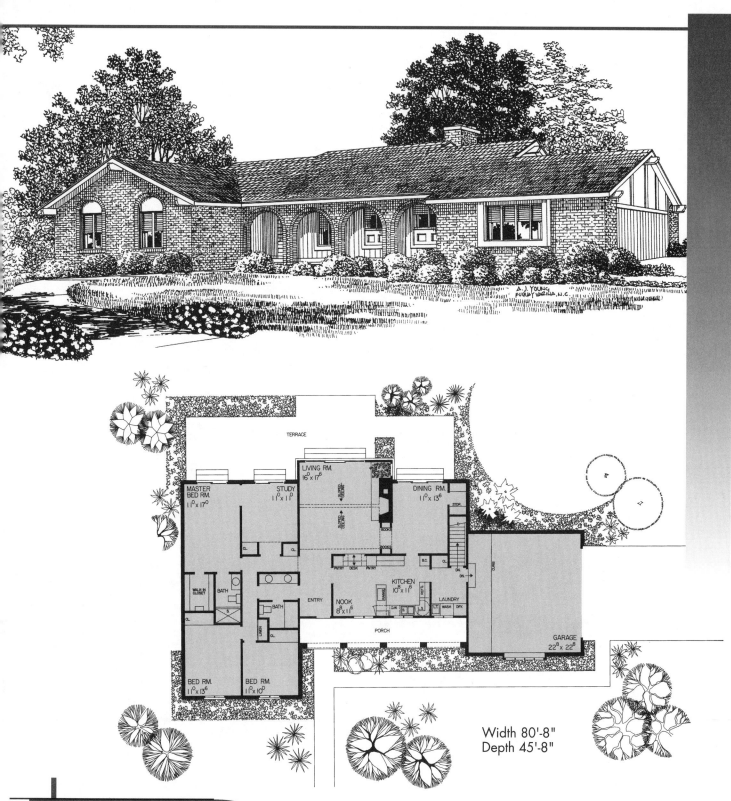

Width 80'-8"
Depth 45'-8"

DESIGN 2557

Square Footage: 1,955

Design by
Home Planners

❏ This eye-catching design with a flavor of the Spanish Southwest will be as interesting to live in as it will be to look at. The character of the exterior is set by the wide overhanging roof with its exposed beams; the massive arched pillars; the arching of the brick over the windows; the panelled door and the horizontal siding that contrasts with the brick. The master bedroom/study suite is a focal point of the interior. However, if neces- sary, the study could become the fourth bedroom. The living and dining rooms are large and are separated by a massive raised-hearth fireplace. Don't miss the planter, the book niches and the china storage. The breakfast nook and the laundry flank the U-shaped kitchen. Notice the twin pantries, the built-in planning desk and the pass-through. A big lazy susan is located to the right of the kitchen sink.

DESIGN 3433

Square Footage: 2,350

L

☐ Santa Fe styling creates interesting angles in this one-story home. A grand entrance leads through a courtyard into the foyer with a circular skylight, closet space, niches and a convenient powder room. Fireplaces in the living room, dining room and on the covered porch create a warming heart of the home. Make note of the island range in the kitchen and the cozy breakfast room adjacent. The master suite has a privacy wall on the covered porch, a deluxe bath and a study close at hand. Two more family bedrooms are placed quietly in the far wing of the house near a segmented family room. The three-car garage offers extra storage.

Design by
Home Planners

QUOTE ONE®

Cost to build? See page 230 to order complete cost estimate to build this house in your area!

Width 92'-7"
Depth 79'

This home, as shown in the photograph, may differ from the actual blueprints. For more detailed information, please check the floor plans carefully.

Photo by Bob Greenspan

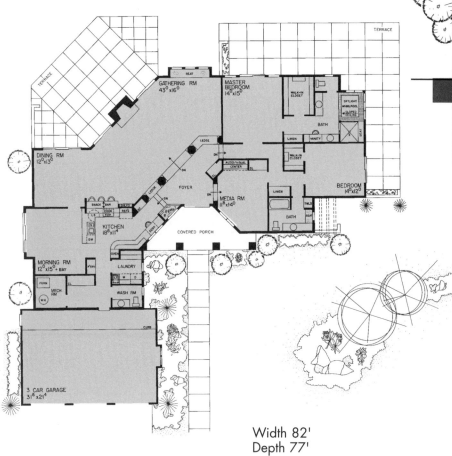

Width 82'
Depth 77'

Design by
Home Planners

DESIGN 2949

Square Footage: 2,922

❏ This one-story matches traditional Southwestern design elements such as stucco, tile and exposed rafters (called vigas) with an up-to-date floor plan. The 43-foot gathering room provides a dramatic multi-purpose living area. Interesting angles highlight the kitchen, which offers plenty of counter and cabinet space, a planning desk, a snack bar pass-through into the gathering room and a morning room with a bumped-out bay. A media room could serve as a third bedroom. The luxurious master bedroom contains a walk-in closet and an amenity-filled bath with a whirlpool tub. A three-car garage easily serves the family fleet.

QUOTE ONE®

Cost to build? See page 230
to order complete cost estimate
to build this house in your area!

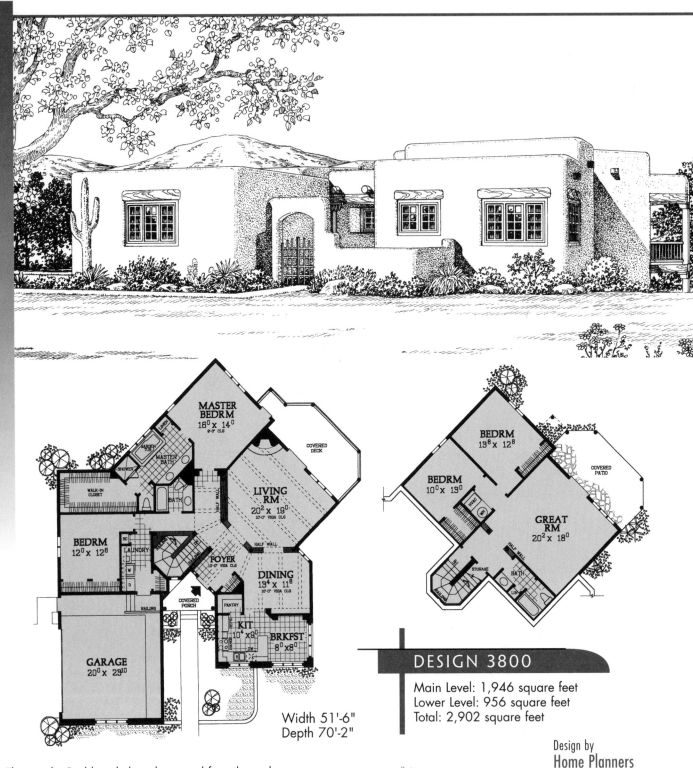

DESIGN 3800

Main Level: 1,946 square feet
Lower Level: 956 square feet
Total: 2,902 square feet

Width 51'-6"
Depth 70'-2"

Design by
Home Planners

❏ The simple, Pueblo-style lines borrowed from the early Native American dwellings combine with contemporary planning for the best possible design. From the front, this home appears to be a one-story. However, a lower level provides a two-story rear elevation, making it ideal for sloping lots. The unique floor plan places a circular staircase to the left of the angled foyer. To the right is an L-shaped kitchen with a walk-in pantry, a sun-filled breakfast room and a formal dining room. Half-walls border the entrance to the formal living room that is warmed by a beehive fireplace. The adjacent covered deck provides shade to the patio below. A roomy master suite, secondary bedroom, full bath and laundry room complete the first floor. The lower level contains a great room, a full bath and two family bedrooms.

Rear Elevation

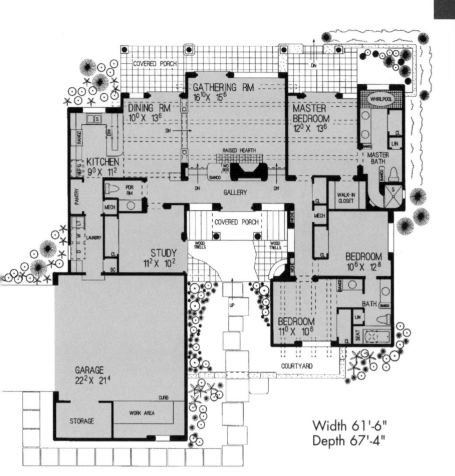

DESIGN 3431

Square Footage: 1,907

❒ Graceful curves welcome you into the courtyard of this Santa Fe home. Inside, a gallery directs traffic to the work zone on the left or the sleeping zone on the right. Straight ahead lies a sunken gathering room with a beam ceiling and a raised-hearth fireplace. A large pantry offers extra storage space for kitchen items. The covered rear porch is accessible from the dining room, gathering room and secluded master bedroom. The master bath has a whirlpool tub, a separate shower, a double vanity and lots of closet space. Two family bedrooms share a compartmented bath.

Width 61'-6"
Depth 67'-4"

Design by
Home Planners

QUOTE ONE®

Cost to build? See page 230
to order complete cost estimate
to build this house in your area!

DESIGN 3403

First Floor: 2,422 square feet
Second Floor: 714 square feet
Total: 3,136 square feet

L

Design by
Home Planners

❐ There is no end to the distinctive features in this Southwestern contemporary. Formal living areas are concentrated in the center of the plan, while the kitchen and family room function well together as an informal living area. The optional guest bedroom or den and the master bedroom are located to the left of the plan. The second floor holds two bedrooms that share a compartmented full bath.

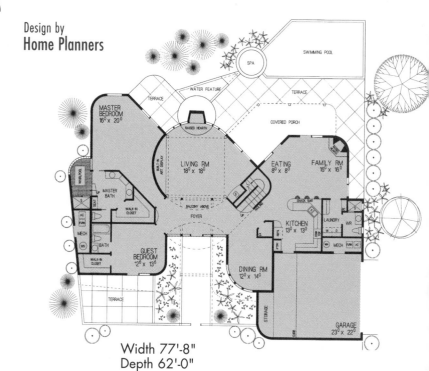

Width 77'-8"
Depth 62'-0"

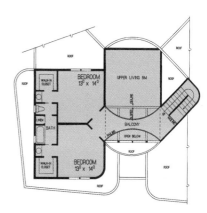

Quote One ®

Cost to build? See page 230 to order complete cost estimate to build this house in your area!

Rear Elevation

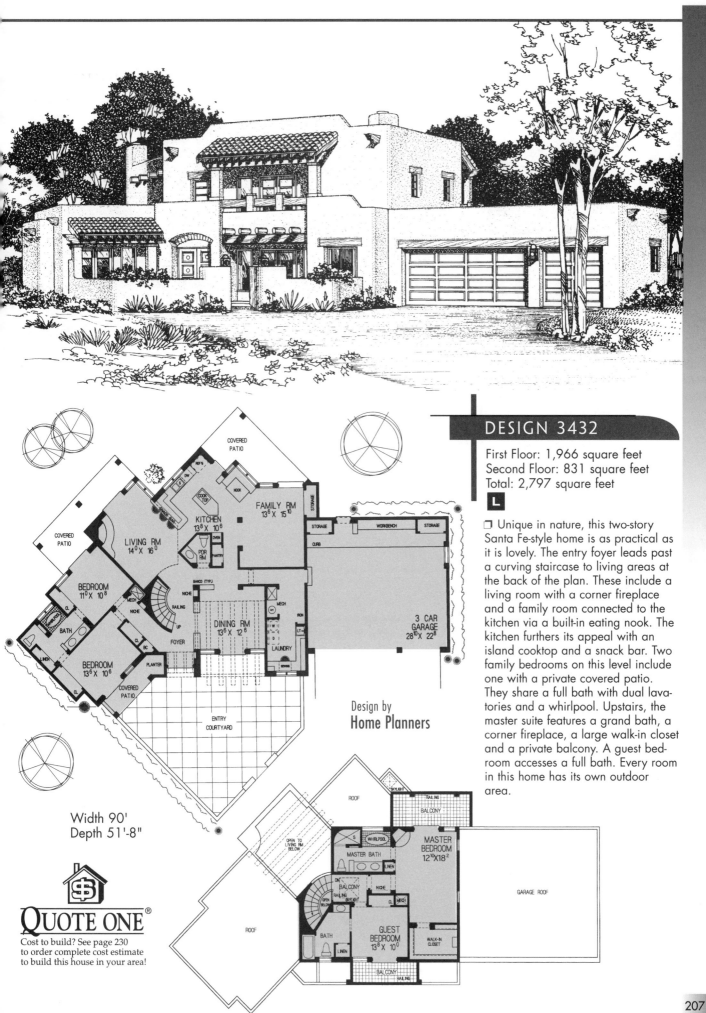

DESIGN 3432

First Floor: 1,966 square feet
Second Floor: 831 square feet
Total: 2,797 square feet

L

❑ Unique in nature, this two-story Santa Fe-style home is as practical as it is lovely. The entry foyer leads past a curving staircase to living areas at the back of the plan. These include a living room with a corner fireplace and a family room connected to the kitchen via a built-in eating nook. The kitchen furthers its appeal with an island cooktop and a snack bar. Two family bedrooms on this level include one with a private covered patio. They share a full bath with dual lavatories and a whirlpool. Upstairs, the master suite features a grand bath, a corner fireplace, a large walk-in closet and a private balcony. A guest bedroom accesses a full bath. Every room in this home has its own outdoor area.

Design by
Home Planners

Width 90'
Depth 51'-8"

QUOTE ONE®

Cost to build? See page 230
to order complete cost estimate
to build this house in your area!

Width 52'
Depth 64'-4"

DESIGN 3425

First Floor: 1,776 square feet
Second Floor: 1,035 square feet
Total: 2,811 square feet

Design by
Home Planners

❏ Here's a two-story Spanish design with an appealing, angled exterior. Inside is an interesting floor plan containing rooms with a variety of shapes. Formal areas are to the right of the entry tower: a sunken living room with a fireplace and a large dining room with access to the rear porch. The kitchen has loads of counter space and is complemented by a bumped-out breakfast room. Note the second fireplace in the family room and the first-floor bedroom which could also be a guest suite. Three second-floor bedrooms radiate around the upper foyer, including the deluxe master suite. Among its many amenities; a private balcony, a walk-in closet and a sumptuous bath.

Quote One®

Cost to build? See page 230 to order complete cost estimate to build this house in your area!

DESIGN 3448

First Floor: 2,495 square feet
Second Floor: 1,080 square feet
Total: 3,575 square feet

L

Width 67'
Depth 72'-6"

❏ The luxurious space provided by each room in this Southwestern design will be the first of many delights. The sunken living room stretches to a full 25 feet, including a romantic bay window. The family room offers entertaining ease with a comfortable fireplace, a wet bar and access to a rear covered patio as well as to the bayed breakfast area (with its coffered ceiling) and the large, well-equipped kitchen. Beyond the dining room is the luxurious master bedroom suite. It features a three-way fireplace, outside access and a master bath with His and Hers walk-in closets and a corner whirlpool. Notice the special amenities found in each of the three upstairs bedrooms. They share a full bath and a sitting area overlooking the upper deck.

QUOTE ONE®

Cost to build? See page 230 to order complete cost estimate to build this house in your area!

Design by
Home Planners

Rear Elevation

This home, as shown in the photograph, may differ from the actual blueprints. For more detailed information, please check the floor plans carefully.

Photo by Bob Greenspan

DESIGN 3441

First Floor: 2,022 square feet
Second Floor: 845 square feet
Total: 2,867 square feet

L

❏ Special details make the difference between a house and this two-story home. A two-story foyer ushers you into a comfortable layout. A snack bar, an audio-visual center, a fireplace and a high, sloped ceiling make the family room a favorite place for informal gathering. A desk, an island cooktop, a bay and skylights enhance the kitchen area. The dining room features two columns and a plant ledge. The formal living room is graced by a sunny bay window, while across the hall a cozy study encourages quiet times. The first-floor master suite includes His and Hers walk-in closets, a spacious bath and a bay window. On the second floor, one bedroom features a walk-in closet and private bath which makes it perfect for a guest suite, while two additional bedrooms share a full bath.

QUOTE ONE®

Cost to build? See page 230 to order complete cost estimate to build this house in your area!

Design by
Home Planners

Width 63'-8"
Depth 56'-2"

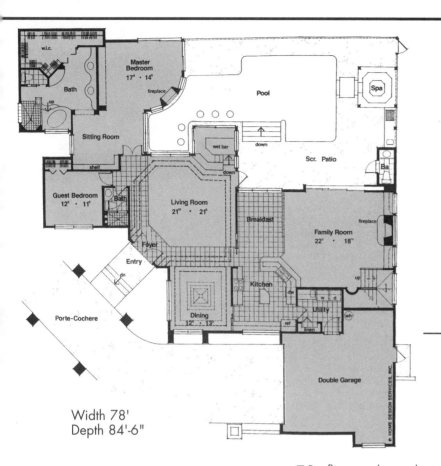

Width 78'
Depth 84'-6"

Design by
**Home Design
Services, Inc.**

DESIGN 8625

First Floor: 2,669 square feet
Second Floor: 621 square feet
Total: 3,290 square feet

❏ Rooflines, arches and corner quoins adorn the facade of this magnificent home. A porte cochere creates a stunning prelude to the double-door entry. A wet bar serves the sunken living room and overlooks the pool area. The dining room has a tray ceiling and is located near the gourmet kitchen with prep island and angled counter. A guest room opens off the living room. The generous family room, warmed by a fireplace, opens to the screened patio. The master bedroom has a sitting room and a fireplace that's set into an angled wall. Its luxurious bath includes a step-up tub. Upstairs, two bedrooms share the oversized balcony and nearby observation room.

This home, as shown in the photograph, may differ from the actual blueprints. For more detailed information, please check the floor plans carefully.

Photo by Home Design Services

DESIGN 3447

First Floor: 1,861 square feet
Second Floor: 1,039 square feet
Total: 2,900 square feet

L D

❏ This classic stucco is designed to make the most of family entertainment. The first floor includes a game room, a front-facing bedroom that would be perfect for out-of-town guests and a large family room with a fireplace and access to a rear covered patio. The spacious, angled kitchen features a snack bar and a corner pantry. It is located conveniently close to both the bay-windowed breakfast room and the combination dining room and living room. The elegant staircase provides a perfect focal point for family portraits or your favorite artist. The master bedroom features a private deck, two closets and a corner whirlpool tub. Two additional bedrooms share a galley-style bath.

Quote One®

Cost to build? See page 230 to order complete cost estimate to build this house in your area!

Design by
Home Planners

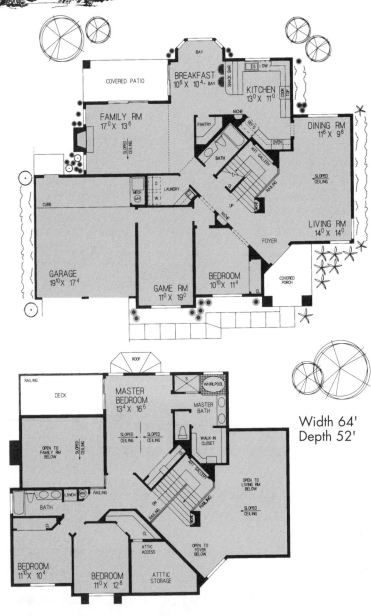

Width 64'
Depth 52'

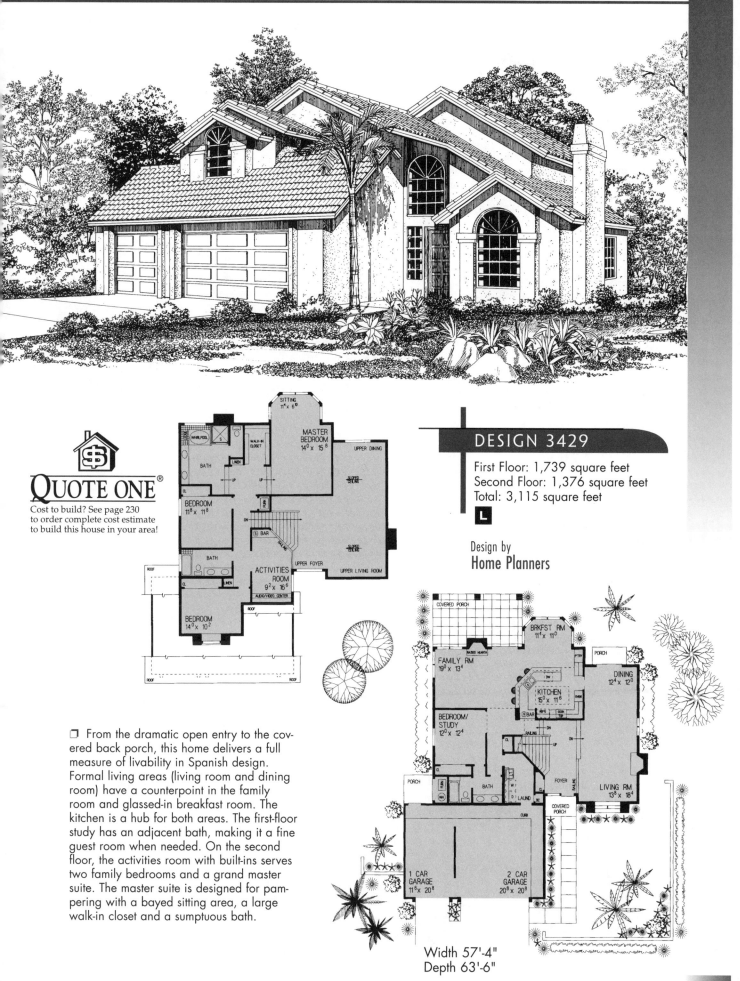

Quote One®

Cost to build? See page 230
to order complete cost estimate
to build this house in your area!

DESIGN 3429

First Floor: 1,739 square feet
Second Floor: 1,376 square feet
Total: 3,115 square feet

L

Design by
Home Planners

❑ From the dramatic open entry to the covered back porch, this home delivers a full measure of livability in Spanish design. Formal living areas (living room and dining room) have a counterpoint in the family room and glassed-in breakfast room. The kitchen is a hub for both areas. The first-floor study has an adjacent bath, making it a fine guest room when needed. On the second floor, the activities room with built-ins serves two family bedrooms and a grand master suite. The master suite is designed for pampering with a bayed sitting area, a large walk-in closet and a sumptuous bath.

Width 57'-4"
Depth 63'-6"

DESIGN 3563

First Floor: 1,023 square feet
Second Floor: 866 square feet
Total: 1,899 square feet

L D

❑ Practical to build, this wonderful transitional plan combines the best of contemporary and traditional styling. Its stucco exterior is enhanced by arched windows and a recessed arched entry plus a lovely balcony off the second-floor master bedroom. A walled entry court extends the living room on the outside. The double front doors open to a foyer with hall closet and powder room. The service entrance is just to the right and accesses the two-car garage. The large living room adjoins directly to the dining room. The family room is set off behind the garage and features a sloped ceiling and fireplace. Sleeping quarters consist of two secondary bedrooms with a shared bath and a generous master suite.

Design by
Home Planners

QUOTE ONE®

Cost to build? See page 230
to order complete cost estimate
to build this house in your area!

Width 52'-4"
Depth 34'-8"

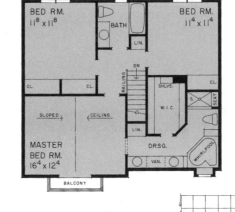

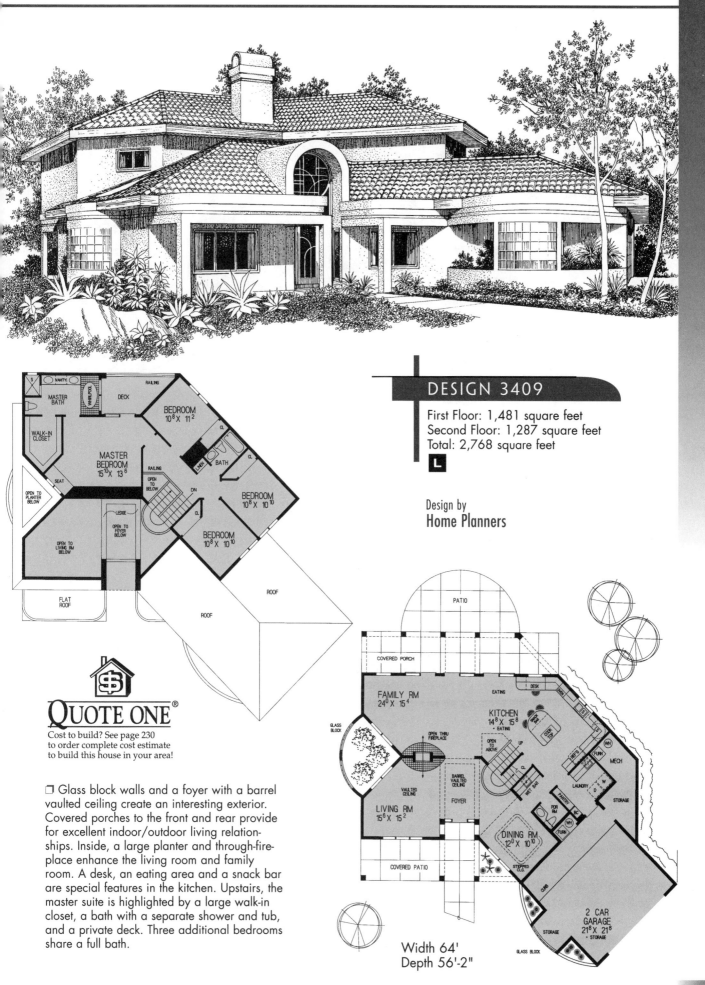

DESIGN 3409

First Floor: 1,481 square feet
Second Floor: 1,287 square feet
Total: 2,768 square feet

L

Design by
Home Planners

QUOTE ONE®

Cost to build? See page 230
to order complete cost estimate
to build this house in your area!

❏ Glass block walls and a foyer with a barrel
vaulted ceiling create an interesting exterior.
Covered porches to the front and rear provide
for excellent indoor/outdoor living relationships. Inside, a large planter and through-fireplace enhance the living room and family
room. A desk, an eating area and a snack bar
are special features in the kitchen. Upstairs, the
master suite is highlighted by a large walk-in
closet, a bath with a separate shower and tub,
and a private deck. Three additional bedrooms
share a full bath.

Width 64'
Depth 56'-2"

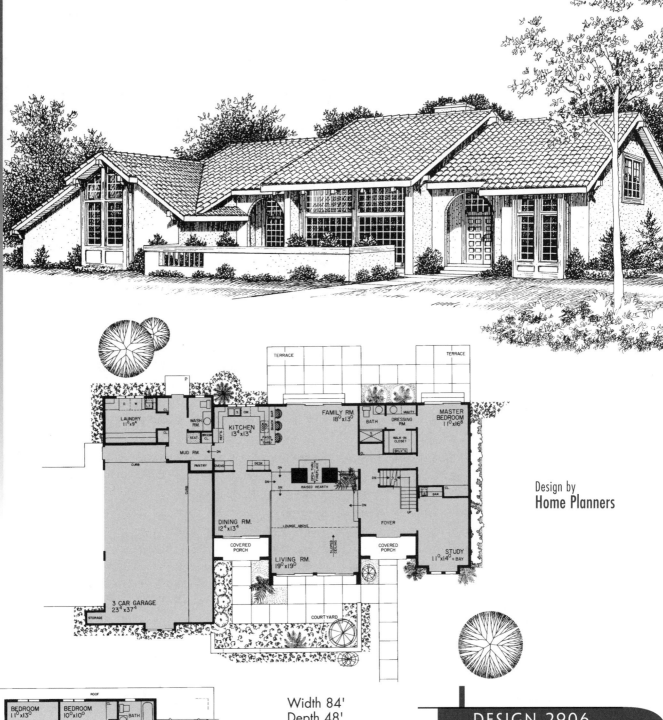

Design by
Home Planners

Width 84'
Depth 48'

DESIGN 2906

First Floor: 2,121 square feet
Second Floor: 913 square feet
Total: 3,034 square feet

L **D**

❒ This striking contemporary design with Spanish good looks offers outstanding livability for today's active lifestyles. A three-car garage opens to a mud room, laundry and wash room. An efficient, spacious kitchen opens to a large dining room, with a pass-through also leading to a family room. The family room and adjoining master bedroom suite overlook a back yard terrace. Just off the master bedroom is a sizable study that opens to a foyer. Stairs just off the foyer make upstairs access quick and easy. The hub of this terrific plan is a living room that faces the front courtyard, and a lounge above the living room. Upstairs, three family bedrooms share a bath and a spacious lounge.

CHAPTER 17

HOMEGROWN RESORTS: *A collection of vacation homes*

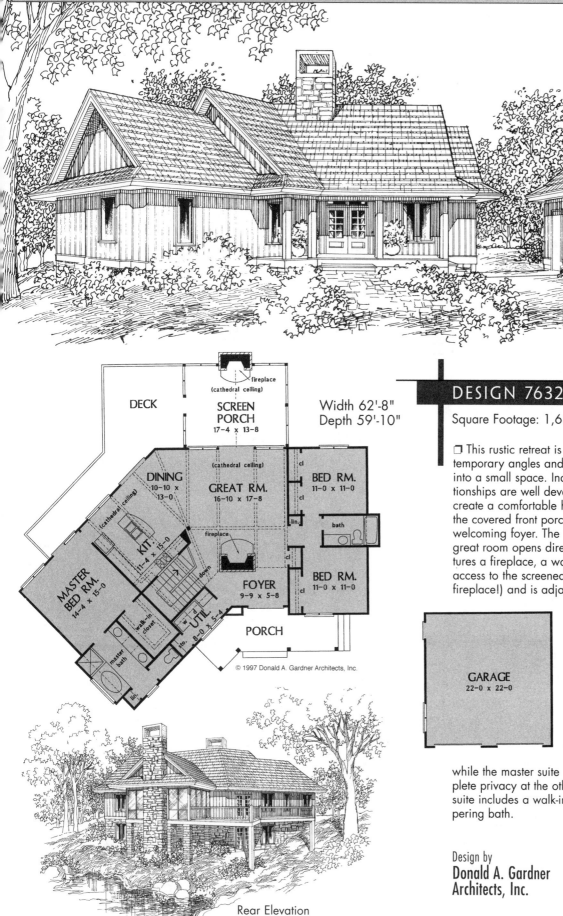

DECK

SCREEN PORCH
17-4 x 13-8

fireplace
(cathedral ceiling)

DINING
10-10 x 13-0

(cathedral ceiling)
GREAT RM.
16-10 x 17-8

KIT.
11-4 x 15-0

fireplace

MASTER BED RM.
14-4 x 15-0

(cathedral ceiling)

walk-in closet

master bath

UTIL
8-0 x 5-4

FOYER
9-9 x 5-8

PORCH

BED RM.
11-0 x 11-0

cl
cl
lin.
bath
cl

BED RM.
11-0 x 11-0

cl

© 1997 Donald A. Gardner Architects, Inc.

Width 62'-8"
Depth 59'-10"

DESIGN 7632

Square Footage: 1,680

❑ This rustic retreat is updated with contemporary angles and packs a lot of living into a small space. Indoor/outdoor relationships are well developed and help to create a comfortable home. Start off with the covered front porch, which leads to a welcoming foyer. The beamed-ceiling great room opens directly ahead and features a fireplace, a wall of windows, access to the screened porch (with its own fireplace!) and is adjacent to the angled dining area. A highly efficient island kitchen is sure to please with a cathedral ceiling, access to the rear deck and tons of counter and cabinet space. Two family bedrooms, sharing a full bath, are located on one end of the plan while the master suite is secluded for complete privacy at the other end. The master suite includes a walk-in closet and a pampering bath.

GARAGE
22-0 x 22-0

Design by
**Donald A. Gardner
Architects, Inc.**

Rear Elevation

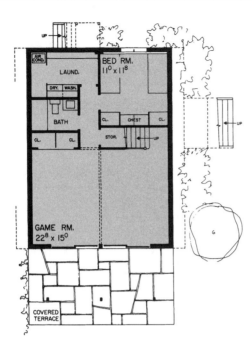

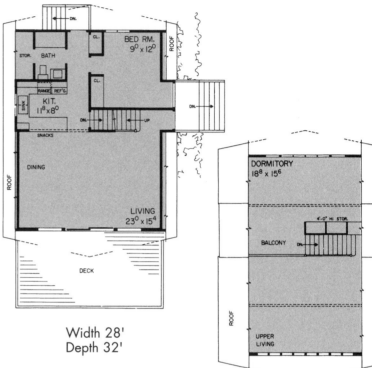

☐ Three levels accommodate family needs with a delightful informality. A dormitory balcony overlooks the main-level living room, which offers deck access. A well-equipped kitchen will easily accommodate meals. The plan offers sleeping quarters on each of the three levels—two bedrooms and a dormitory—plus extra space for games and recreation. Two full baths, a laundry room and extra storage space complete the plan.

DESIGN 1499

Main Level: 896 square feet
Upper Level: 298 square feet
Lower Level: 896 square feet
Total: 2,090 square feet

Design by
Home Planners

Width 28'
Depth 32'

Design by
Home Planners

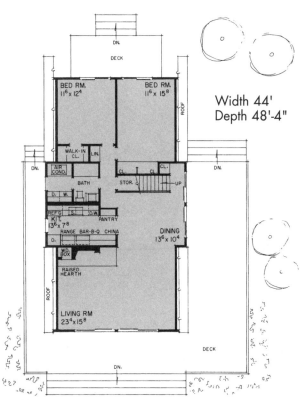

Width 44'
Depth 48'-4"

❒ This dramatic A-frame will surely command its share of attention wherever located. Its soaring roof and large glass areas put this design in a class all on its own. Raised wood decks on all sides provide delightful outdoor living areas. In addition, there is a balcony outside the second floor master bedroom. The living room is the focal point of the interior. The attractive raised-hearth fireplace is a favorite feature. Another favored highlight is the lounge area of the second floor overlooking the living room. The kitchen work center has all the conveniences of home. Note the barbecue unit, pantry and china cabinet which are sure to make living easy. Two secondary bedrooms complete this plan.

DESIGN 1451

First Floor: 1,224 square feet
Second Floor: 464 square feet
Total: 1,688 square feet

DESIGN 1491

First Floor: 576 square feet
Second Floor: 234 square feet
Total: 810 square feet

☐ Wherever situated—in the northern woods, or on the southern coast—this enchanting A-frame will function as a perfect retreat. Whether called upon to serve as a ski lodge or a summer haven, it will perform admirably. The large living/dining room area offers direct access to a huge outdoor deck and an efficient kitchen fulfills all family meal needs. A bedroom and full bath complete this floor. Upstairs is a large loft perfect for bunks or use as a game room.

Design by
Home Planners

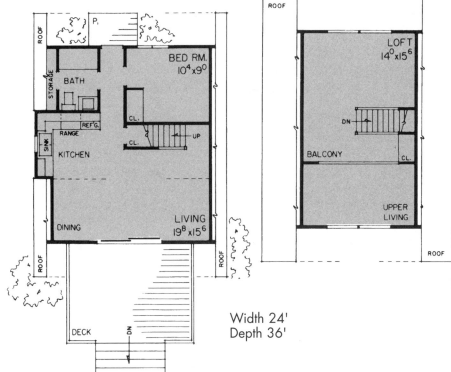

Width 24'
Depth 36'

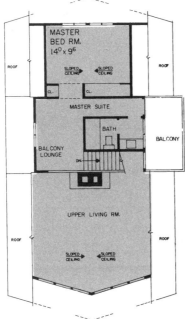

DESIGN 2431

First Floor: 1,057 square feet
Second Floor: 406 square feet
Total: 1,463 square feet

Design by
Home Planners

MASTER
BED RM.
14⁰ x 9⁶

ROOF

ROOF

SLOPED
CEILING

SLOPED
CEILING

CL.

CL.

MASTER SUITE

BATH

BALCONY

BALCONY
LOUNGE

DN.

UPPER LIVING RM.

ROOF

ROOF

SLOPED
CEILING

SLOPED
CEILING

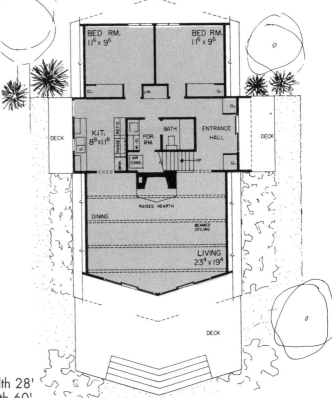

BED RM.
11⁶ x 9⁶

BED RM.
11⁶ x 9⁶

DECK

DECK

CL.

LIN.

CL.

CL.

KIT.
8⁸ x 11⁸

RANGE

REF'S

PDR.
RM.

BATH

ENTRANCE
HALL

W. D.

AIR
COND.

BRM.

UP

RAISED HEARTH

DINING

BEAMED
CEILING

LIVING
23⁴ x 19⁴

DECK

Width 28'
Depth 60'

❒ Dramatic use of glass and sweeping lines characterize a classic favorite—the A-frame. The sloped ceiling
and exposed beams in the living room are gorgeous
touches complemented by a wide deck for enjoying
fresh air. The convenience of the central bath with
attached powder room is accentuated by space here
for washer and dryer. The truly outstanding feature of
this plan, however, is its magnificent master suite.
There's a private balcony outside and a balcony lounge
inside—the scenery is splendid from every angle.

B. NATHAN.

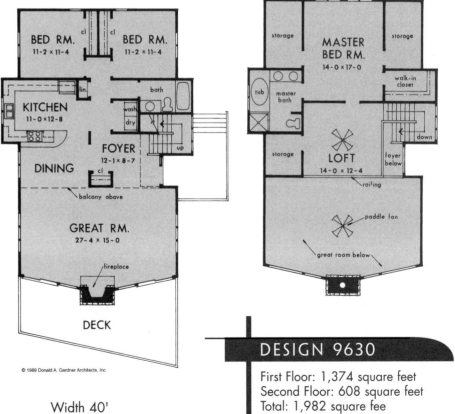

BED RM.
11-2 × 11-4

BED RM.
11-2 × 11-4

KITCHEN
11-0 × 12-8

bath

wash
dry

FOYER
12-1 × 8-7

up

DINING

cl

balcony above

GREAT RM.
27-4 × 15-0

fireplace

DECK

© 1989 Donald A. Gardner Architects, Inc.

Width 40'
Depth 60'-8"

storage

MASTER
BED RM.
14-0 × 17-0

storage

tub

master
bath

walk-in
closet

storage

LOFT
14-0 × 12-4

down

foyer
below

railing

paddle fan

great room below

Design by
Donald A. Gardner
Architects, Inc.

❏ This rustic three-bedroom vacation home allows for casual living both inside and out. The two-level great room offers dramatic space for entertaining with windows to the roof that maximize the outdoor view. A stone fireplace dominates this room. Bedrooms on the first floor share a full bath. The second floor holds the master bedroom with spacious master bath and walk-in closet. A large loft area overlooks the great room and entrance foyer.

DESIGN 9630

First Floor: 1,374 square feet
Second Floor: 608 square feet
Total: 1,982 square fee

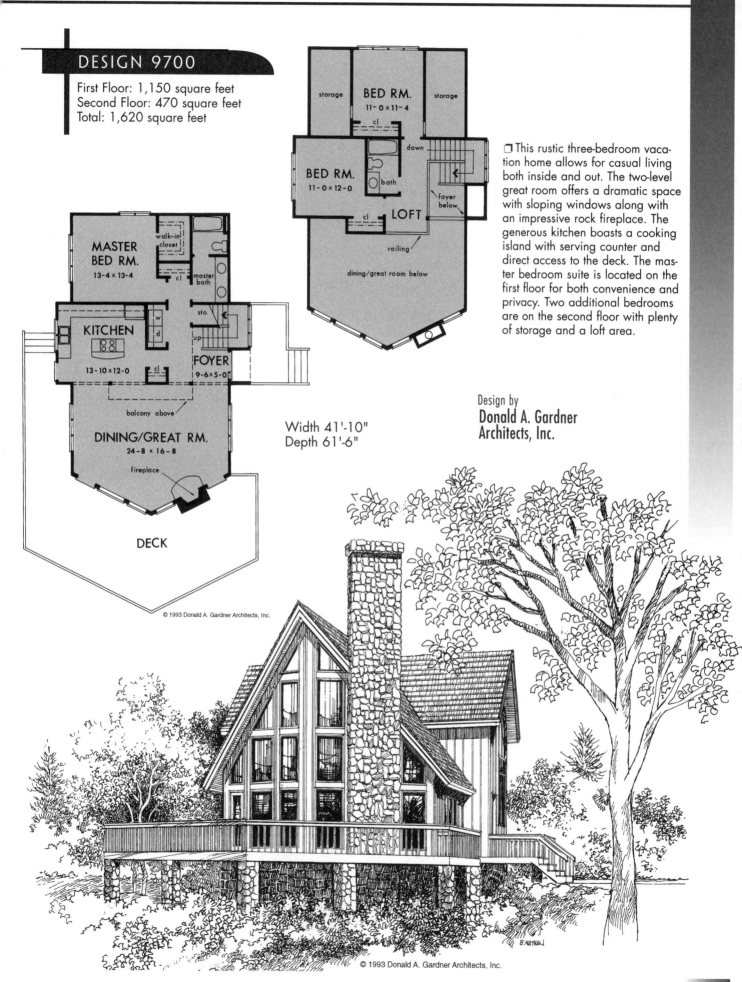

DESIGN 9700

First Floor: 1,150 square feet
Second Floor: 470 square feet
Total: 1,620 square feet

BED RM.
11-0 x 11-4

storage

storage

cl

down

BED RM.
11-0 x 12-0

bath

foyer below

cl

LOFT

railing

dining/great room below

❏ This rustic three-bedroom vacation home allows for casual living both inside and out. The two-level great room offers a dramatic space with sloping windows along with an impressive rock fireplace. The generous kitchen boasts a cooking island with serving counter and direct access to the deck. The master bedroom suite is located on the first floor for both convenience and privacy. Two additional bedrooms are on the second floor with plenty of storage and a loft area.

MASTER BED RM.
13-4 x 13-4

walk-in closet

cl

master bath

KITCHEN
13-10 x 12-0

w

d

sto.

up

cl

FOYER
9-6 x 5-0

balcony above

DINING/GREAT RM.
24-8 x 16-8

fireplace

DECK

Width 41'-10"
Depth 61'-6"

Design by
Donald A. Gardner Architects, Inc.

B.NATHAN

Design by
Home Planners

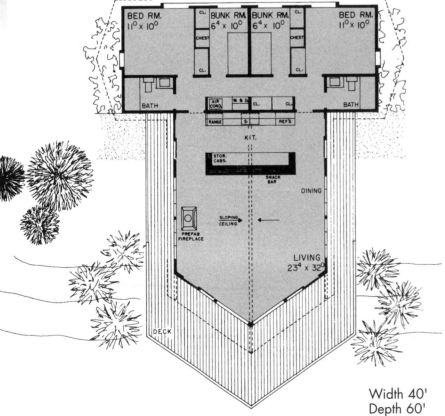

BED RM.
11⁰ x 10⁰

BUNK RM.
6⁴ x 10⁰

BUNK RM.
6⁴ x 10⁰

BED RM.
11⁰ x 10⁰

CHEST

CHEST

BATH

BATH

AIR COND.

W. & D.

RANGE

REF'G.

KIT.

STOR. CABS.

SNACK BAR

DINING

PREFAB FIREPLACE

SLOPING CEILING

LIVING
23⁴ x 32⁰

DECK

Width 40'
Depth 60'

DESIGN 2439

Square Footage: 1,312

❏ Here is a wonderfully organized plan with an exterior that will command the attention of each and every passerby. The rooflines and the pointed glass gable-end wall will be noticed immediately—the delightful deck will be quickly noticed, too. Inside visitors will be thrilled by the spaciousness of the huge living room. The ceilings slope upward to the exposed ridge beam. A free-standing fireplace will make its contribution to a cheerful atmosphere. The sleeping zone has two bedrooms, two bunk rooms, two full baths, two built-in chests and fine closet space.

DESIGN 2423

Square Footage: 864

❏ A true vacationer's delight, this two-bedroom home extends the finest contemporary livability. Two sets of sliding glass doors open off the kitchen and living room where a sloped ceiling lends added dimension. In the kitchen, full counter space and cabinetry assure ease in meal preparation. A pantry stores all of your canned and boxed goods. In the living room, a fireplace serves as a nice design as well as a practical feature. The rear of the plan is comprised of two bedrooms of identical size. A nearby full bath holds a washer/dryer unit. Two additional closets, as well as two linen closets, add to storage capabilities.

Design by
Home Planners

Width 34'-8"
Depth 48'

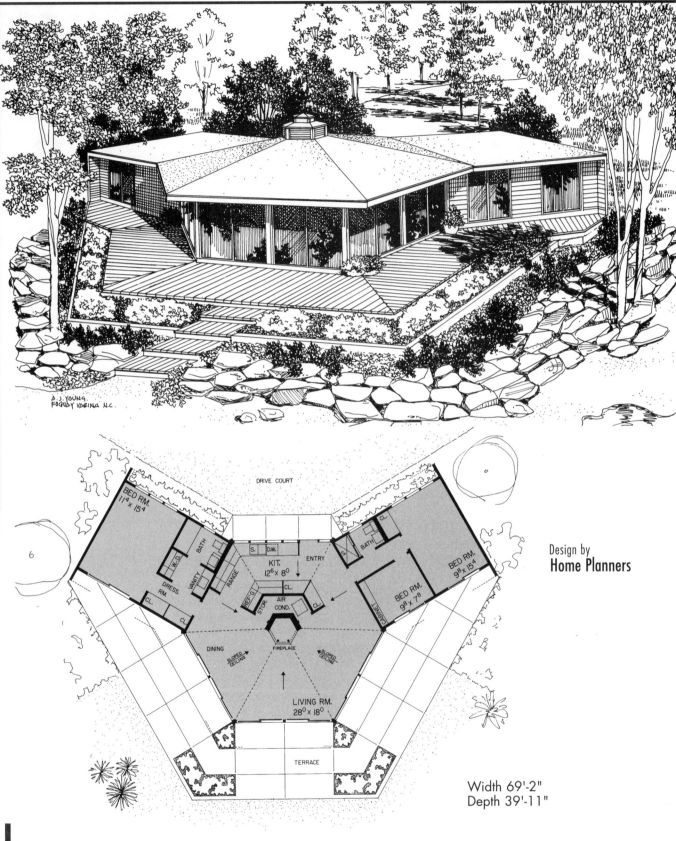

A.J. YOUNG
FUQUAY VARINA N.C.

DRIVE COURT

BED RM.
11⁴ x 15⁴

BATH

CL.

BATH

W.D.

VANITY

RANGE

S.

D.W.

KIT.
12⁶ x 8⁰

ENTRY

CL.

S.

CABINET

CL.

BED RM.
9⁸ x 15⁴

DRESS.
RM.

REF'G.

STOR.

AIR
COND.

CL.

BED RM.
9⁸ x 7⁸

CL.

CL.

DINING

SLOPED
CEILING

FIREPLACE

SLOPED
CEILING

6

Design by
Home Planners

LIVING RM.
28⁰ x 18⁰

TERRACE

Width 69'-2"
Depth 39'-11"

DESIGN 1404

Square Footage: 1,336

❏ Here is an exciting design, unusual in character, yet fun to live in. This design, with its frame exterior and large glass areas, has as its dramatic focal point a hexagonal living area that gives way to interesting angles. The spacious living area features sliding glass doors through which traffic may pass to the terrace stretching across the entire length of the house. The wide overhanging roofs project over the terraces, thus providing partial protection from the weather. The sloping ceilings converge above the unique, open fireplace. The sleeping areas are located in each wing from the hexagonal center.

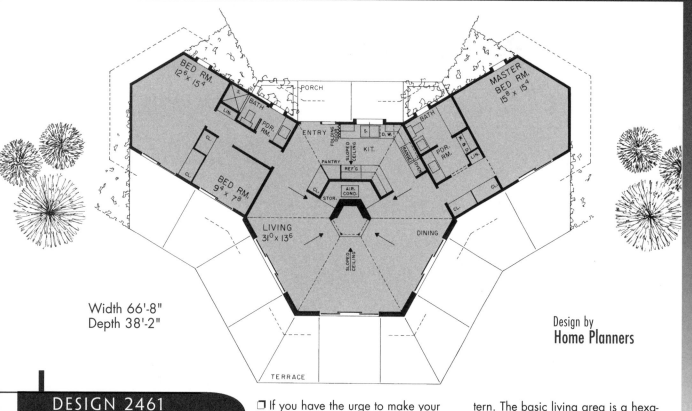

Width 66'-8"
Depth 38'-2"

Design by
Home Planners

DESIGN 2461

Square Footage: 1,400

❒ If you have the urge to make your vacation home one that has a distinctive flair of individuality, definite consideration should be given to the design illustrated here. Not only does this plan present a unique exterior, but it also offers an exceptional living pattern. The basic living area is a hexagon. To this space, conscious geometric shape is incorporated with the sleeping wings and baths. The center of the living area enjoys a warming fireplace as its focal point.

When You're Ready To Order . . .

Let Us Show You Our Home Blueprint Package.

Building a home? Planning a home? Our Blueprint Package has nearly everything you need to get the job done right, whether you're working on your own or with help from an architect, designer, builder or subcontractors. Each Blueprint Package is the result of many hours of work by licensed architects or professional designers.

QUALITY

Hundreds of hours of painstaking effort have gone into the development of your blueprint set. Each home has been quality-checked by professionals to insure accuracy and buildability.

VALUE

Because we sell in volume, you can buy professional-quality blueprints at a fraction of their development cost. With our plans, your dream home design costs only a few hundred dollars, not the thousands of dollars that custom architects charge.

SERVICE

Once you've chosen your favorite home plan, you'll receive fast, efficient service whether you choose to mail or fax your order to us or call us toll free at 1-800-521-6797. For customer service, call toll free 1-888-690-1116.

SATISFACTION

Over 50 years of service to satisfied home plan buyers provide us unparalleled experience and knowledge in producing quality blueprints. What this means to you is satisfaction with our product and performance.

ORDER TOLL FREE 1-800-521-6797

After you've looked over our Blueprint Package and Important Extras on the following pages, simply mail the order form on page 237 or call toll free on our Blueprint Hotline: 1-800-521-6797. We're ready and eager to serve you. For customer service, call toll free 1-888-690-1116.

Each set of blueprints is an interrelated collection of detail sheets which includes components such as floor plans, interior and exterior elevations, dimensions, cross-sections, diagrams and notations. These sheets show exactly how your house is to be built.

Among the sheets included may be:

Frontal Sheet
This artist's sketch of the exterior of the house gives you an idea of how the house will look when built and landscaped. Large ink-line floor plans show all levels of the house and provide an overview of your new home's livability, as well as a handy reference for deciding on furniture placement.

Foundation Plans
These plans show the foundation layout

SAMPLE PACKAGE

including support walls, excavated and unexcavated areas, if any, and foundation notes. If slab construction rather than basement, the plan shows footings and details for a monolithic slab. This page, or another in the set, may include a sample plot plan for locating your house on a building site.

Detailed Floor Plans

These plans show the layout of each floor of the house. Rooms and interior spaces are carefully dimensioned and keys are given for cross-section details provided later in the plans. The positions of electrical outlets and switches are shown.

House Cross-Sections

Large-scale views show sections or cut-aways of the foundation, interior walls, exterior walls, floors, stairways and roof details. Additional cross-sections may show important changes in floor, ceiling or roof heights or the relationship of one level to another. Extremely valuable for construction, these sections show exactly how the various parts of the house fit together.

Interior Elevations

Many of our drawings show the design and placement of kitchen and bathroom cabinets, laundry areas, fireplaces, bookcases and other built-ins. Little "extras," such as mantelpiece and wainscoting drawings, plus moulding sections, provide details that give your home that custom touch.

Exterior Elevations

These drawings show the front, rear and sides of your house and give necessary notes on exterior materials and finishes. Particular attention is given to cornice detail, brick and stone accents or other finish items that make your home unique.

Frontal Sheet

Foundation Plans

Detailed Floor Plans

Exterior Elevations

Interior Elevations

House Cross-Sections

Important Extras To Do The Job Right!

Introducing eight important planning and construction aids developed by our professionals to help you succeed in your home-building project.

MATERIALS LIST

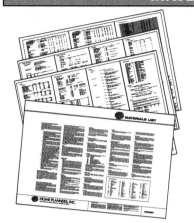

(Note: Because of the diversity of local building codes, our Materials List does not include mechanical materials.)

For many of the designs in our portfolio, we offer a customized materials take-off that is invaluable in planning and estimating the cost of your new home. This Materials List outlines the quantity, type and size of materials needed to build your house (with the exception of mechanical system items). Included are framing lumber, windows and doors, kitchen and bath cabinetry, rough and finish hardware, and much more. This handy list helps you or your builder cost out materials and serves as a reference sheet when you're compiling bids. A Materials List cannot be ordered before blueprints are ordered.

SPECIFICATION OUTLINE

This valuable 16-page document is critical to building your house correctly. Designed to be filled in by you or your builder, this book lists 166 stages or items crucial to the building process. It provides a comprehensive review of the construction process and helps in choosing materials. When combined with the blueprints, a signed contract, and a schedule, it becomes a legal document and record for the building of your home.

QUOTE ONE®

Summary Cost Report / Materials Cost Report

A new service for estimating the cost of building select designs, the Quote One® system is available in two separate stages: The Summary Cost Report and the Materials Cost Report.

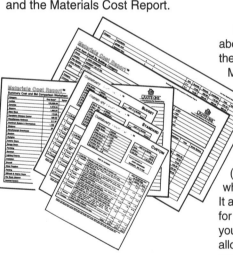

The Summary Cost Report is the first stage in the package and shows the total cost per square foot for your chosen home in your zip-code area and then breaks that cost down into various categories showing the costs for building materials, labor and installation. The total cost for the report (which includes three grades: Budget, Standard and Custom) is just $29.95 for one home, and additionals are only $14.95. These reports allow you to evaluate your building budget and compare the costs of building a variety of homes in your area.

Make even more informed decisions about your home-building project with the second phase of our package, our Materials Cost Report. This tool is invaluable in planning and estimating the cost of your new home. The material and installation (labor and equipment) cost is shown for each of over 1,000 line items provided in the Materials List (Standard grade), which is included when you purchase this estimating tool. It allows you to determine building costs for your specific zip-code area and for your chosen home design. Space is allowed for additional estimates from contractors and subcontractors, such as for mechanical materials, which are not included in our packages. This invaluable tool is available for a price of $120 ($130 for Schedules C4-L4 plans), which includes a Materials List. A Materials Cost Report cannot be ordered before blueprints are ordered.

The Quote One® program is continually updated with new plans. If you are interested in a plan that is not indicated as Quote One®, please call and ask our sales reps. They will be happy to verify the status for you. To order these invaluable reports, use the order form on page 237 or call 1-800-521-6797.

CONSTRUCTION INFORMATION

If you want to know more about techniques—and deal more confidently with subcontractors—we offer these useful sheets. Each set is an excellent tool that will add to your understanding of these technical subjects.

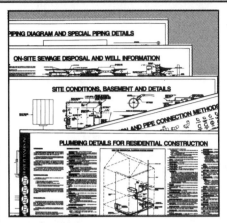

PLUMBING

The Blueprint Package includes locations for all the plumbing fixtures in your new house, including sinks, lavatories, tubs, showers, toilets, laundry trays and water heaters. However, if you want to know more about the complete plumbing system, these 24x36-inch detail sheets will prove very useful. Prepared to meet requirements of the National Plumbing Code, these six fact-filled sheets give general information on pipe schedules, fittings, sump-pump details, water-softener hookups, septic system details and much more. Color-coded sheets include a glossary of terms.

ELECTRICAL

The locations for every electrical switch, plug and outlet are shown in your Blueprint Package. However, these Electrical Details go further to take the mystery out of household electrical systems. Prepared to meet requirements of the National Electrical Code, these comprehensive 24x36-inch drawings come packed with helpful information, including wire sizing, switch-installation schematics, cable-routing details, appliance wattage, door-bell hookups, typical service panel circuitry and much more. Six sheets are bound together and color-coded for easy reference. A glossary of terms is also included.

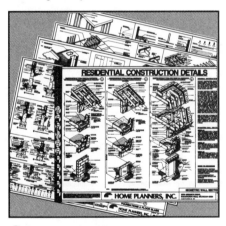

CONSTRUCTION

The Blueprint Package contains everything an experienced builder needs to construct a particular house. However, it doesn't show all the ways that houses can be built, nor does it explain alternate construction methods. To help you understand how your house will be built—and offer additional techniques—this set of drawings depicts the materials and methods used to build foundations, fireplaces, walls, floors and roofs. Where appropriate, the drawings show acceptable alternatives. These six sheets will answer questions for the advanced do-it-yourselfer or home planner.

MECHANICAL

This package contains fundamental principles and useful data that will help you make informed decisions and communicate with subcontractors about heating and cooling systems. The 24x36-inch drawings contain instructions and samples that allow you to make simple load calculations and preliminary sizing and costing analysis. Covered are today's most commonly used systems from heat pumps to solar fuel systems. The package is packed full of illustrations and diagrams to help you visualize components and how they relate to one another.

Plan-A-Home®

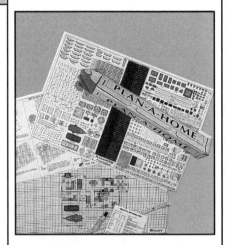

Plan-A-Home® is an easy-to-use tool that helps you design a new home, arrange furniture in a new or existing home, or plan a remodeling project. Each package contains:

- **More than 700 reusable peel-off planning symbols** on a self-stick vinyl sheet, including walls, windows, doors, all types of furniture, kitchen components, bath fixtures and many more.

- **A reusable, transparent, ¼-inch scale planning grid** that matches the scale of actual working drawings (¼-inch equals one foot). This grid provides the basis for house layouts of up to 140x92 feet.

- **Tracing paper** and a protective sheet for copying or transferring your completed plan.

- **A felt-tip pen,** with water-soluble ink that wipes away quickly.

Plan-A-Home® lets you lay out areas as large as a 7,500 square foot, six-bedroom, seven-bath house.

To Order, Call Toll Free 1-800-521-6797

To add these important extras to your Blueprint Package, simply indicate your choices on the order form on page 237 or call us Toll Free 1-800-521-6797 and we'll tell you more about these exciting products. For Customer Service, call toll free 1-888-690-1116.

◨ *The Deck Blueprint Package*

Many of the homes in this book can be enhanced with a professionally designed Home Planners Deck Plan. Those home plans highlighted with a ◨ have a matching or corresponding deck plan available which includes a Deck Plan Frontal Sheet, Deck Framing and Floor Plans, Deck Elevations and a Deck Materials List. A Standard Deck Details Package, also available, provides all the how-to information necessary for building *any* deck. Our Complete Deck Building Package contains one set of Custom Deck Plans of your choice, plus one set of Standard Deck Building Details all for one low price. Our plans and details are carefully prepared in an easy-to-understand format that will guide you through every stage of your deck-building project. This page contains a sampling of 12 of the 25 different Deck layouts to match your favorite house. See page 234 for prices and ordering information.

SPLIT-LEVEL SUN DECK
Deck Plan D100

BI-LEVEL DECK WITH COVERED DINING
Deck Plan D101

WRAPAROUND FAMILY DECK
Deck Plan D104

DECK FOR DINING AND VIEWS
Deck Plan D107

TREND-SETTER DECK
Deck Plan D110

TURN-OF-THE-CENTURY DECK
Deck Plan D111

WEEKEND ENTERTAINER DECK
Deck Plan D112

CENTER-VIEW DECK
Deck Plan D114

KITCHEN-EXTENDER DECK
Deck Plan D115

SPLIT-LEVEL ACTIVITY DECK
Deck Plan D117

TRI-LEVEL DECK WITH GRILL
Deck Plan D119

CONTEMPORARY LEISURE DECK
Deck Plan D120

⊞ *The Landscape Blueprint Package*

For the homes marked with an ⊞ in this book, Home Planners has created a front-yard landscape plan that matches or is complementary in design to the house plan. These comprehensive blueprint packages include a Frontal Sheet, Plan View, Regionalized Plant & Materials List, a sheet on Planting and Maintaining Your Landscape, Zone Maps and Plant Size and Description Guide. These plans will help you achieve professional results, adding value and enjoyment to your property for years to come. Each set of blueprints is a full 18" x 24" in size with clear, complete instructions and easy-to-read type. Six of the forty front-yard Landscape Plans to match your favorite house are shown below.

Regional Order Map

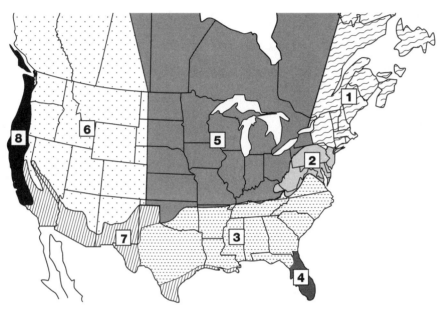

Most of the Landscape Plans shown on these pages are available with a Plant & Materials List adapted by horticultural experts to 8 different regions of the country. Please specify Geographic Region when ordering your plan. See pages 234-235 for prices, ordering information and regional availability. When you're ready to order, please turn to page 237.

Region	1	Northeast
Region	2	Mid-Atlantic
Region	3	Deep South
Region	4	Florida & Gulf Coast
Region	5	Midwest
Region	6	Rocky Mountains
Region	7	Southern California & Desert Southwest
Region	8	Northern California & Pacific Northwest

CAPE COD COTTAGE
Landscape Plan L202

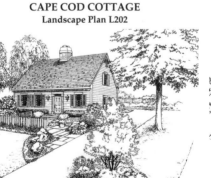

GAMBREL-ROOF COLONIAL
Landscape Plan L203

CENTER-HALL COLONIAL
Landscape Plan L204

CLASSIC NEW ENGLAND COLONIAL
Landscape Plan L205

COUNTRY-STYLE FARMHOUSE
Landscape Plan L207

TRADITIONAL SPLIT-LEVEL
Landscape Plan L228

Price Schedule & Plans Index

Blueprint Price Schedule
(Prices guaranteed through December 31, 2000)

Tiers	1-set Study Package	4-set Building Package	8-set Building Package	1-set Reproducible Sepias	Home Customizer® Package
P1	$20	$50	$90	N/A	N/A
P2	$40	$70	$110	N/A	N/A
P3	$60	$90	$130	N/A	N/A
P4	$80	$110	$150	N/A	N/A
P5	$100	$130	$170	N/A	N/A
P6	$120	$150	$190	N/A	N/A
A1	$400	$440	$500	$600	$650
A2	$440	$480	$540	$660	$710
A3	$480	$520	$580	$720	$770
A4	$520	$560	$620	$780	$830
C1	$560	$600	$660	$840	$890
C2	$600	$640	$700	$900	$950
C3	$650	$690	$750	$950	$1000
C4	$700	$740	$800	$1000	$1050
L1	$750	$790	$850	$1050	$1100
L2	$800	$840	$900	$1100	$1150
L3	$900	$940	$1000	$1200	$1250
L4	$1000	$1040	$1100	$1300	$1350

Options for plans in Tiers A1–A4
Additional Identical Blueprints in same order for "A1–L4" price plans....................$50 per set
Reverse Blueprints (mirror image) with 4- or 8-set order for "A1–L4" price plans............$50 fee per order
Specification Outlines...............................$10 each
Materials Lists for "A1–C3" price plans..........$60 each
Materials Lists for "C4–L4" price plans...........$70 each

Options for plans in Tiers P1–P6
Additional Identical Blueprints in same order for "P1–P6" price plans.....................................$10 per set
Reverse Blueprints (mirror image) for "P1–P6" price plans..$10 per set
1 Set of Deck Construction Details...............$14.95 each
Deck Construction Package............add $10 to Building Package price
   (1 set of "P1–P6" price plans, plus 1 set Standard Deck Construction Details)
1 Set of Gazebo Construction Details..........$14.95 each
Gazebo Construction Package.......add $10 to Building Package price
   (1 set of "P1–P6" price plans, plus 1 set Standard Gazebo Construction Details)

IMPORTANT NOTES
The 1-set study package is marked "not for construction." Prices for 4- or 8-set Building Packages honored only at time of original order.

Index

To use the Index below, refer to the design number listed in numerical order (a helpful page reference is also given). Note the price index letter and refer to the House Blueprint Price Schedule above for the cost of one, four or eight sets of blueprints or the cost of a reproducible sepia. Additional prices are shown for identical and reverse blueprint sets, as well as other very useful products for many of the plans. Also note in the Index below those plans that have matching or complementary Deck Plans or Landscape Plans. Refer to the schedules above for prices of these plans. All plans in this publication are customizable. However, only Home Planners plans can be customized with Home Planners Home Customizer® Package. These plans are indicated below with this symbol: ♠. See page 237 for information. Some plans are also part of our Quote One® estimating service and are indicated by this symbol: ⌂. Many plans offer Materials Lists and are indicated by this symbol: ✓. See page 230 for more information.

To Order: Fill in and send the order form on page 237—or call toll free 1-800-521-6797 or 520-297-8200. Fax: 1-800-224-6699 or 520-544-3086.

Before You Order . . .

Before filling out the coupon at right or calling us on our Toll-Free Blueprint Hotline, you may want to learn more about our services and products. Here's some information you will find helpful.

Quick Turnaround
We process and ship every blueprint order from our office within two business days. Because of this quick turnaround, we won't send a formal notice acknowledging receipt of your order.

Our Exchange Policy
Since blueprints are printed in response to your order, we cannot honor requests for refunds. However, we will exchange your entire first order for an equal number of blueprints at a price of $50 for the first set and $10 for each additional set; $70 total exchange fee for 4 sets; $100 total exchange fee for 8 sets . . . *plus* the difference in cost if exchanging for a design in a higher price bracket or *less* the difference in cost if exchanging for a design in lower price bracket. One exchange is allowed within a year of purchase date. **(Sepias and reproducibles are not refundable, returnable or exchangeable.)** All sets from the first order must be returned before the exchange can take place. Please add $18 for postage and handling via Regular Service; $30 via Priority Service; $40 via Express Service. Returns and cancellations are subject to a 20% restocking fee, and shipping and handling charges are not refundable.

About Reverse Blueprints
If you want to build in reverse of the plan as shown, we will include an extra set of reverse blueprints (mirror image) for an additional fee of $50. Although lettering and dimensions will appear backward, reverses will be a useful aid if you decide to flop the plan.

Revising, Modifying and Customizing Plans
The wide variety of designs available in this publication allows you to select ideas and concepts for a home to fit your building site and match your family's needs, wants and budget. Like many homeowners who buy these plans, you and your builder, architect or engineer may want to make changes to them. Some minor changes may be made by your builder, but we recommend that most changes be made by a licensed architect or engineer. If you need to make alterations to a design that is customizable, you need only order our Home Customizer® Package to get you started. As set forth below, we cannot assume any responsibility for blueprints which have been changed, whether by you, your builder or by professionals selected by you or referred to you by us, because such individuals are outside our supervision and control.

Architectural and Engineering Seals
Some cities and states are now requiring that a licensed architect or engineer review and "seal" a blueprint, or officially approve it, prior to construction due to concerns over energy costs, safety and other factors. Prior to application for a building permit or the start of actual construction, we strongly advise that you consult your local building official who can tell you if such a review is required.

About the Designers
The architects and designers whose work appears in this publication are among America's leading residential designers. Each plan was designed to meet the requirements of a nationally recognized model building code in effect at the time and place the plan was drawn. Because national building codes change from time to time, plans may not comply with any such code at the time they are sold to a customer. In addition, building officials may not accept these plans as final construction documents of record as the plans may need to be modified and additional drawings and details added to suit local conditions and requirements. We strongly advise that purchasers consult a licensed architect or engineer, and their local building official, before starting any construction related to these plans.

Local Building Codes and Zoning Requirements
At the time of creation, our plans are drawn to specifications published by the Building Officials and Code Administrators (BOCA) International, Inc.; the Southern Building Code Congress (SBCCI) International, Inc.; the International Conference of Building Officials; or the Council of American Building Officials (CABO). Our plans are designed to meet or exceed national building standards. Because of the great differences in geography and climate throughout the United States and Canada, each state, county and municipality has its own building codes, zone requirements, ordinances and building regulations. Your plan may need to be modified to comply with local requirements regarding snow loads, energy codes, soil and seismic conditions and a wide range of other matters. In addition, you may need to obtain permits or inspections from local governments before and in the course of construction. Prior to using blueprints ordered from us, we strongly advise that you consult a licensed architect or engineer—and speak with your local building official—before applying for any permit or beginning construction. We authorize the use of our blueprints on the express condition that you strictly comply with all local building codes, zoning requirements and other applicable laws, regulations, ordinances and requirements. **Notice: Plans for homes to be built in Nevada must be redrawn by a Nevada-registered professional. Consult your building official for more information on this subject.**

Foundation and Exterior Wall Changes
Most of our plans are drawn with either a full or partial basement foundation. Depending on your specific climate or regional building practices, you may wish to change this basement to a slab or crawlspace. Most professional contractors and builders can easily adapt your plans to alternate foundation types. Likewise, most can easily change 2x4 wall construction to 2x6, or vice versa.

Disclaimer
We and the designers we work with have put substantial care and effort into the creation of our blueprints. However, because we cannot provide on-site consultation, supervision and control over actual construction, and because of the great variance in local building requirements, building practices and soil, seismic, weather and other conditions, WE CANNOT MAKE ANY WARRANTY, EXPRESS OR IMPLIED, WITH RESPECT TO THE CONTENT OR USE OF OUR BLUEPRINTS, INCLUDING BUT NOT LIMITED TO ANY WARRANTY OF MERCHANTABILITY OR OF FITNESS FOR A PARTICULAR PURPOSE.

Terms and Conditions
These designs are protected under the terms of United States Copyright Law and may not be copied or reproduced in any way, by any means, unless you have purchased Sepias or Reproducibles which clearly indicate your right to copy or reproduce. We authorize the use of your chosen design as an aid in the construction of one single family home only. You may not use this design to build a second or multiple dwellings without purchasing another blueprint or blueprints or paying additional design fees.

How Many Blueprints Do You Need?
A single set of blueprints is sufficient to study a home in greater detail. However, if you are planning to obtain cost estimates from a contractor or subcontractors—or if you are planning to build immediately—you will need more sets. Because additional sets are cheaper when ordered in quantity with the original order, make sure you order enough blueprints to satisfy all requirements. The following checklist will help you determine how many you need:

____ Owner

____ Builder (generally requires at least three sets; one as a legal document, one to use during inspections, and at least one to give to subcontractors)

____ Local Building Department (often requires two sets)

____ Mortgage Lender (usually one set for a conventional loan; three sets for FHA or VA loans)

____ TOTAL NUMBER OF SETS

Have You Seen Our Newest Designs?

Home Planners is one of the country's most active home design firms, creating nearly 100 new plans each year. At least 50 of our latest creations are featured in each edition of our New Design Portfolio. You may have received a copy with your latest purchase by mail. If not, or if you purchased this book from a local retailer, just return the coupon below for your FREE copy. Make sure you consider the very latest of what Home Planners has to offer.

Yes! Please send my FREE copy of your latest New Design Portfolio.

Offer good to U.S. shipping address only.

Name _____

Address _____

City_____State_____Zip _____

Order Form Key
| TB53 |

HOME PLANNERS, LLC
Wholly owned by Hanley-Wood, LLC
3275 WEST INA ROAD, SUITE 110
TUCSON, ARIZONA 85741

Toll Free 1-800-521-6797
Regular Office Hours:
8:00 a.m. to 8:00 p.m. Eastern Time, Monday through Friday
Our staff will gladly answer any questions during regular office hours. Our answering service can place orders after hours or on weekends.

If we receive your order by 4:00 p.m. Eastern Time, Monday through Friday, we'll process it and ship within two business days. When ordering by phone, please have your credit card ready. We'll also ask you for the Order Form Key Number at the bottom of the coupon.

By FAX: Copy the Order Form on the next page and send it on our FAX line: 1-800-224-6699 or 520-544-3086.

Canadian Customers
Order Toll-Free 1-877-223-6389

For faster service, Canadian customers may now call in orders directly to our Canadian supplier of plans and charge the purchase to a credit card. Or, you may complete the order form at right, adding the current exchange rate to all prices, and mail in Canadian funds to:

Home Planners Canada   301-611 Alexander Street
c/o Select Home Designs   Vancouver, B.C., Canada
V6A 1E1

OR: Copy the Order Form and send it via our FAX line: 1-800-224-6699.

The Home Customizer®

"This house is perfect...if only the family room were two feet wider." Sound familiar? In response to the numerous requests for this type of modification, Home Planners has developed **The Home Customizer® Package**. This exclusive package offers our top-of-the-line materials to make it easy for anyone, anywhere to customize any Home Planners design to fit their needs. Check the index on pages 234-235 for those plans which are customizable.

Some of the changes you can make to any of our plans include:

- exterior elevation changes
- kitchen and bath modifications
- roof, wall and foundation changes
- room additions and more!

The Home Customizer® Package includes everything you'll need to make the necessary changes to your favorite Home Planners design. The package includes:

- instruction book with examples
- architectural scale and clear work film
- erasable red marker and removable correction tape
- 1/4"-scale furniture cutouts
- 1 set reproducible, erasable Sepias
- 1 set study blueprints for communicating changes to your design professional
- a copyright release letter so you can make copies as you need them
- referral letter with the name, address and telephone number of the professional in your region who is trained in modifying Home Planners designs efficiently and inexpensively.

The price of the **Home Customizer® Package** ranges from $650 to $1350, depending on the price schedule of the design you have chosen. **The Home Customizer® Package** will not only save you 25% to 75% of the cost of drawing the plans from scratch with a custom architect or engineer, it will also give you the flexibility to have your changes and modifications made by our referral network or by the professional of your choice. Now it's even easier and more affordable to have the custom home you've always wanted.

☎ ORDER TOLL FREE!
For information about any of our services or to order call 1-800-521-6797 or 520-297-8200 Browse our website: www.homeplanners.com

BLUEPRINTS ARE NOT REFUNDABLE EXCHANGES ONLY

For Customer Service, call toll free 1-888-690-1116.

ORDER FORM

HOME PLANNERS, LLC
Wholly owned by Hanley-Wood, LLC
3275 WEST INA ROAD, SUITE 110
TUCSON, ARIZONA 85741

THE BASIC BLUEPRINT PACKAGE
Rush me the following (please refer to the Plans Index and Price Schedule in this section):

_____ Set(s) of blueprints for plan number(s) _____.	$_____
_____ Set(s) of sepias for plan number(s) _____.	$_____
_____ Home Customizer® Package for plan(s)_____.	$_____
_____ Additional identical blueprints in same order @ $50 per set.	$_____
_____ Reverse blueprints @ $50 per set.	$_____

IMPORTANT EXTRAS
Rush me the following:

_____ Materials List: $60 (Must be purchased with Blueprint set.) Add $10 for a Schedule C4-L4 plan.	$_____
_____ **Quote One®** Summary Cost Report @ $29.95 for one, $14.95 for each additional, for plans _____ Building location: City _____Zip Code _____	$_____
_____ **Quote One®** Materials Cost Report @ $120 Schedule P1-C3; $130 Schedules C4-L4, for plan_____ (Must be purchased with Blueprints set.) Building location: City _____Zip Code _____	$_____
_____ Specification Outlines @ $10 each.	$_____
_____ Detail Sets @ $14.95 each; any two for $22.95; any three for $29.95; all four for $39.95 (save $19.85). ❑ Plumbing ❑ Electrical ❑ Construction ❑ Mechanical (These helpful details provide general construction advice and are not specific to any single plan.)	$_____
_____ Plan-A-Home® @ $29.95 each.	$_____
DECK BLUEPRINTS	
_____ Set(s) of Deck Plan _____.	$_____
_____ Additional identical blueprints in same order @ $10 per set.	$_____
_____ Reverse blueprints @ $10 per set.	$_____
_____ Set of Standard Deck Details @ $14.95 per set.	$_____
_____ Set of Complete Building Package (Best Buy!) Includes Custom Deck Plan _____. (See Index and Price Schedule) Plus Standard Deck Details	$_____
LANDSCAPE BLUEPRINTS	
_____ Set(s) of Landscape Plan _____.	$_____
_____ Additional identical blueprints in same order @ $10 per set.	$_____
_____ Reverse blueprints @ $10 per set.	$_____

Please indicate the appropriate region of the country for Plant & Material List. (See Map on page 233): Region _____

POSTAGE AND HANDLING	1–3 sets	4+ sets
Signature is required for all deliveries. **DELIVERY** (No CODs) (Requires street address—No P.O. Boxes)		
• Regular Service (Allow 7–10 business days delivery)	❑ $15.00	❑ $18.00
• Priority (Allow 4–5 business days delivery)	❑ $20.00	❑ $30.00
• Express (Allow 3 business days delivery)	❑ $30.00	❑ $40.00
CERTIFIED MAIL If no street address available. (Allow 7–10 days delivery)	❑ $20.00	❑ $30.00
OVERSEAS DELIVERY Note: All delivery times are from date Blueprint Package is shipped.	fax, phone or mail for quote	

POSTAGE (From box above) $_____
SUBTOTAL $_____
SALES TAX (AZ, MI, & WA residents, please add appropriate state and local sales tax.) $_____
TOTAL (Subtotal and tax) $_____

YOUR ADDRESS (please print)

Name _____

Street _____

City _____State_____Zip _____

Daytime telephone number (_____) _____

FOR CREDIT CARD ORDERS ONLY
Please fill in the information below:
Credit card number _____
Exp. Date: Month/Year _____
Check one ❑ Visa ❑ MasterCard ❑ Discover Card ❑ American Express

Signature _____

Please check appropriate box: ❑ Licensed Builder-Contractor
              ❑ Homeowner

☎ ORDER TOLL FREE!
1-800-521-6797 or 520-297-8200

Order Form Key
TB53

Helpful Books & Software

Home Planners wants your building experience to be as pleasant and trouble-free as possible. That's why we've expanded our library of Do-It-Yourself titles to help you along. In addition to our beautiful plans books, we've added books to guide you through specific projects as well as the construction process. In fact, these are titles that will be as useful after your dream home is built as they are right now.

ONE-STORY

1 448 designs for all lifestyles. 860 to 5,400 square feet. 384 pages $9.95

TWO-STORY

2 460 designs for one-and-a-half and two stories. 1,245 to 7,275 square feet. 384 pages $9.95

VACATION

3 345 designs for recreation, retirement and leisure. 312 pages $8.95

MULTI-LEVEL

4 214 designs for split-levels, bi-levels, multi-levels and walkouts. 224 pages $8.95

COUNTRY

5 200 country designs from classic to contemporary by 7 winning designers. 224 pages $8.95

MOVE-UP

6 200 stylish designs for today's growing families from 9 hot designers. 224 pages $8.95

NARROW-LOT

7 200 unique homes less than 60' wide from 7 designers. Up to 3,000 square feet. 224 pages $8.95

SMALL HOUSE

8 200 beautiful designs chosen for versatility and affordability. 224 pages $8.95

BUDGET-SMART

9 200 efficient plans from 7 top designers, that you can really afford to build! 224 pages $8.95

EXPANDABLES

10 200 flexible plans that expand with your needs from 7 top designers. 240 pages $8.95

ENCYCLOPEDIA

11 500 exceptional plans for all styles and budgets—the best book of its kind! 352 pages $9.95

AFFORDABLE

12 Completely revised and updated, featuring 300 designs for modest budgets. 256 pages $9.95

ENCYCLOPEDIA 2

13 500 completely new plans. Spacious and stylish designs for every budget and taste. 352 pages $9.95

VICTORIAN

14 160 striking Victorian and Farmhouse designs from three leading designers. 192 pages $12.95

ESTATE

15 Dream big! Twenty-one designers showcase their biggest and best plans. 208 pages. $15.95

LUXURY

16 154 fine luxury plans—loaded with luscious amenities! 192 pages $14.95

COTTAGES

17 25 fresh new designs that are warm as a tropical breeze. A blend of the best aspects of many coastal styles. 64 pages. $19.95

BEST SELLERS

18 Our 50th Anniversary book with 200 of our very best designs in full color! 224 pages $12.95

SPECIAL COLLECTION
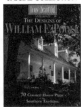
19 70 romantic house plans that capture the classic tradition of home design. 160 pages $17.95

COUNTRY HOUSES

20 208 unique home plans that combine traditional style and modern livability. 224 pages $9.95

CLASSIC

21 Timeless, elegant designs that always feel like home. Gorgeous plans that are as flexible and up-to-date as their occupants. 240 pages. $9.95

CONTEMPORARY

22 The most complete and imaginative collection of contemporary designs available anywhere. 240 pages. $9.95

EASY-LIVING

23 200 efficient and sophisticated plans that are small in size, but big on livability. 224 pages $8.95

SOUTHERN

24 207 homes rich in Southern styling and comfort. 240 pages $8.95

SUNBELT

25 215 designs that capture the spirit of the Southwest. 208 pages $10.95

WESTERN

26 215 designs that capture the spirit and diversity of the Western lifestyle. 208 pages $9.95

ENERGY GUIDE

27 The most comprehensive energy efficiency and conservation guide available. 280 pages $35.00

Design Software

BOOK & CD-ROM
28 Both the Home Planners Gold book and matching Windows™ CD-ROM with 3D floorplans. $24.95

3D DESIGN SUITE
29 Home design made easy! View designs in 3D, take a virtual reality tour, add decorating details and more. $59.95

Outdoor Projects

OUTDOOR
30 42 unique outdoor projects. Gazebos, strombellas, bridges, sheds, playsets and more! 96 pages $7.95

GARAGES & MORE
31 101 multi-use garages and outdoor structures to enhance any home. 96 pages $7.95

DECKS

32 25 outstanding single-, double- and multi-level decks you can build. 112 pages $7.95

Landscape Designs

EASY CARE	FRONT & BACK	BACKYARDS	BEDS & BORDERS	BATHROOMS	KITCHENS	HOUSE CONTRACTING	WINDOWS & DOORS

     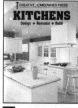  

33 41 special landscapes designed for beauty and low maintenance. 160 pages $14.95

34 The first book of do-it-yourself landscapes. 40 front, 15 backyards. 208 pages $14.95

35 40 designs focused solely on creating your own specially themed backyard oasis. 160 pages $14.95

36 Practical advice and maintenance techniques for a wide variety of yard projects. 160 pages. $14.95

37 An innovative guide to organizing, remodeling and decorating your bathroom. 96 pages $10.95

38 An imaginative guide to designing the perfect kitchen. Chock full of bright ideas to make your job easier. 176 pages $14.95

39 Everything you need to know to act as your own general contractor...and save up to 25% off building costs. 134 pages $14.95

40 Installation techniques and tips that make your project easier and more professional looking. 80 pages $7.95

ROOFING	FRAMING	VISUAL HANDBOOK	BASIC WIRING	PATIOS & WALKS	TILE	TRIM & MOLDING

41 Information on the latest tools, materials and techniques for roof installation or repair. 80 pages $7.95

42 For those who want to take a more hands-on approach to their dream. 319 pages $19.95

43 A plain-talk guide to the construction process; financing to final walk-through, this book covers it all. 498 pages $19.95

44 A straightforward guide to one of the most misunderstood systems in the home. 160 pages $12.95

45 Clear step-by-step instructions take you from the basic design stages to the finished project. 80 pages $7.95

46 Every kind of tile for every kind of application. Includes tips on use installation and repair. 176 pages $12.95

47 Step-by-step instructions for installing baseboards, window and door casings and more. 80 pages $7.95

Additional Books Order Form

To order your books, just check the box of the book numbered below and complete the coupon. We will process your order and ship it from our office within two business days. Send coupon and check (in U.S. funds).

YES! Please send me the books I've indicated:

☐ 1:VO	$9.95	☐ 25:SW	$10.95
☐ 2:VT	$9.95	☐ 26:WH	$9.95
☐ 3:VH	$8.95	☐ 27:RES	$35.00
☐ 4:VS	$8.95	☐ 28:HPGC	$24.95
☐ 5:FH	$8.95	☐ 29:PLANSUITE	$59.95
☐ 6:MU	$8.95	☐ 30:YG	$7.95
☐ 7:NL	$8.95	☐ 31:GG	$7.95
☐ 8:SM	$8.95	☐ 32:DP	$7.95
☐ 9:BS	$8.95	☐ 33:ECL	$14.95
☐ 10:EX	$8.95	☐ 34:HL	$14.95
☐ 11:EN	$9.95	☐ 35:BYL	$14.95
☐ 12:AF	$9.95	☐ 36:BB	$14.95
☐ 13:E2	$9.95	☐ 37:CDB	$10.95
☐ 14:VDH	$12.95	☐ 38:CKI	$14.95
☐ 15:EDH	$15.95	☐ 39:SBC	$14.95
☐ 16:LD2	$14.95	☐ 40:CGD	$7.95
☐ 17:CTG	$19.95	☐ 41:CGR	$7.95
☐ 18:HPG	$12.95	☐ 42:SRF	$19.95
☐ 19:WEP	$17.95	☐ 43:RVH	$19.95
☐ 20:CN	$9.95	☐ 44:CBW	$12.95
☐ 21:CS	$9.95	☐ 45:CGW	$7.95
☐ 22:CM	$9.95	☐ 46:CWT	$12.95
☐ 23:EL	$8.95	☐ 47:CGT	$7.95
☐ 24:SH	$8.95		

Canadian Customers
Order Toll-Free 1-877-223-6389

Additional Books Subtotal $_____
ADD Postage and Handling $ 4.00
Sales Tax: (AZ, MI, & WA residents, please add appropriate state and local sales tax.) $_____
YOUR TOTAL (Subtotal, Postage/Handling, Tax) $_____

YOUR ADDRESS (Please print)

Name _____

Street _____

City _____ State_____ Zip _____

Phone (_____) _____—_____

YOUR PAYMENT
Check one: ☐ Check ☐ Visa ☐ MasterCard ☐ Discover Card ☐ American Express
Required credit card information:

Credit Card Number_____

Expiration Date (Month/Year) _____/_____

Signature Required _____

 Home Planners, LLC
Wholly owned by Hanley-Wood, LLC
3275 W. Ina Road, Suite 110, Dept. BK, Tucson, AZ 85741

TB53

Design 3636, page18

OVER 3 MILLION BLUEPRINTS SOLD

'We instructed our builder to follow the plans including all of the many details which make this house so elegant…Our home is a fine example of the results one can achieve by purchasing and following the plans which you offer…Everyone who has seen it has assured us that it belongs in 'a picture book.' I truly mean it when I say that my home 'is a DREAM HOUSE.'"

S.P.
Anderson, SC

"We have had a steady stream of visitors, many of whom tell us this is the most beautiful home they've seen. Everyone is amazed at the layout and remarks on how unique it is. Our real estate attorney, who is a Chicago dweller and who deals with highly valued properties, told me this is the only suburban home he has seen that he would want to live in."

W. & P.S.
Flossmoor, IL

"Your blueprints saved us a great deal of money. I acted as the general contractor and we did a lot of the work ourselves. We probably built it for half the cost! We are thinking about more plans for another home. I purchased a competitor's book but my husband wants only your plans!"

K.M.
Grovetown, GA

"We are very happy with the product of our efforts. The neighbors and passersby appreciate what we have created. We have had many people stop by to discuss our house and kindly praise it as being the nicest house in our area of new construction. We have even had one person stop and make us an unsolicited offer to buy the house for much more than we have invested in it."

K. & L.S.
Bolingbrook, IL

"The traffic going past our house is unbelievable. On several occasions, we have heard that it is the 'prettiest house in Batvia.' Also, when meeting someone new and mentioning what street we live on, quite often we're told, 'Oh, you're the one in the yellow house with the wrap-around porch! I love it!'"

A.W.
Batvia, NY

"I have been involved in the building trades my entire life…Since building our home we have built two other homes for other families. Their plans from local professional architects were not nearly as good as yours. For that reason we are ordering additional plan books from you."

T.F.
Kingston, WA

"The blueprints we received from you were of excellent quality and provided us with exactly what we needed to get our successful home-building project underway. We appreciate your invaluable role in our home-building effort."

T.A.
Concord, TN